AF469067

Victoria & Albert

Our Lives in Watercolour

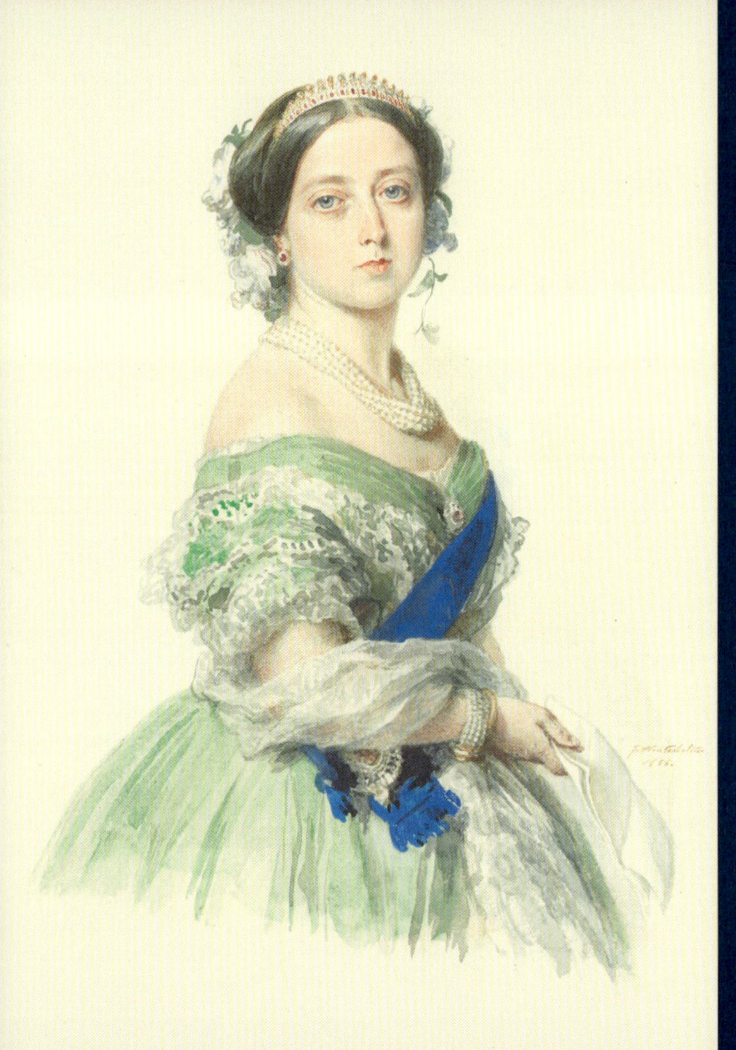

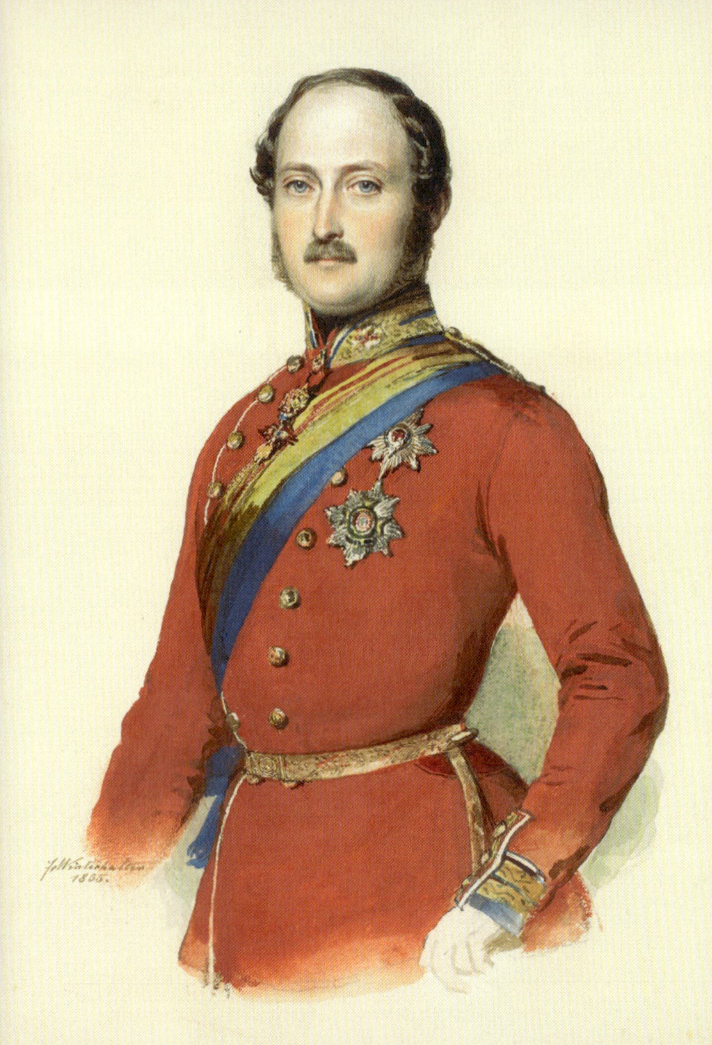

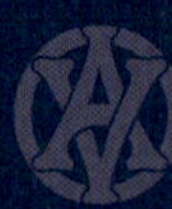

Victoria & Albert

Our Lives in Watercolour

Carly Collier

ROYAL COLLECTION TRUST

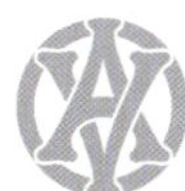

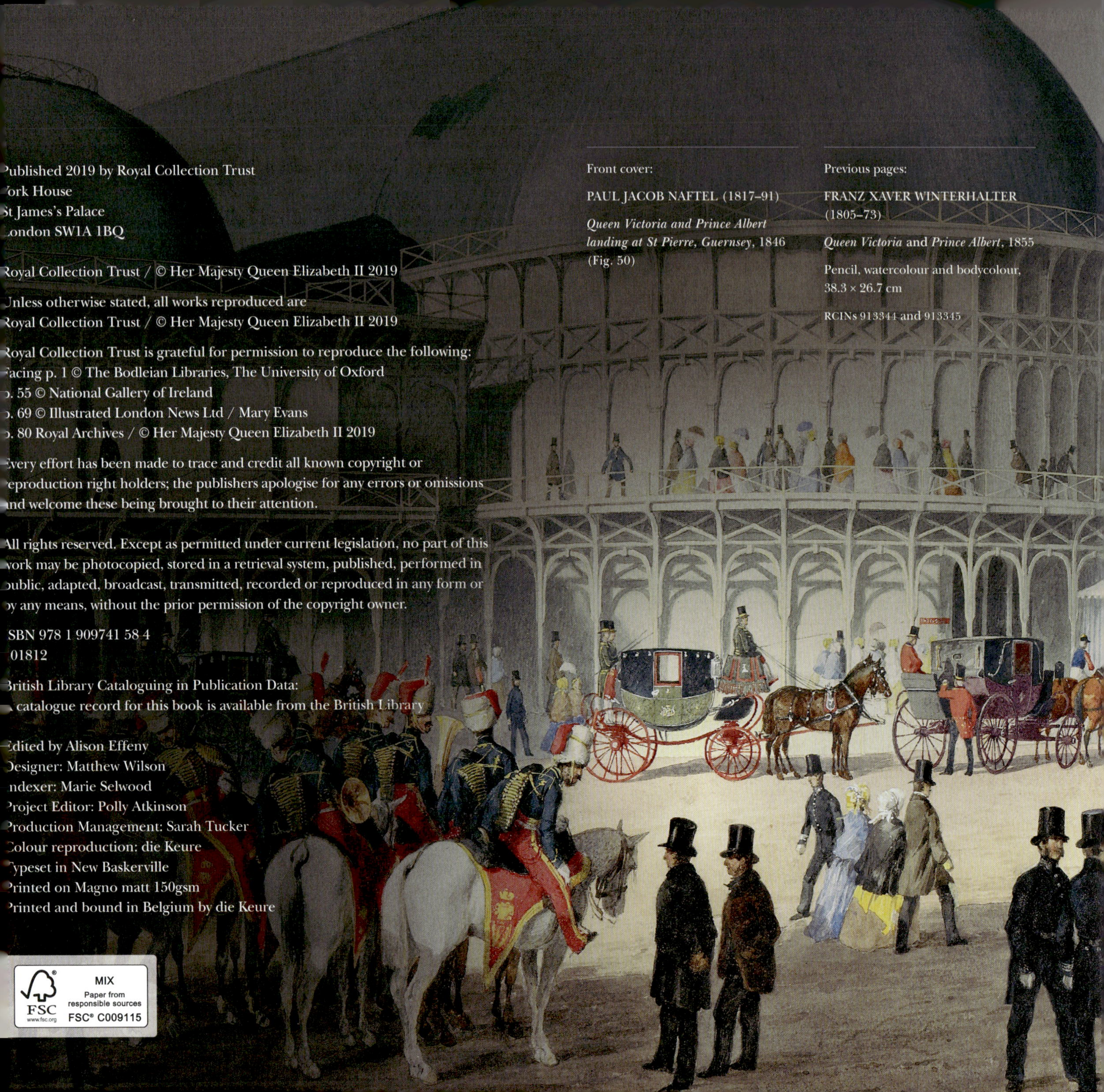

Published 2019 by Royal Collection Trust
York House
St James's Palace
London SW1A 1BQ

ISBN 978 1 909741 58 4
101812

British Library Cataloguing in Publication Data:
A catalogue record for this book is available from the British Library

Edited by Alison Effeny
Designer: Matthew Wilson
Indexer: Marie Selwood
Project Editor: Polly Atkinson
Production Management: Sarah Tucker
Colour reproduction: die Keure
Typeset in New Baskerville
Printed on Magno matt 150gsm
Printed and bound in Belgium by die Keure

MIX
Paper from responsible sources
FSC® C009115
FSC www.fsc.org

Front cover:

PAUL JACOB NAFTEL (1817–91)

Queen Victoria and Prince Albert landing at St Pierre, Guernsey, 1846 (Fig. 50)

Previous pages:

FRANZ XAVER WINTERHALTER (1805–73)

Queen Victoria and *Prince Albert*, 1855

Pencil, watercolour and bodycolour, 38.3 × 26.7 cm

RCINs 913344 and 913345

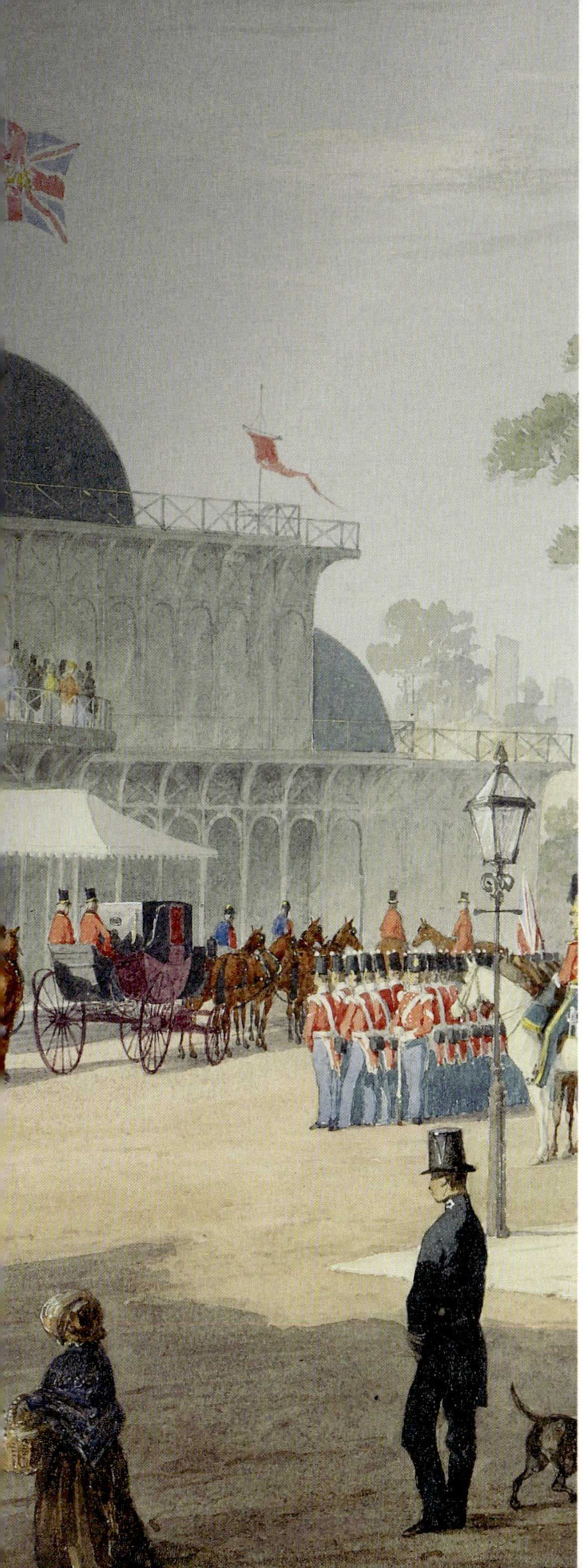

Contents

Family Tree

George III (1738–1820) *=1761* Charlotte (1744–1818), Queen

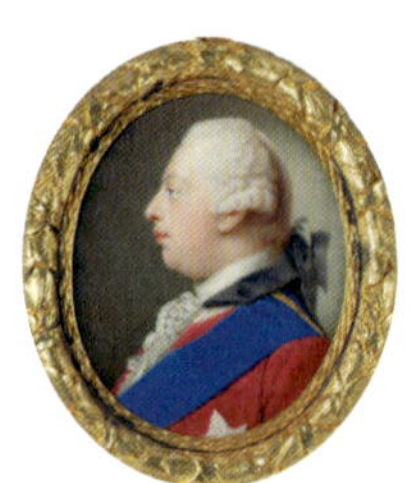

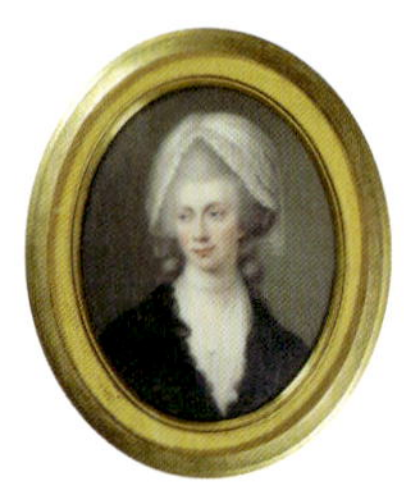

Edward (1767–1820), Duke of Kent *=1818* Victoria (1786–1861), Duchess of Kent

Leopold I (1790–1865), from 1831, King of the Belgians

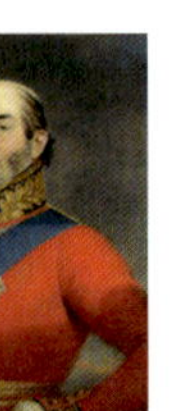

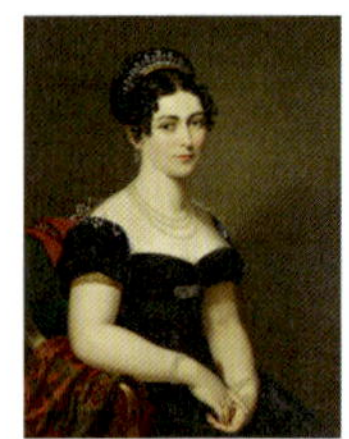

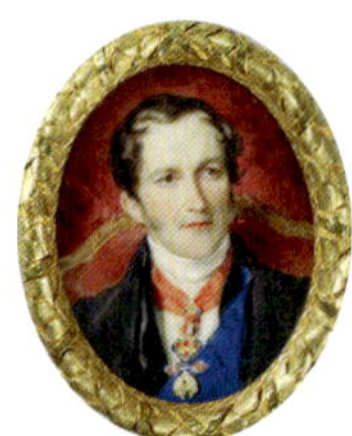

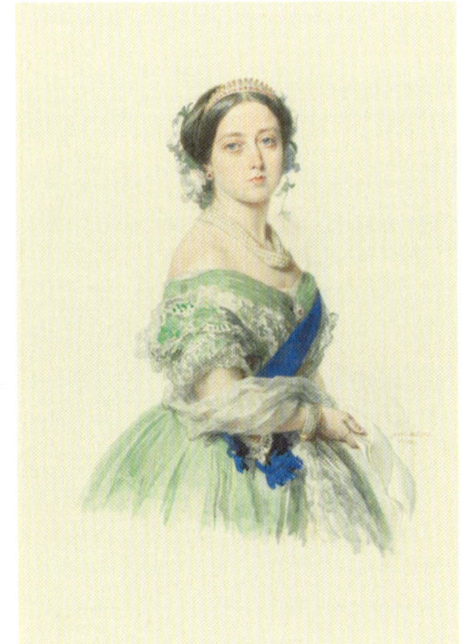

VICTORIA (1819–1901)

Victoria (1840–1901), Princess Royal

Albert Edward (1841–1910), Prince of Wales; from 1901, Edward VII

Alice (1843–78)

Alfred (1844–1900), Duke of Edinburgh

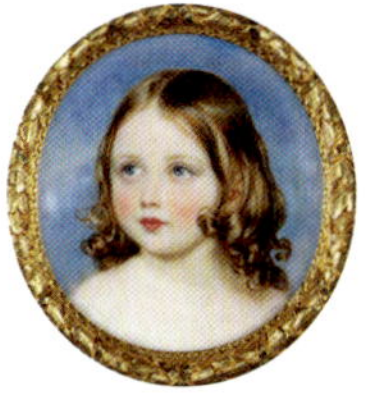

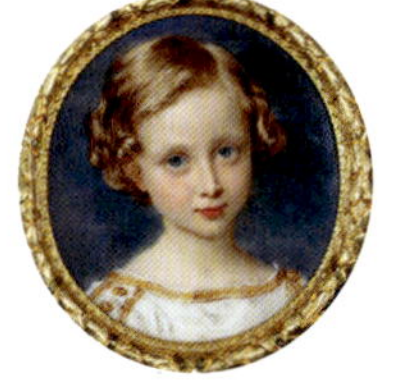

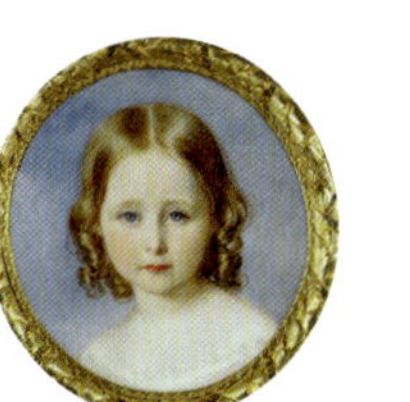

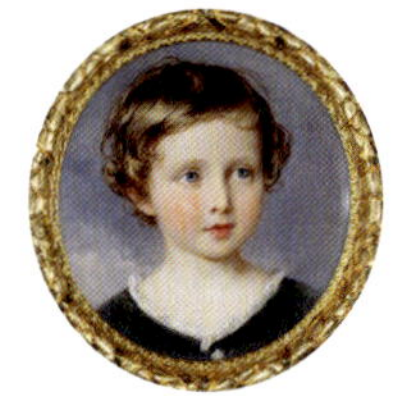

Francis (1750–1806), from 1800, Duke of Saxe-Coburg-Saalfeld

= 1777

Augusta (1757–1831), Duchess of Saxe-Coburg-Saalfeld

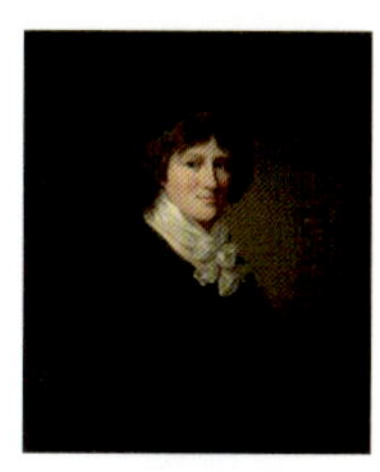

=1832

Louise Marie (1812–50), d. of Louis-Philippe, King of the French

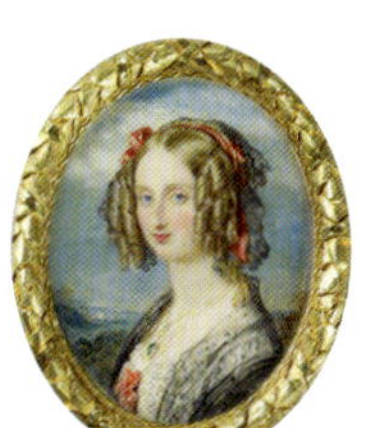

Ernest I (1784–1844), from 1826, Duke of Saxe-Coburg and Gotha

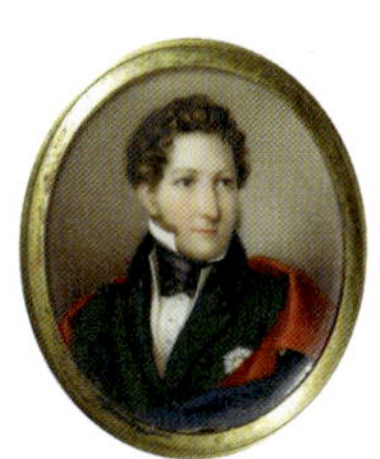

=1817 (diss. 1826)

Louise (1800–31), Duchess of Saxe-Coburg and Gotha

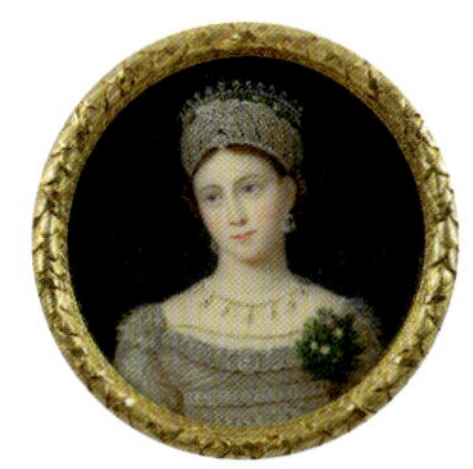

=1840

ALBERT (1819–61), from 1857, Prince Consort

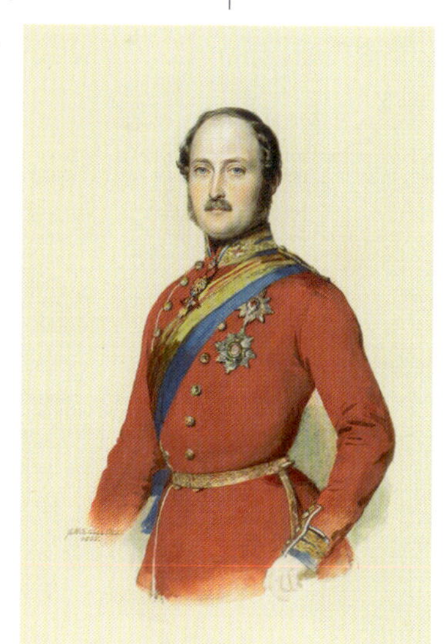

Helena (1846–1923)

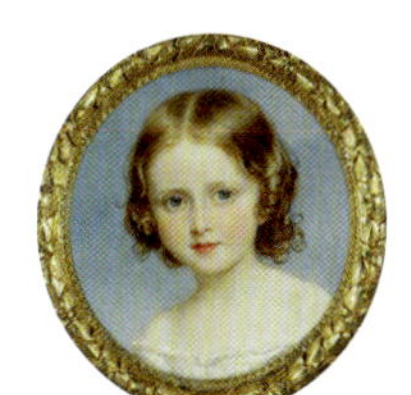

Louise (1848–1939)

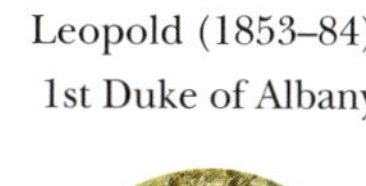

Arthur (1850–1941), 1st Duke of Connaught

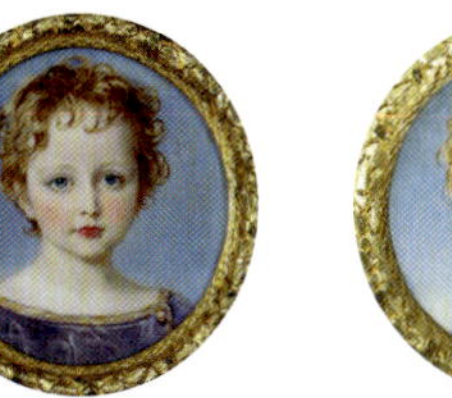

Leopold (1853–84), 1st Duke of Albany

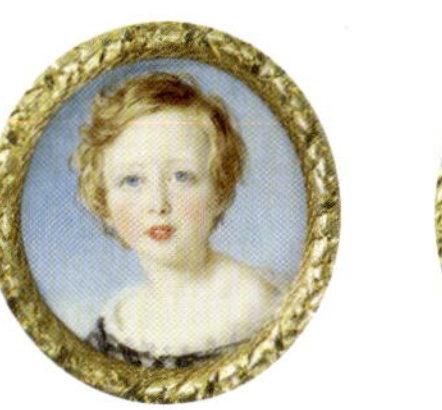

Beatrice (1857–1944)

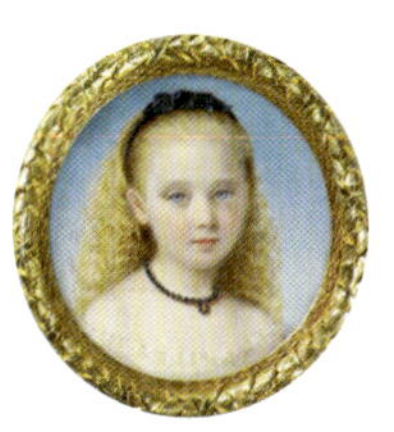

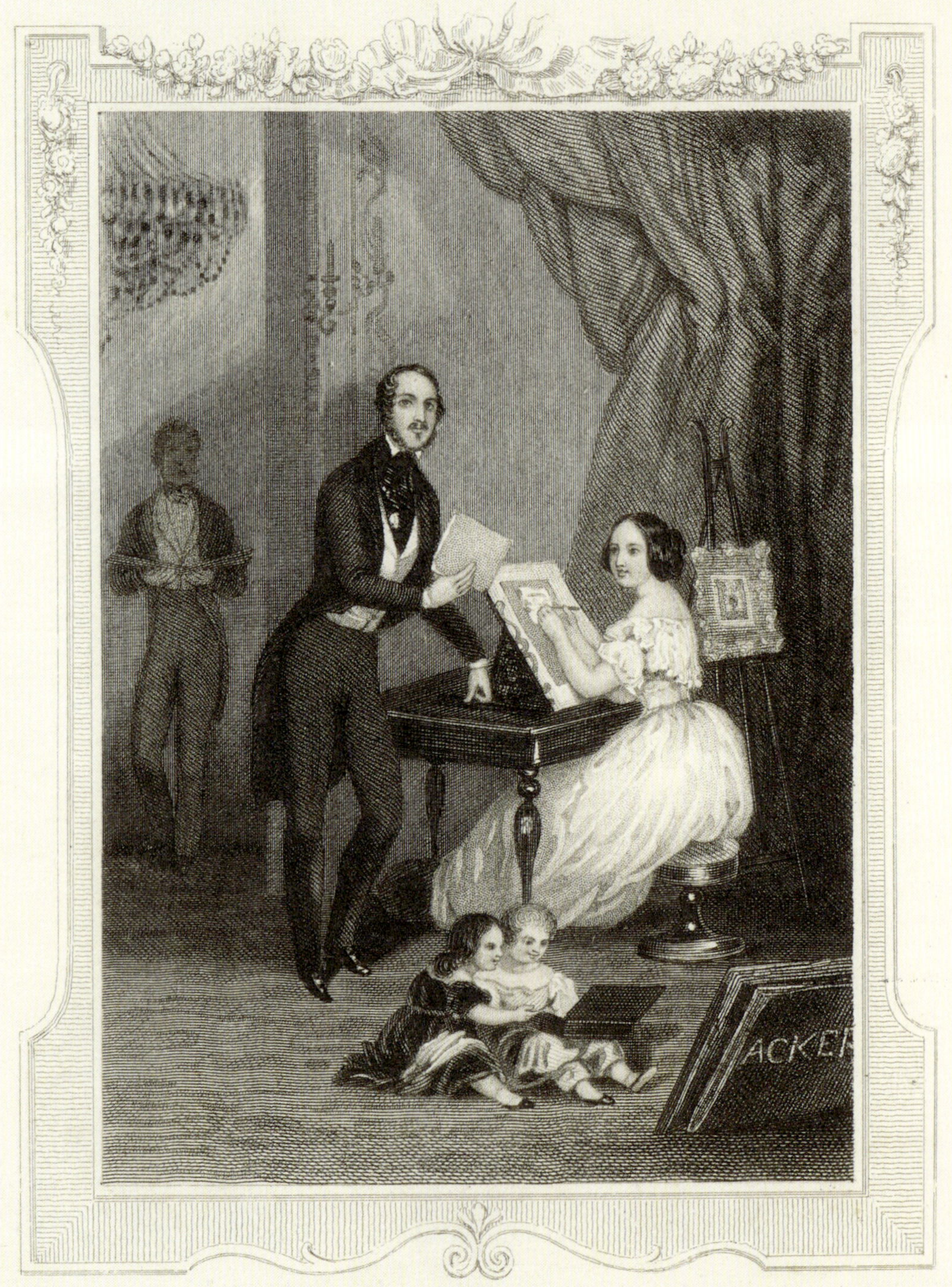

Fig. 1

THEODORE HENRY ADOLPHUS FIELDING (1781–1851)

Frontispiece to *Ackermann's Manual of Colours used in the Different Branches of Watercolour Painting*, 1844

Introduction

In 1844, the eighth year of Queen Victoria's reign and the fifth of her married life, *Ackermann's Manual of Colours used in the Different Branches of Watercolour Painting* was published.[1] Ackermann & Co. were well-established publishers, printsellers and suppliers of artists' colours who advertised as 'Manufacturer of Superfine Water-Colours to Her Majesty and the Royal Family'.[2] Queen Victoria (1819–1901) did indeed use the company's products and equipment.[3] Of particular interest is the illustration that serves as a frontispiece (fig. 1) to Ackermann's manual, which demonstrates that early in their marriage the young Queen Victoria and her husband Prince Albert (1819–61) were publicly known for their love of painting in watercolours and general interest in the medium.[4]

The royal couple are depicted within a domestic (though clearly palatial) interior, Victoria seemingly in the midst of painting with Albert leaning on the table at which she works. Sitting on the floor are two young children – presumably the Princess Royal (1840–1901) and the Prince of Wales (1841–1910), who were then aged about four and three years old – handling, with some fascination, a colour box (a not especially subtle reference on the part of Ackermann & Co. to a hope for future royal patronage). Two large portfolios inscribed with the beginning of the word 'Ackermann' lie in the foreground, and a framed work sits on an easel to the right of the group. The message is clear – the royal family are a paragon of domestic harmony and contentment, engrossed in the practice and appreciation of watercolour painting. Furthermore, in the title lettered below the image – *Artium protectores*, or 'Protectors of Art' – the monarchy is designated the most important patron of watercolour painting. As the Surveyor of The Queen's Pictures Richard Redgrave (1804–88) asserted in 1860, watercolour was 'a truly national art'.[5] This belief was already prevalent in the 1840s when *Ackermann's Manual* appeared. In the frontispiece, then, the monarchy, one of the most visible and potent symbols of the nation, is explicitly identified with the artistic medium widely considered by the British as their own.

'Protectors of Art'

Throughout their marriage of almost twenty-two years, Victoria and Albert were keen patrons of the fine and decorative arts as well as enthusiastic amateur artists themselves.[6] From the age of thirteen onwards Victoria kept a journal, writing in it almost every day of her life, and between her marriage in 1840 and Albert's unexpected death in 1861 she recorded hundreds of instances of the royal couple looking at, commissioning and acquiring works of art of all kinds, from oil paintings to photographs, sculpture, jewellery, furniture and watercolours.[7]

Victoria and Albert were greatly interested in the historic royal collection inherited by the Queen on her accession in 1837, which contained innumerable treasures including paintings in a variety of media. In April 1841, for example, Victoria recorded that she was writing a (now untraced) catalogue of her miniatures, and in early 1844 Albert was occupied with hanging pictures in Windsor Castle.[8] From the mid-1840s the growth of their family necessitated the building and renovating of various domestic spaces, and the decoration and furnishing of these residences led to the acquisition of more works of art. A characteristic and personal feature of Victoria and Albert's patronage was their exchanging of gifts on birthdays, anniversaries, Christmases and other significant occasions.[9] Palpable in all of their own writings on the subject, and reinforced by the testimony of members of the court, is the shared pleasure that the royal couple took in the arts.

Beyond their commissions and acquisitions, the royal couple's encouragement of contemporary art manifested itself in other ways. The national press celebrated the example Victoria and Albert set through their attendance at the major London exhibitions, and they themselves loaned many works both nationally and internationally. They also gave a warm welcome to new technologies such as photography. Underpinning this pattern of interest and support was Prince Albert's involvement with some of the most significant artistic projects of the mid-nineteenth century, including the decoration of the Palace of Westminster, begun in the 1840s, the Great Exhibition of 1851 and the Manchester Art Treasures exhibition in 1857.[10]

'The Arts – how wonderful was his knowledge & judgement of them & taste!'[11] In her private papers and in correspondence and conversation with others, the Queen repeatedly stressed Prince Albert's intellectual appreciation of the arts, which she perceived to be far greater than her own. In the case of watercolour painting, however, Victoria's artistic efforts and output – for it appears to have been her favourite medium – surpassed those of her husband, and there is strong evidence of her interest in watercolour, as a patron and practitioner, prior to her marriage.[12]

The young Princess Victoria began taking drawing lessons at the age of eight with the Royal Academician Richard Westall (1765–1836), a portrait and history painter whose large-scale watercolours were particularly esteemed.[13] Such tuition was a common component of royal and aristocratic education. Westall taught the Princess for almost a decade, encouraging her draughtsmanship and use of colour by providing works for her to copy; praise was accompanied with suggestions for improvement. An obituary published in the *Gentleman's Magazine* celebrated Westall's success as royal drawing master, with 'the very beautiful drawings of his Royal pupil' furnishing 'abundant' proof of the effectiveness of his lessons.[14]

In addition to learning to draw and paint herself, the Princess was also taken to exhibitions in London, enabling her to appreciate at first hand works by many professional artists. The earliest record of such a visit in her journal is dated 3 May 1833, when she went with her governess and others to the annual Royal Academy exhibition. The thirteen-year-old Princess noted works by artists including the President Sir Martin Archer Shee (1769–1850), her drawing master Westall, David Wilkie (1785–1841) and George Hayter (1792–1871); overall, she judged the exhibition to be 'very good'. Two months later Victoria visited an

'The Arts – how wonderful was his knowledge & judgement of them & taste!'

– Queen Victoria

exhibition of watercolours, and although she did not describe any individual contributors or their works, on this occasion the Princess wrote enthusiastically that it was a 'very fine' display.[15] Which of the two major watercolour societies held this exhibition is unclear, but the archives of the older of the two, the Old (now Royal) Watercolour Society, note a visit made by Victoria and her mother, the Duchess of Kent (1786–1861), the following year, after which an annual private viewing was arranged.[16] In 1836 Princess Victoria recorded that a group of artists were in attendance during her visit.[17] On her first visit to the Old Watercolour Society's exhibition as queen in 1838, Victoria purchased paintings by Anthony Copley Fielding (1787–1855), John Frederick Tayler (1802–89), Peter De Wint (1784–1849) and Samuel Prout (1783–1852).[18]

In Prince Albert Queen Victoria found another watercolour enthusiast, and he was to be a regular and welcome visitor to both watercolour societies. The landscape painter William Callow (1812–1908) remembered having 'a long conversation' with Prince Albert about art at the Old Watercolour Society's exhibition of 1852, which included a discussion on the display of watercolours, and being asked 'many questions relative to my painting' by Victoria.[19] A few years later, Copley Fielding reassured the institution's secretary about a royal visit, stating that the Prince 'never fails to make it agreeable to those who accompany him through the Exhibition'.[20] On returning to the Society's exhibition rooms after many years, the royal couple's eldest child Victoria (known to her family as Vicky), then Crown Princess of Prussia, recalled happy memories of frequent childhood visits made in company with her father.[21] Both Victoria and Albert made purchases on these occasions. They gave many of these to one another as gifts, and Albert explained to Vicky that by doing so his and Victoria's pleasure in watercolours was 'doubled'.[22] Artists who attracted royal attention in this way were aware of the significance of such patronage; Edward Corbould (1815–1905), whose large work *The Woman taken in Adultery* was bought by Albert at the New Society of Painters in Watercolours exhibition of 1842, later told the Queen that he 'owed all his success' to the Prince.[23]

> '[Prince Albert] never fails to make it agreeable to those who accompany him through the Exhibition.'
>
> – Copley Fielding

'She paints too well for an amateur'[24]

Victoria and Albert's appreciation of watercolour as a medium was undoubtedly enhanced by their own practice of the technique, and the acquaintance with professional watercolour painters that resulted. The royal couple were adventurous in the breadth of their artistic experimentation. Together, they learned to etch in the first year of their marriage and produced prints based on their own and each other's drawings as well as works in the Royal Collection.[25] Both painted in oils, with Albert giving Victoria tuition in technique; the Queen took lessons in drawing with chalks with Edwin Landseer (1802–73), though did not highly rate her own productions in that medium; and in 1852 Albert's librarian Ernst Becker (1826–88) recorded that he and his master had been taught the calotype photographic process by a Captain Scott.[26] Albert, like his wife, had been given drawing lessons as a child, and Victoria remembered him being 'much taken up with painting' in their first year of marriage, though the time available to him to pursue this interest dwindled.[27] The Queen specifically mentioned the Prince working in watercolour only once in her journals, on 4 July 1844: 'Read to Albert out of Adolphus, whilst he painted in water colours.'[28]

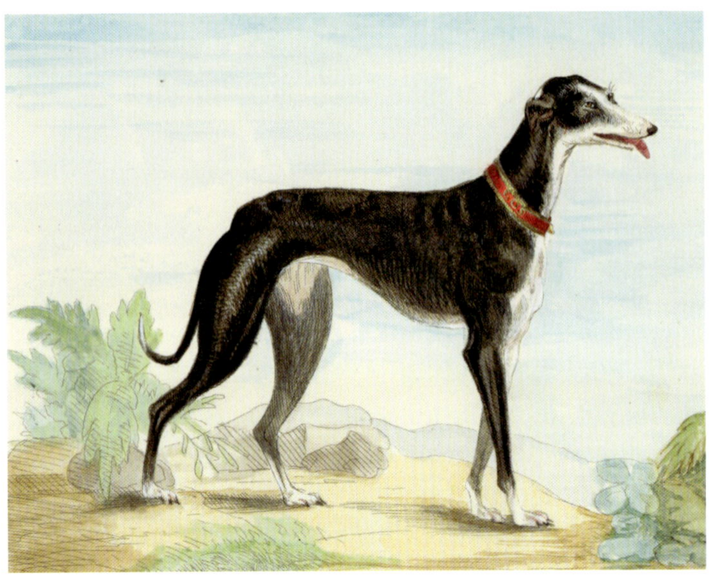

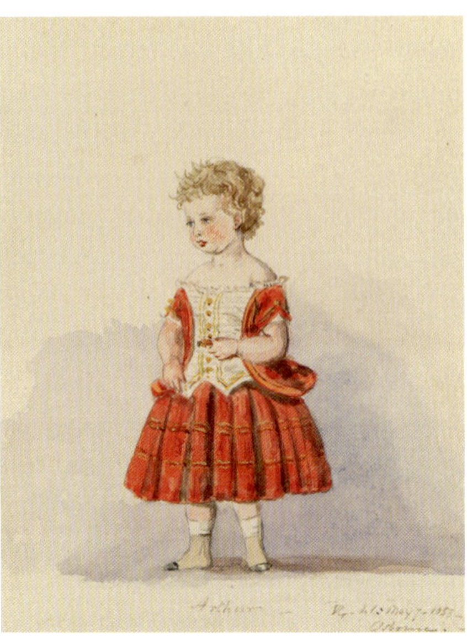

Fig. 3

QUEEN VICTORIA

Arthur, 7 May 1853

Pencil, watercolour and ink, 16.6 × 12.8 cm

RCIN 980024.dk

Fig. 2

QUEEN VICTORIA (1819–1901)

Eos, 4 October 1840

Hand-coloured etching, 11.6 × 15.2 cm

RCIN 816796

In the mid-1840s Queen Victoria's own skills in watercolour painting developed significantly. The majority of the works from Victoria's youth and the early years of her marriage are figurative. She took as her subjects those close to her, including her pets (fig. 2), family (fig. 3) and acquaintances, and also frequently sketched actors, dancers and singers whom she saw at the theatre and admired intensely. Over the summer of 1846, Victoria took twelve lessons with the artist Edward Lear (1812–88) who, she thought, 'teaches remarkably well, in landscape painting in water colours'.[29] The Queen was partly inspired by the examples of two of her ladies who were especially artistic, Viscountess Charlotte Canning (1817–61) and the Hon. Eleanor Stanley (1821–1903), both of whose landscape watercolours she admired and acquired. After her lessons with Lear, Victoria began receiving tuition from another landscape painter, introduced to her by Lady Canning. William Leighton Leitch taught the Queen for almost twenty years, as well as some of the royal children and, in the 1860s, the Princess of Wales (later Queen Alexandra, 1844–1925). He undoubtedly had the most significant influence on Victoria's painting style and her understanding of watercolour technique; surviving in the Royal Collection are demonstration sheets made by Leitch

Fig. 4

QUEEN VICTORIA, probably copying WILLIAM LEIGHTON LEITCH (1804–83)

Watercolour practice sheet, *c.*1846–50

Pencil and watercolour, 45.2 × 30.4 cm

RCIN 981350

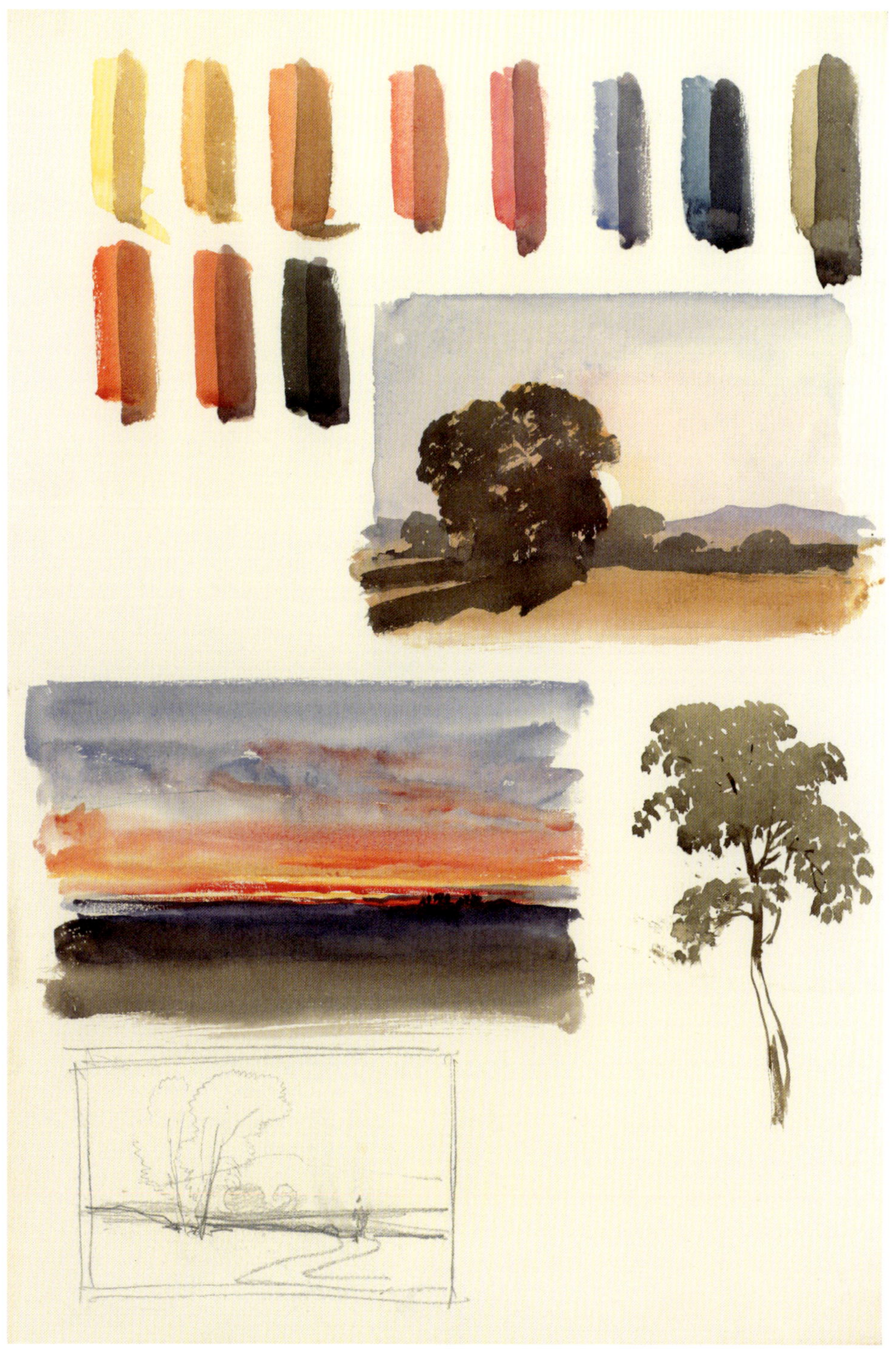

for the Queen, designed to teach aspects of colouring, building up compositions and mark-making, and practice sheets made by his pupil (fig. 4). There is also a manuscript (fig. 5a) in which Leitch explains in detail the stages of executing a watercolour (figs 5b–d).

The sketchbooks and albums of Victoria's middle and later years are heavily populated with landscape views, of both the familiar and the unfamiliar (fig. 6).[30] From the 1840s onwards the ever-increasing periods spent by the royal family at their private residences on the Isle of Wight and in Scotland – Osborne House and Balmoral Castle – provided a continual stimulus to the Queen's pencil and colour box. The deep love for painting in nature that Victoria developed came to offer some solace in her widowhood, and her artistic efforts were often praised by those who saw them. Her second daughter, Alice (1843–78), while holidaying in the Swiss Alps, wrote to her mother of her frustration at what she perceived to be her own limitations in capturing her beautiful surroundings, compared to what Victoria was capable of: 'I am enchanted, delighted with this magnificent scenery. Oh, how you would admire it! When I am sketching, I keep telling Louis [Alice's husband] how much more like you would make the things; one can always recognise the places when you draw them.'[31]

The Moonlight Lesson.

No 1.

After the outline is done. wash the whole over with yellow oker. let the wash dry. then go over the region of the Castle with yellow oker and a little Cobalt & light red added. let that likewise dry. & go over the foreground. with burnt Sienna & french blue added. the B. Sienna predominating as it comes forward. let this also dry & then begin with

No 2.

Begin with putting in the Sky, Cobalt with a little indigo mixed. laid on with a.

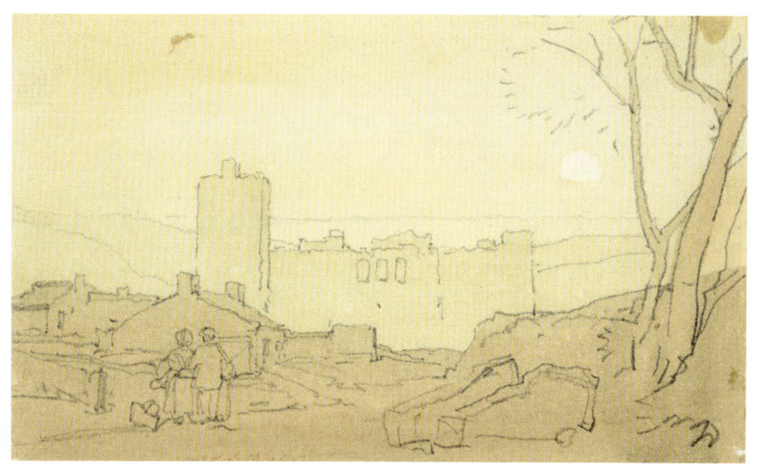

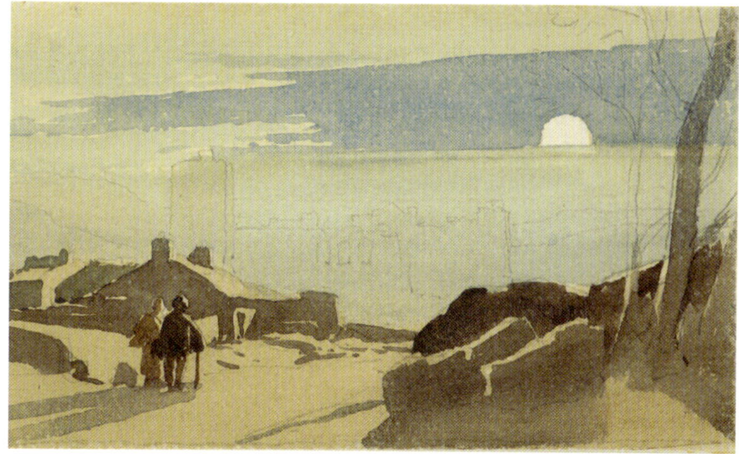

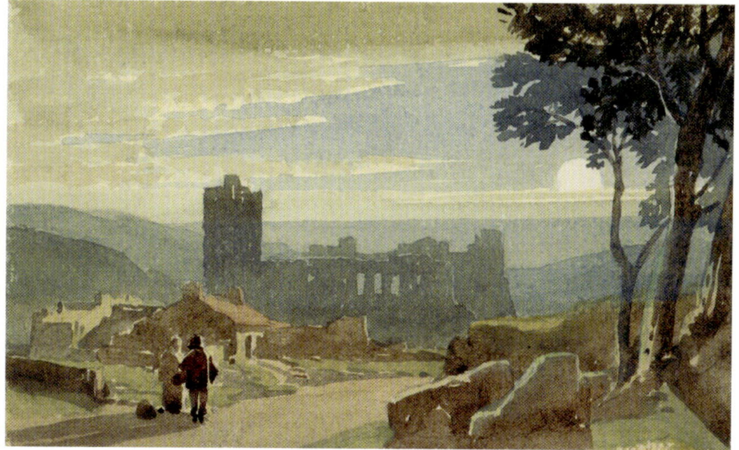

Figs 5a–d

WILLIAM LEIGHTON LEITCH

The Moonlight Lesson: a three-stage watercolour demonstration, *c.*1846–65

Ink, 20.1 × 11.7 cm (manuscript)

Pencil and wash, 8.0 × 14.0 cm (each watercolour)

RCINs 919718.a and .b, 919719 and 919720

Just a month after Prince Albert died in December 1861 at the age of forty-two, Victoria began committing her 'recollections & reminiscences' of her husband to paper.[32] Much of the couple's married life had taken place in the public eye, and there is a poignancy to the Queen's memories of her private time with Albert: 'When we dined alone … [which] we generally did twice a week & generally on Sundays – we 1st arranged Albums or looked at them; I always kept for those Eve[nin]gs the placing [of] any new Drawings … & photographs into the various Albums – wh[ich] my beloved Angel always did himself.'[33]

The act of compiling albums together was clearly given much importance by both Victoria and Albert, and some of the volumes of prints, photographs and watercolours they made survive in the Royal Collection today. These albums took on an even greater significance to the widowed Victoria, functioning as both a tangible memory of time she spent alone with her beloved husband and a pictorial record of significant moments in their lives. While their many albums incorporated a variety of media, the Queen seems to have most prized a sequence of nine volumes containing watercolours, organised chronologically, which she called her 'View Albums'. That these albums do not survive in their original form, having been disbound and reorganised in the 1930s, is probably testament to her heavy consultation of them in the second half of the nineteenth century; along with other

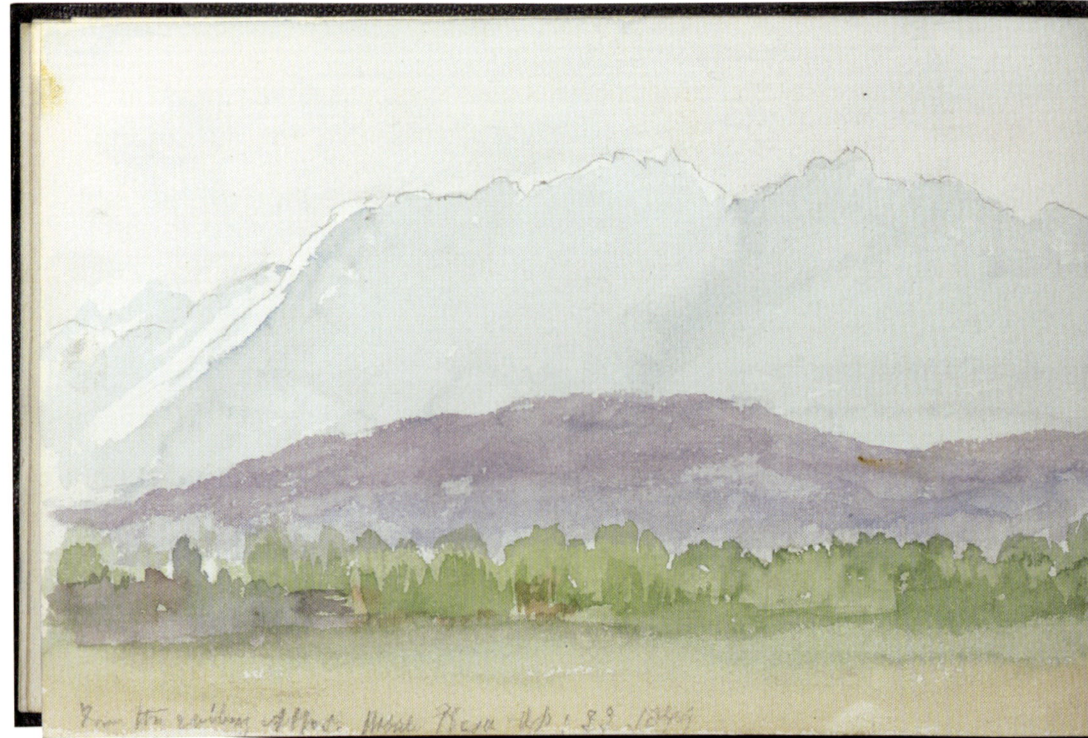

Fig. 6

QUEEN VICTORIA

From the railway Monte Rosa, 23 April 1879

Pencil and watercolour, 13.9 × 45.4 cm

RCIN 980050.q

objects of particular sentimental significance, they travelled with the Queen from residence to residence.[34] Victoria herself also ensured that they appeared as the first item on a list of albums she wished to be deposited in the Print Room at Windsor Castle after her death to become part of the Royal Collection. The View Albums were described on this list as the Queen's 'valuable albums'.[35]

It is these very personal albums, and Queen Victoria and Prince Albert's taste for watercolours more generally, that are the subject of this book. The thousands of watercolours that the royal couple commissioned and acquired give us an intimate insight into the private and public life they shared. This is enriched by the survival of Victoria and Albert's own thoughts, opinions and feelings about the scenes depicted and the artists charged with illustrating them, which are known to us through Victoria's journal, the couple's private correspondence and other writings, and in the accounts of those who knew and served them. The watercolours show us some of the pomp and spectacle of the British court, the intricacies of foreign diplomacy and the exploration and shaping of a modern nation – and, importantly, the close-knit family at the heart of, in Victoria's words, 'the excitement & the bustle we are living in'.[36]

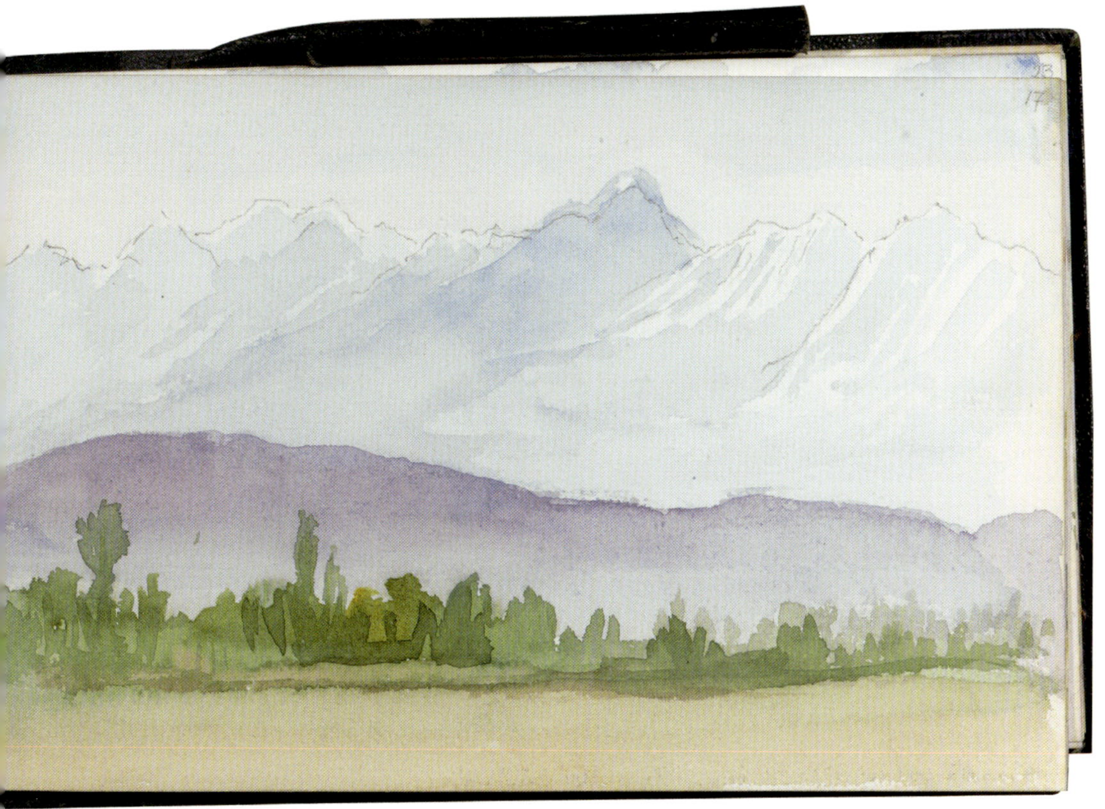

'When we dined alone … we 1st arranged Albums or looked at them; I always kept for those Eve[nin]gs the placing [of] any new Drawings … & photographs into the various Albums – wh[ich] my beloved Angel always did himself.'

– Queen Victoria

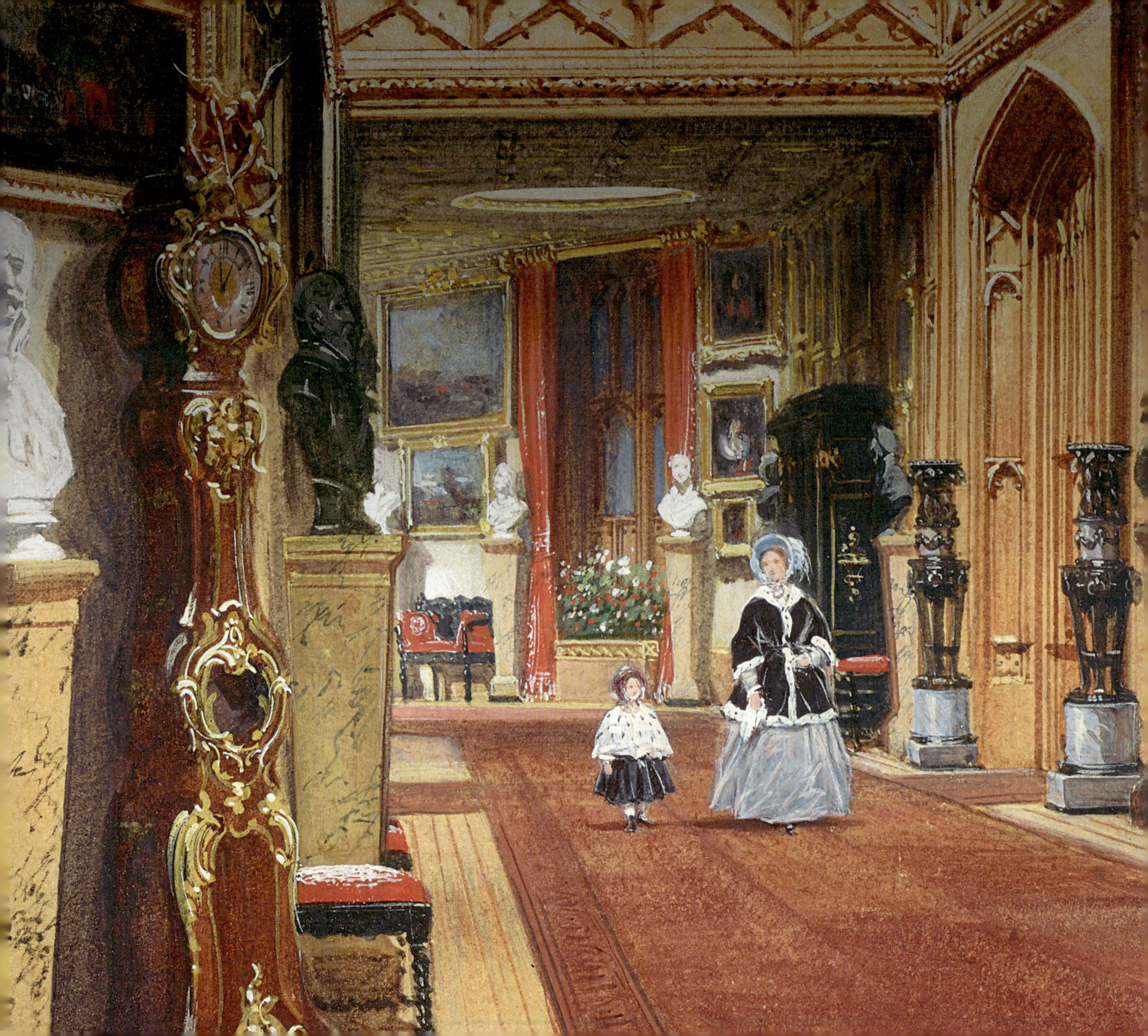

CHAPTER 1

HOME & FAMILY

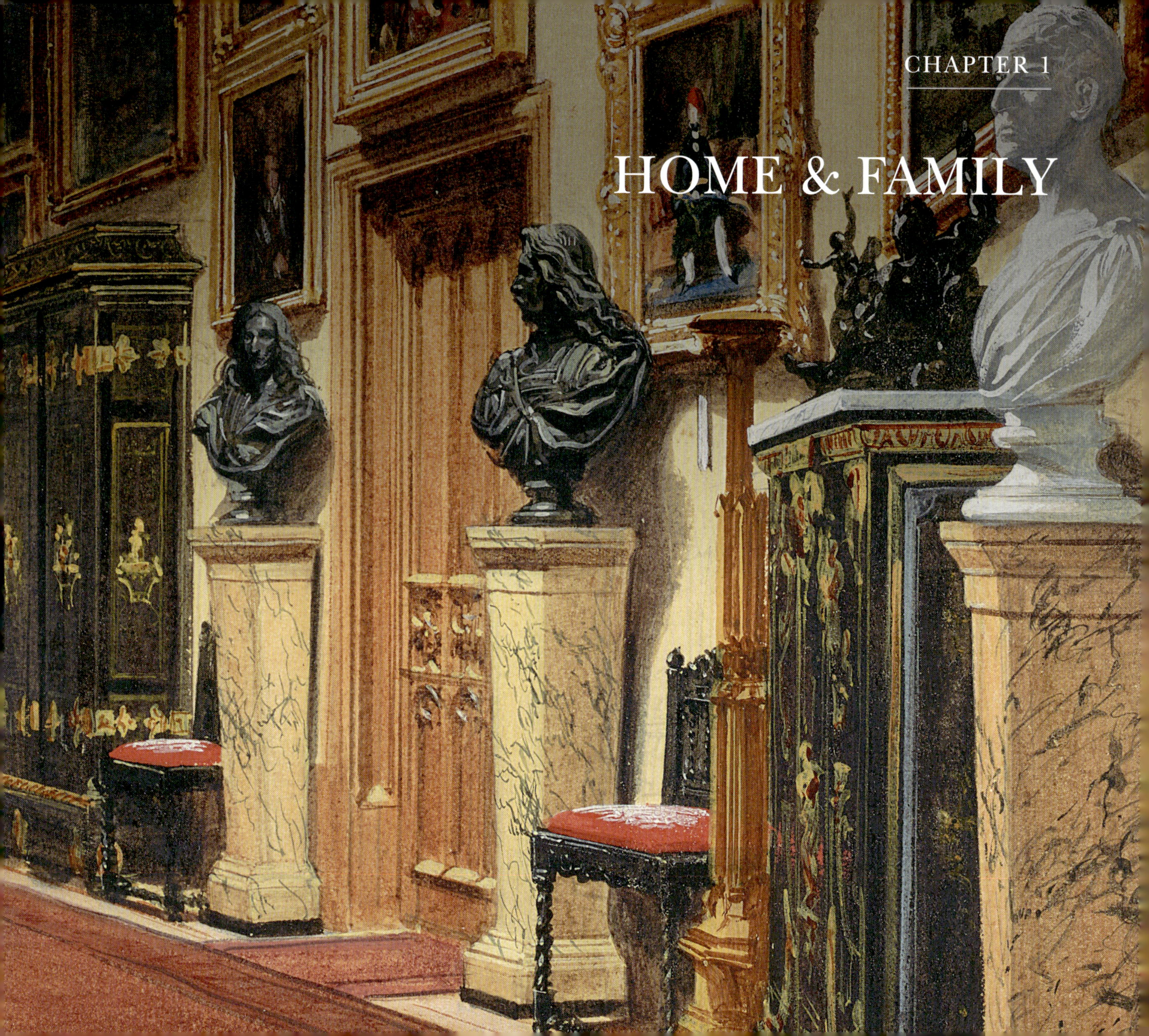

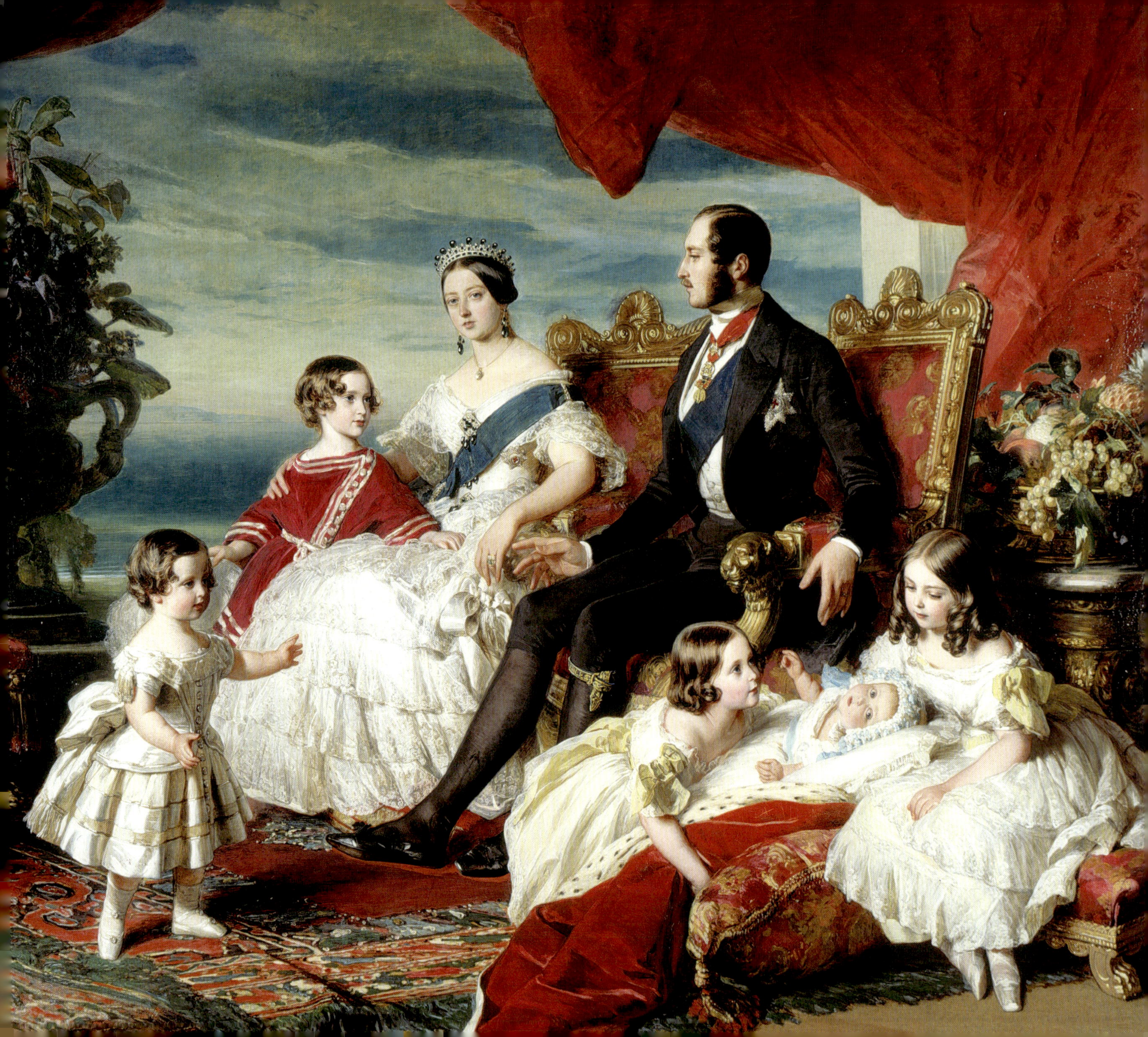

CHAPTER 1

Home & Family

'*They say* no *Sovereign* was more *loved than I am (I am bold enough to say), and* that *from our* happy domestic home *– which gives such a good example.*'[1]

– Queen Victoria

Fig. 7

FRANZ XAVER WINTERHALTER (1805–73)

The Royal Family in 1846, 1846

Oil on canvas, 250.5 × 317.3 cm

RCIN 405413

Queen Victoria married her first cousin Prince Albert of Saxe-Coburg and Gotha on 10 February 1840, when they were both twenty years old. The couple were to have nine children, five girls and four boys. Both Victoria and Albert prized their happy family and domestic life highly, and at their command it was captured on numerous occasions in paint. Some of these images were intended for the public domain, and thus served to both project and reinforce the notion of the royal family's domestic harmony – as recorded by both Victoria and Albert, with delight, in their private correspondence.

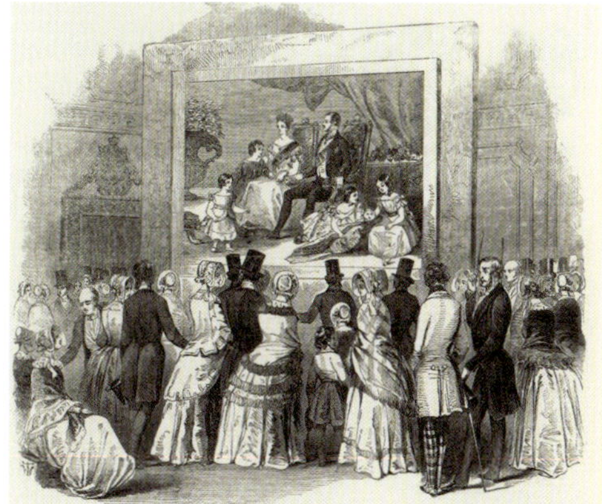

Fig. 8

Exhibition at St James's Palace of Winterhalter's pictures, painted for Her Majesty

Illustrated London News, 8 May 1847, p. 300

The Royal Family in 1846 (fig. 7), painted by the couple's favourite portraitist, Franz Xaver Winterhalter, is perhaps the most arresting and successful expression of these values. In this painting, which Victoria referred to as 'the Family picture', she and Albert are seated on throne-like chairs. The Queen, looking out at the viewer, has her arm around her first-born son and heir, Prince Albert Edward (later King Edward VII, known within the family as Bertie), with the two elder princesses – Vicky and Alice – cuddling the infant Princess Helena (1846–1923, also looking outwards) in the right foreground, as Prince Alfred (1844–1900) toddles towards them. Despite the grand interior in which they are situated and the evening dress worn by the royal couple, there is a strong sense of intimacy and

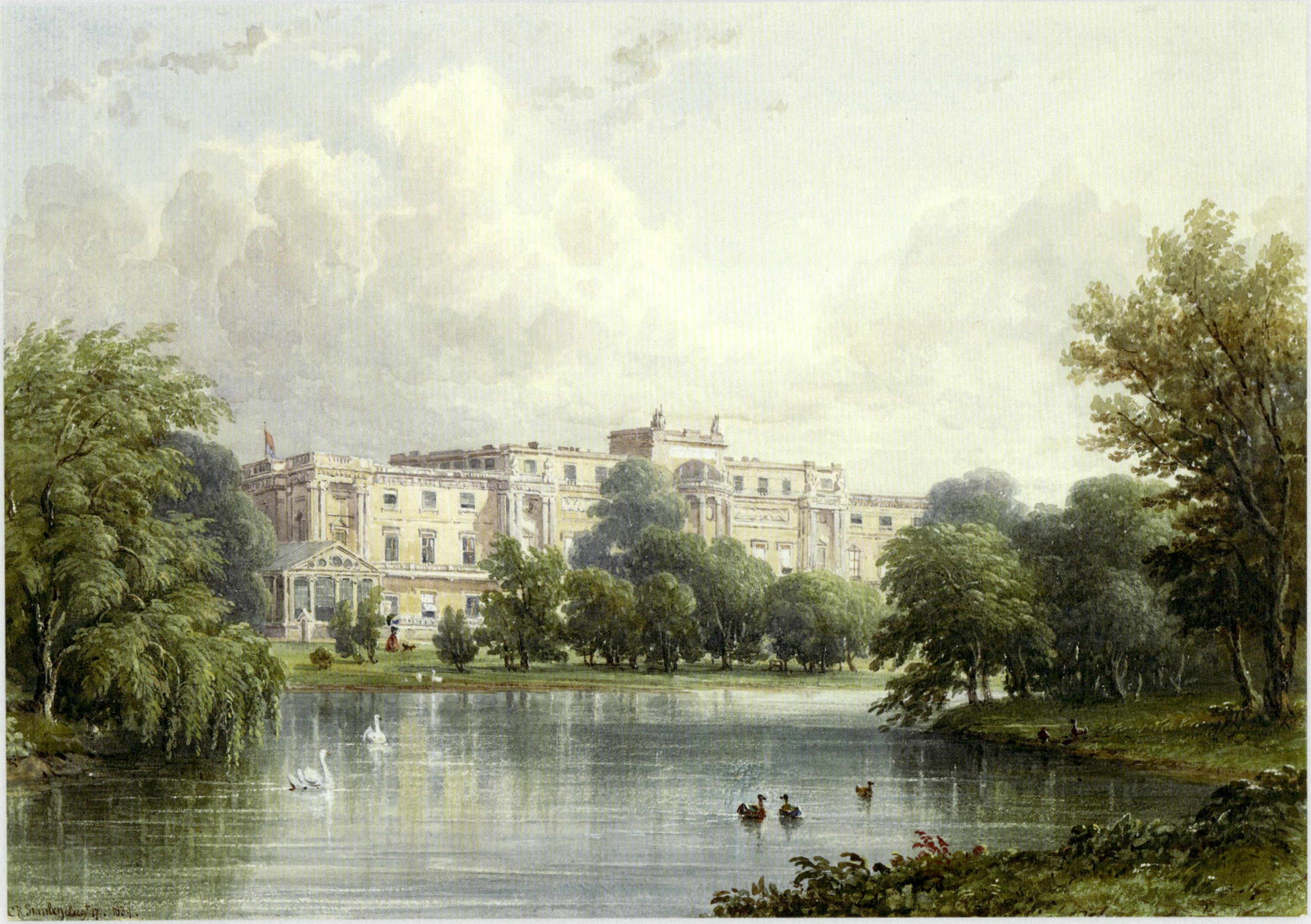

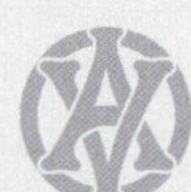

ordinary family life, conveyed through the naturalness of the poses and interaction of the figures, the majority of whom seem oblivious to the viewer.[2]

Though commissioned to hang at Osborne House on the Isle of Wight, Winterhalter's painting was exhibited first at St James's Palace in London, where it was seen by over 100,000 people (fig. 8), and then reproduced and made widely available as a print. More private were the hundreds of watercolours that the royal couple commissioned from a variety of artists to record, in Victoria's own words, 'views of all the places we visited – sketches of rooms – & events wh[ich] took place in our lives'.[3] These works were intended for the pages of the albums Victoria and Albert compiled together. Victoria refers several times in her journal to looking at albums, either alone with Albert, with their children or with members of their wider family, and it was presumably the watercolours within them illustrating the family's homes and the milestones of their personal lives that were of the greatest significance.[4]

'Your very dear and comfortable home'[5]

The watercolour chosen by Victoria and Albert to open the first of their View Albums was a prospect of the garden front of Buckingham Palace from across the lake by Caleb Robert Stanley (fig. 9). Its primary position in one of the Queen's most important albums may, perhaps, reflect the fact that moving into the palace on her accession in 1837 was an important sign of Victoria's independence. Also significant is the fact that this watercolour was given to her as a gift by her mother, the Duchess of Kent, in 1839. Victoria described the drawing as 'very pretty', and it probably prompted her to commission Stanley, a landscape painter in both oils and watercolour, to make a series of exterior views in watercolours of Windsor Castle a couple of months later.[6] Along with depictions of other royal residences and places visited by the royal couple that Stanley painted over the following few years, the views of Windsor formed a significant group of works in Victoria and Albert's first View Album. Of the sixty-four drawings and watercolours mounted in it, twenty-one were by Stanley.

A well-developed tradition in Britain for topographical watercolour – and particularly for views of country houses – was complemented from the beginning of the nineteenth century by a new, fashionable genre in watercolour painting, the 'interior view' of the rooms in a home. Queen Victoria has been described as 'one of the most ardent admirers of interior views' because of the numerous watercolours of this type she and Albert commissioned, compiling a visual record of the spaces they inhabited.[7] There was a significant – and public – precedent for such illustrations of royal spaces in William Henry Pyne's *The History of the Royal Residences* (1819), which comprised descriptive text accompanied by exterior and interior views.[8]

Some of the views commissioned by Victoria and Albert circulated more widely than the albums for which they were originally commissioned. Twenty-five watercolours of Windsor Castle by Joseph Nash were exhibited first in London and then Belfast in 1847, before being reproduced in Thomas McLean's *Views of the Interior and Exterior of Windsor Castle* (1848).[9] Nash dedicated the *Views* to Queen Victoria, and in an advertisement in the *Morning Chronicle* announcing the exhibition of Nash's watercolours at McLean's London gallery, both the Queen's patronage and 'her gracious permission' in allowing them to be exhibited

Fig. 9

CALEB ROBERT STANLEY (1795–1868)

The garden front of Buckingham Palace,
17 August 1839

Watercolour and bodycolour, 27.8 × 40.8 cm

RCIN 919891

are stressed.[10] Nash had clearly pleased his royal patrons with his work.

Nash was a member of the Old Watercolour Society, and presumably Victoria and Albert encountered his work at one of its annual exhibitions. Having studied architectural drawing and colouring at a school established by Augustus Charles Pugin (1769–1832), Nash's specialism was exploited by Victoria and Albert in the many interior and exterior views of their residences they commissioned in the 1840s and 1850s.[11] Their appreciation of Nash's skill in the rendering of architecture and furniture and his deft inclusion of figures was shared by many art critics. The *Athenaeum*'s view in 1843 that Nash had 'a feeling … for old English architecture' may, perhaps, have been of particular interest to his royal patrons.[12] Nash was first employed by Victoria and Albert to sketch scenes from the visit of Emperor Nicholas I of Russia (1789–1855) to Windsor in June 1844, when the Queen recorded in her journal that he had 'made some slight, but very nice water colour sketches [of the visit]… They are intended for our album & will be charming souvenirs.'[13] One watercolour by Nash, depicting Victoria and Nicholas entering the Waterloo Chamber for a state dinner, was mounted in the second View Album, and a replica of it was also commissioned from the artist as a gift for the Emperor.[14]

Many of the interior and exterior views that Victoria and Albert commissioned are populated with figures or with personal belongings. The overriding impression is of spaces that – while clearly palatial and (in many cases) having a ceremonial function – served as settings for domestic activity. This accords with contemporary tourist accounts; during a tour of the private apartments at Windsor, the American author Harriet Beecher Stowe (1811–96) particularly recalled seeing 'a baby's wicker wagon … such a carriage as all mothers are familiar with; such as figures largely in the history of almost every family'.[15] Almost all the watercolours reproduced in Nash's *Views* include figures. A number illustrate events during state visits in the 1840s, but there are also some which portray members of the royal family at leisure. The two figures walking into view in Nash's depiction of the Grand Corridor in the castle (fig. 10), for example, are the Queen herself and her second daughter, Princess Alice, who would have been three or four years old when this watercolour was painted. Several of these views are important documents not only of

> '*[Nash has] made some slight, but very nice water colour sketches … They are intended for our album & will be charming souvenirs.*'
>
> – Queen Victoria

Fig. 10

JOSEPH NASH (1809–78)

The Grand Corridor, Windsor Castle, 1846

Pencil, watercolour and bodycolour, 33.0 × 41.5 cm

RCIN 919781

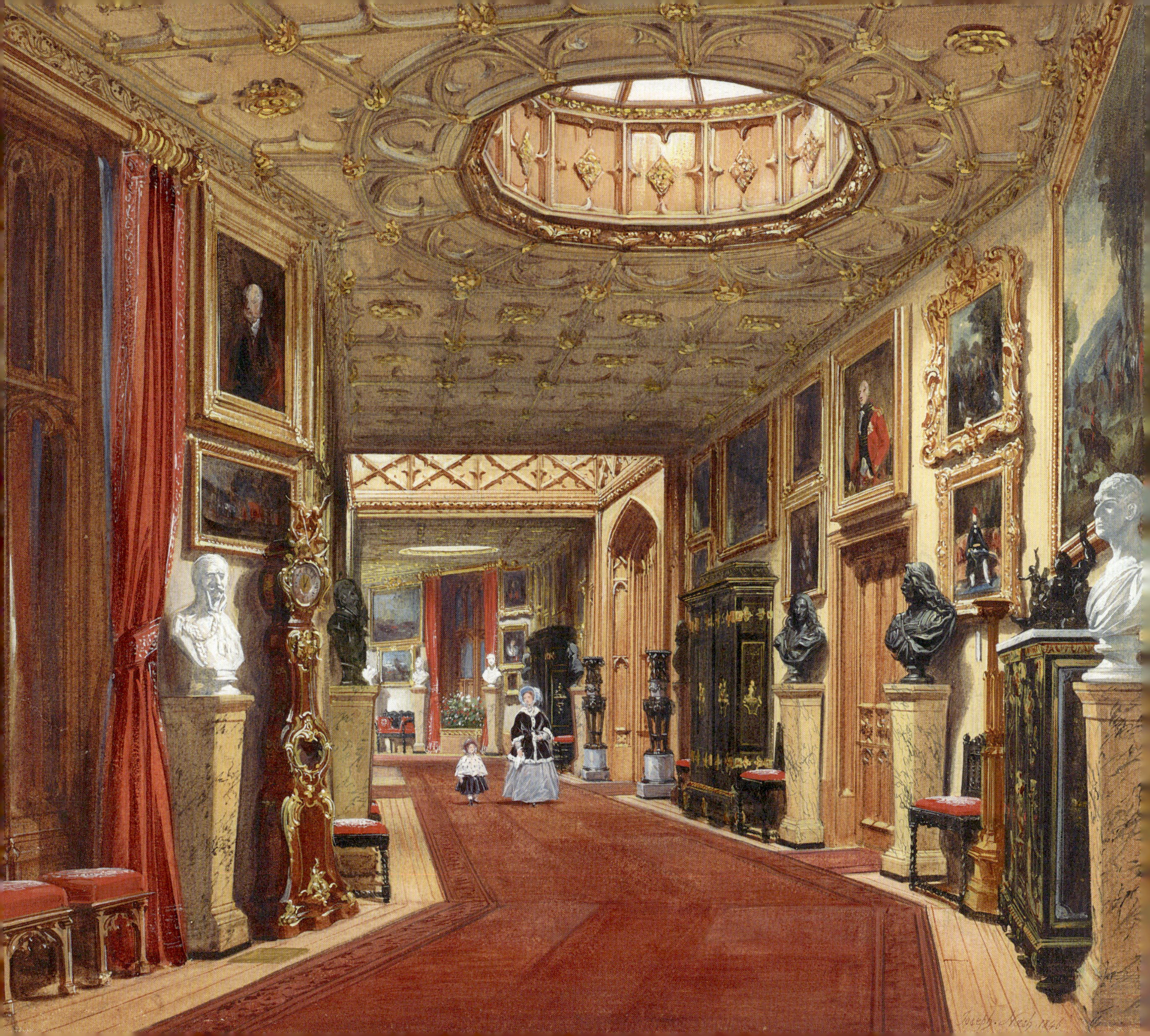

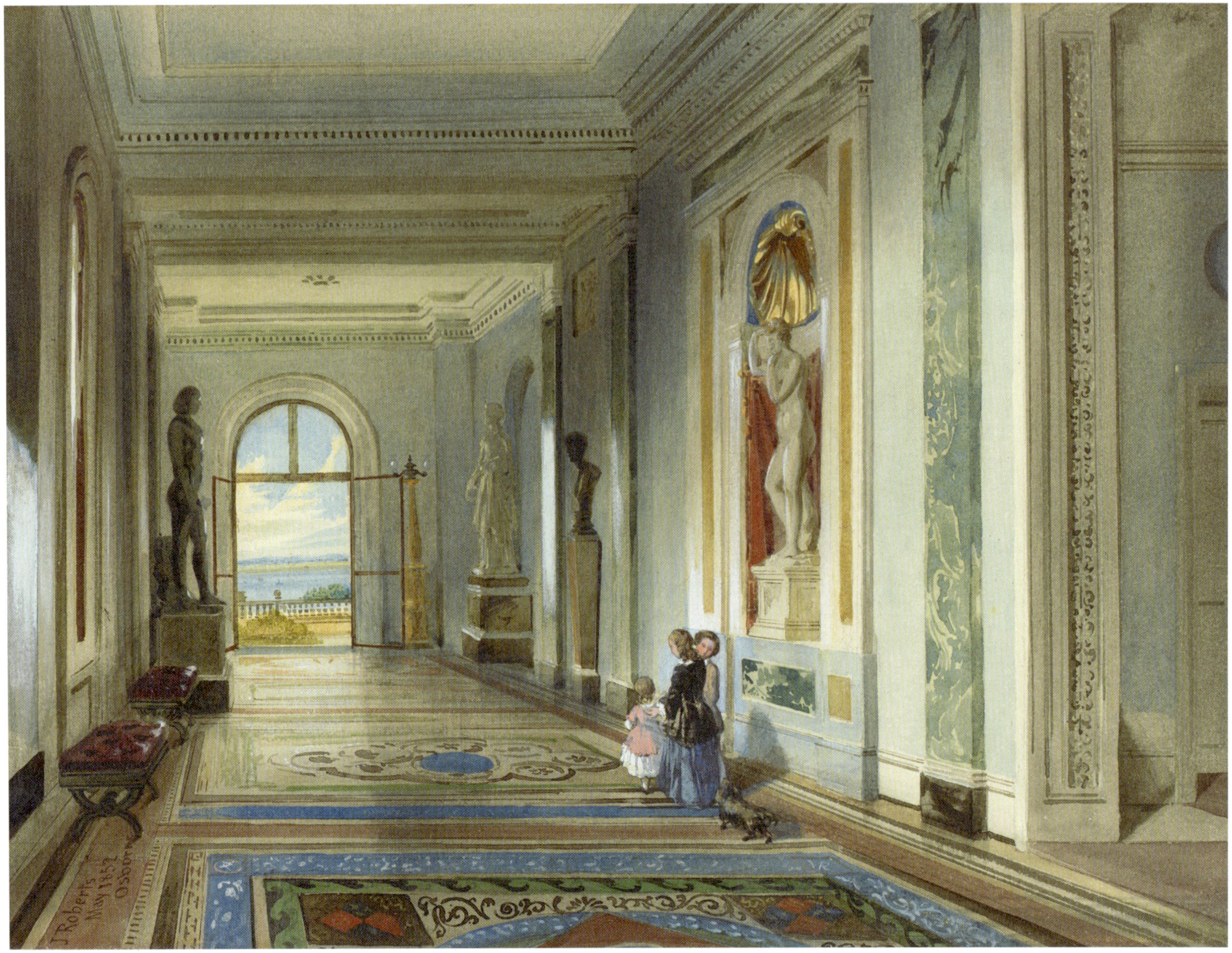
J Roberts
May 1852
Osborne

royal family life but also of interior decorative schemes – recorded here is a picture hang and arrangement of sculpture from the reign of George IV (r.1820–30) which had been changed by late 1847, when Victoria commented that the 'general rearrangement [was] very successful'.[16]

A similar view of the marble corridor at Osborne House (fig. 11) made a few years later shows three children – probably the Princesses Louise (1848–1939) and Alice with their brother Prince Alfred – and a dachshund, one of Victoria's favourite breeds of dog. James Roberts, painter of this watercolour and another interior view specialist, did not usually include figures in the many such scenes he produced for his royal patrons, and it has been argued that the inclusion of the children in this instance may have been a device to give a sense of the large scale of the sculptures in the corridor.[17] The lack of furniture in the corridor may also have demanded figures to break up the space. The detail below shows that the children were painted over the floor pattern, and thus were added later by the artist, probably at the behest of his patrons. The many letters surviving in the Royal Archives between the Queen's dresser Marianne Skerrett (1793–1887), who often liaised with artists on her mistress's behalf, and one of Victoria and Albert's favourite painters, Edwin Landseer, demonstrate that the couple were engaged patrons who frequently gave specific instructions about the subject of a commission, and did not refrain from suggesting compositional alterations when they deemed them necessary.[18] Although Roberts

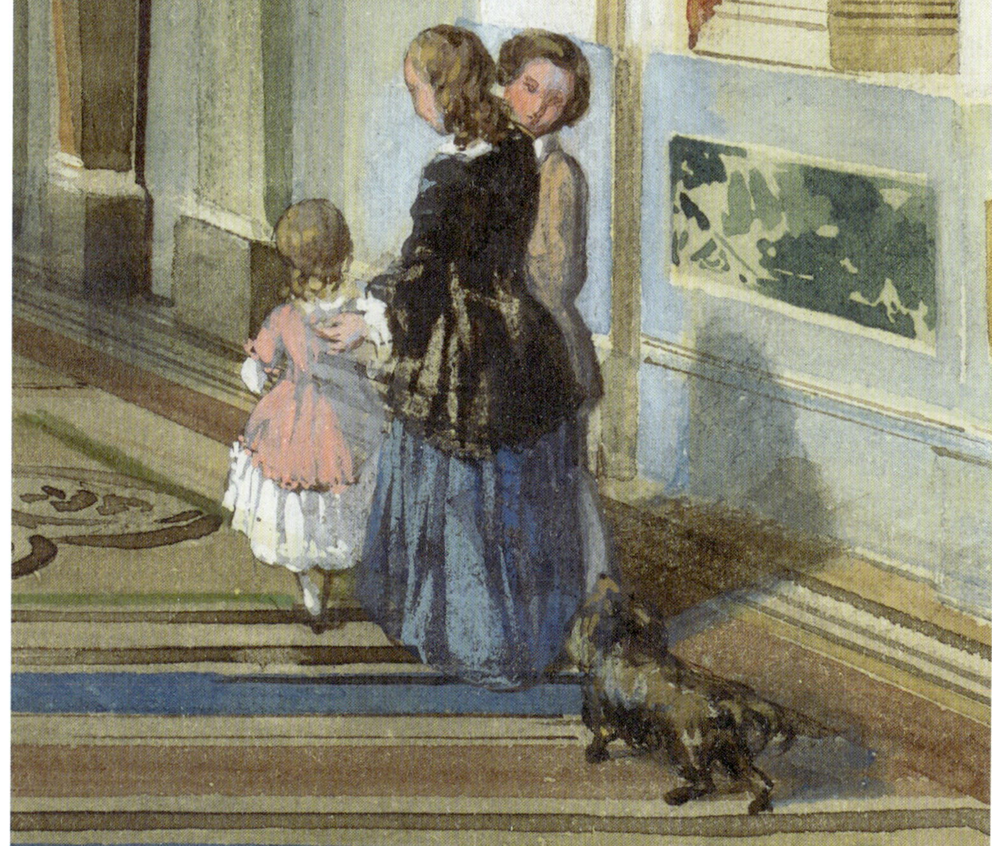

Fig. 11

JAMES ROBERTS (*c.*1800–67)

The Marble Corridor, Osborne House, 1852

Pencil, watercolour and bodycolour, 26.0 × 36.5 cm

RCIN 923463

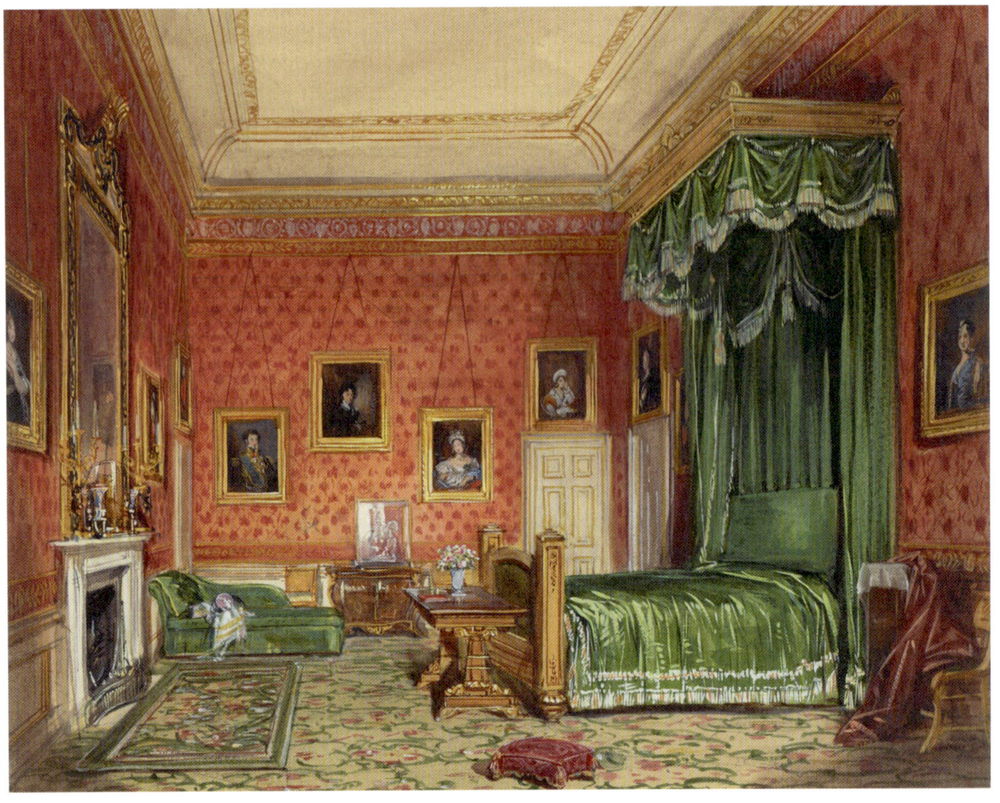

Fig.12

JOSEPH NASH

*Queen Victoria's bedroom, Windsor Castle, c.*1847

Pencil, watercolour and bodycolour with gum arabic, 25.7 × 32.7 cm

RCIN 919810

specified in a list of prices he provided via Skerrett in 1848 that 'complicating' a watercolour with 'figures and family groups' incurred a higher fee (if not doubled it), that does not seem to have been the case for his view of the marble corridor.[19] Roberts was often paid 7 guineas (£7 7s) for his unpopulated interior views for Victoria and Albert, and the most likely payment associated with this work is the £14 paid to Roberts in June 1852 – for two watercolours made at Osborne.[20]

Though unpopulated, Nash's interior view of the royal bedroom at Windsor Castle (fig. 12) still strongly illustrates the importance of family to Victoria and Albert. On 31 March 1847, Victoria wrote in her journal that they had looked at a number of newly rearranged rooms within the private apartments at Windsor: 'our bedroom ... looks very handsome, papered with crimson & gold, & all the portraits, from our former bedroom, are hung up here again.'[21] There are several portraits visible in Nash's watercolour, and using nineteenth-century inventories the full original hang of the room can be recreated, including the works on the fourth wall not depicted here.[22] The portraits in this most private of rooms were of Victoria and Albert's immediate forebears. The largest two on the facing wall were of the Prince's parents, Duke Ernest I of Saxe-Coburg and Gotha (1784–1844) and Duchess Louise (1800–31), and on the opposite wall (unseen in the watercolour) were the Queen's parents, Victoria, Duchess of Kent (and sister of Ernest), and Prince Edward, Duke of Kent (1767–1820). The other especially prominent portraits in the room were depictions of Queen Victoria's favourite uncle, Leopold I, King of the Belgians (1790–1865), his first wife Princess Charlotte (1796–1817, daughter of George IV and heir to the British throne before her death in childbirth), and the couple's grandmother, Augusta of Saxe-Coburg-Saalfeld (1757–1831). The couple's Coburg aunts were the subjects of the remainder of the portraits decorating the room. The majority of these works were copies of paintings in other European collections, ordered by Victoria and Albert from two artists who were used frequently for this type of commission, Herbert Luther Smith (1809–69) and William Corden the Younger (1819–1900). These are mostly dated 1844; it seems likely that the catalyst for the creation of this decorative scheme was the death of Albert's father on 29 January of that year.[23] Victoria and Albert mounted Nash's watercolour of the bedroom in the fourth View Album, and it unsurprisingly remained a private image, not reproduced in *Views* or elsewhere.

The royal children

With their large family, Victoria and Albert kept many artists busy recording the changing appearances, life events and daily activities of the princes and princesses. Often artists were patronised over a period of years, allowing them to develop familiarity with the physical features and personalities of the children – which undoubtedly served them well in pleasing the Queen, for whom a good likeness was paramount.[24] Franz Xaver Winterhalter and Sir William Ross both depicted the growing brood of royal children on many occasions and in diverse forms. Double portraits of the two eldest girls (Vicky and Alice) by Winterhalter (fig. 13) and the two eldest boys (Bertie and Alfred, known as Affie) by Ross (fig. 14) were mounted in a watercolour album that was devoted to portraits of family. In the work by Winterhalter, Vicky and Alice wear the eighteenth-century costumes in which they performed a dance on their mother's birthday on 24 May 1850 – a surprise organised by Prince Albert. The Queen's delight on the occasion, clearly expressed in her journal, is also demonstrated by the rapid commissioning (by either her or Albert) of this souvenir from

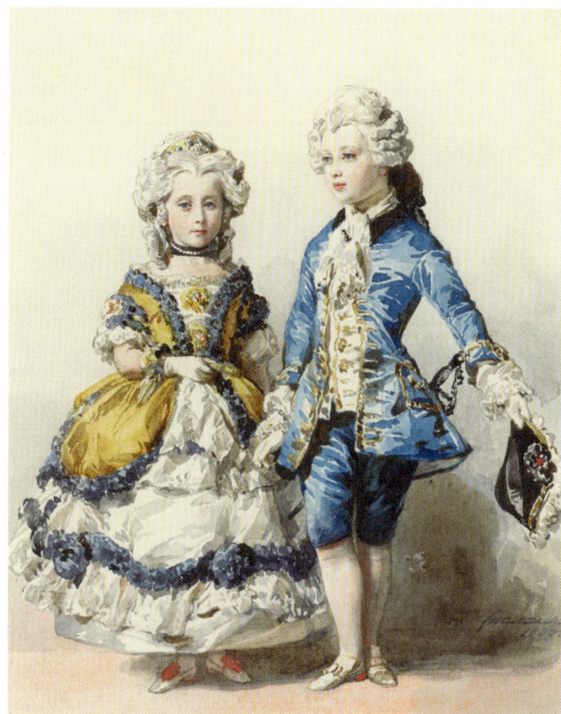

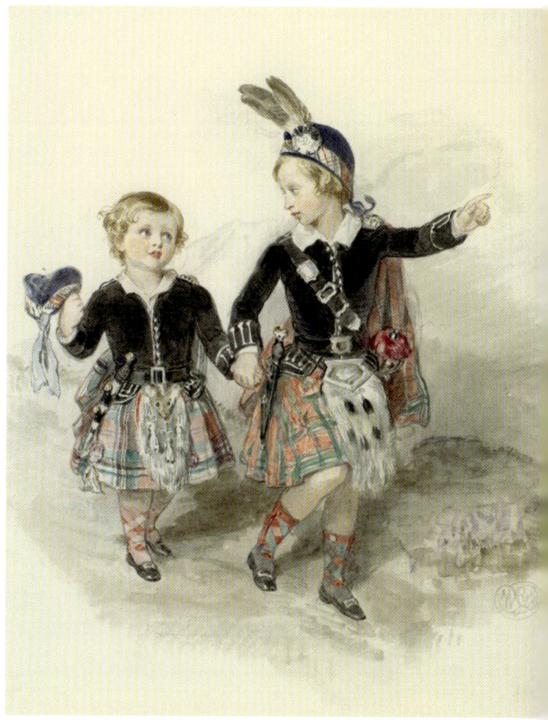

Fig. 13 (above left)

FRANZ XAVER WINTERHALTER

Victoria, Princess Royal, and Princess Alice in eighteenth-century costume, 1850

Pencil, watercolour and bodycolour, 28.8 × 23.8 cm

RCIN 913335

Fig. 14 (above right)

SIR WILLIAM ROSS (1794–1860)

Albert Edward, Prince of Wales, and Prince Alfred, 1847

Watercolour, 25.8 × 21.1 cm

RCIN 913818

'… he [Haghe] is one of the boldest of our water-colour painters, the most powerful in his effects of light and shade, and in his combination of figures and architecture.'

– Tom Taylor

Winterhalter. He had finished the watercolour by 23 July, when Victoria described it as 'such a beautiful sketch'.[25] When added to the portrait album it joined two watercolours by Louis Haghe of Victoria and Albert in the eighteenth-century costumes they themselves had worn to a Buckingham Palace ball in 1845.[26]

Ross's double portrait of Bertie and Affie does not record a specific moment in the same way as the Winterhalter, but it does reflect Victoria's growing love for Scotland, which she first visited in 1842. This watercolour was lithographed by Thomas Fairland (1804–52), and Eleanor Stanley, a maid of honour, recorded that the ladies and gentlemen of the royal household were given an impression of the print as a Christmas present from Victoria and Albert in 1847, though she thought that the boys had 'hardly [been] done justice to' by Ross.[27] Repeated commissions clearly allowed a rapport to develop between some artists and their royal subjects. Writing to her mother after Ross's death in 1860, Vicky (who had married and left home two years previously), remembered the artist as 'such a good kind simple hearted old man … I shall never forget his funny voice and ways.'[28]

Some of the watercolours commissioned by Victoria and Albert for their albums combined multiple functions, such as *The banquet for Prince Leopold's christening* by Louis Haghe and *The children's costume ball at Buckingham Palace* by Eugenio Agneni. In both cases, the watercolours simultaneously record a family milestone, a court function and interior decoration schemes in Buckingham Palace that no longer survive.

Louis Haghe was a much-favoured artist, commissioned by both Victoria and Albert to paint a wide variety of events and occasions. Born in the Low Countries, he spent much of his career in England, first working as a printmaker and then concentrating on watercolour painting as a founder member and later president of the New Watercolour Society.[29] In both fields he was highly esteemed by the critical establishment. Writing about his watercolours shown at the 1857 Art Treasures exhibition at Manchester, the journalist Tom Taylor (1817–80) declared that had Haghe 'lived in the days of Rubens, he might have been one of the greatest of his scholars. As it is, he is one of the boldest of our water-colour painters, the most powerful in his effects of light and shade, and in his combination of figures and architecture.'[30] Queen Victoria particularly noticed his works at some New Watercolour Society exhibitions, and during her visit to the Manchester exhibition it was reported that she expressed 'a most marked and gracious expression of approbation' on seeing a watercolour by Haghe of the exhibition's opening ceremony (fig. 15), over which Prince Albert had presided.[31] She purchased the watercolour in question some thirty years later.[32]

The choice of viewpoint in Haghe's depiction of the banquet held to celebrate Prince Leopold's christening (fig. 16) is somewhat unusual, in that it makes the servants in attendance the most prominent figures in the composition, rather than Victoria and Albert or any of their guests. However, the magnificent long banquet table stretching off into the distance, decorated

Fig. 15

LOUIS HAGHE (1806–85)

Prince Albert at the opening of the Manchester Art Treasures exhibition, 1857

Pencil, watercolour and bodycolour, 76.2 × 105.8 cm

RCIN 921500

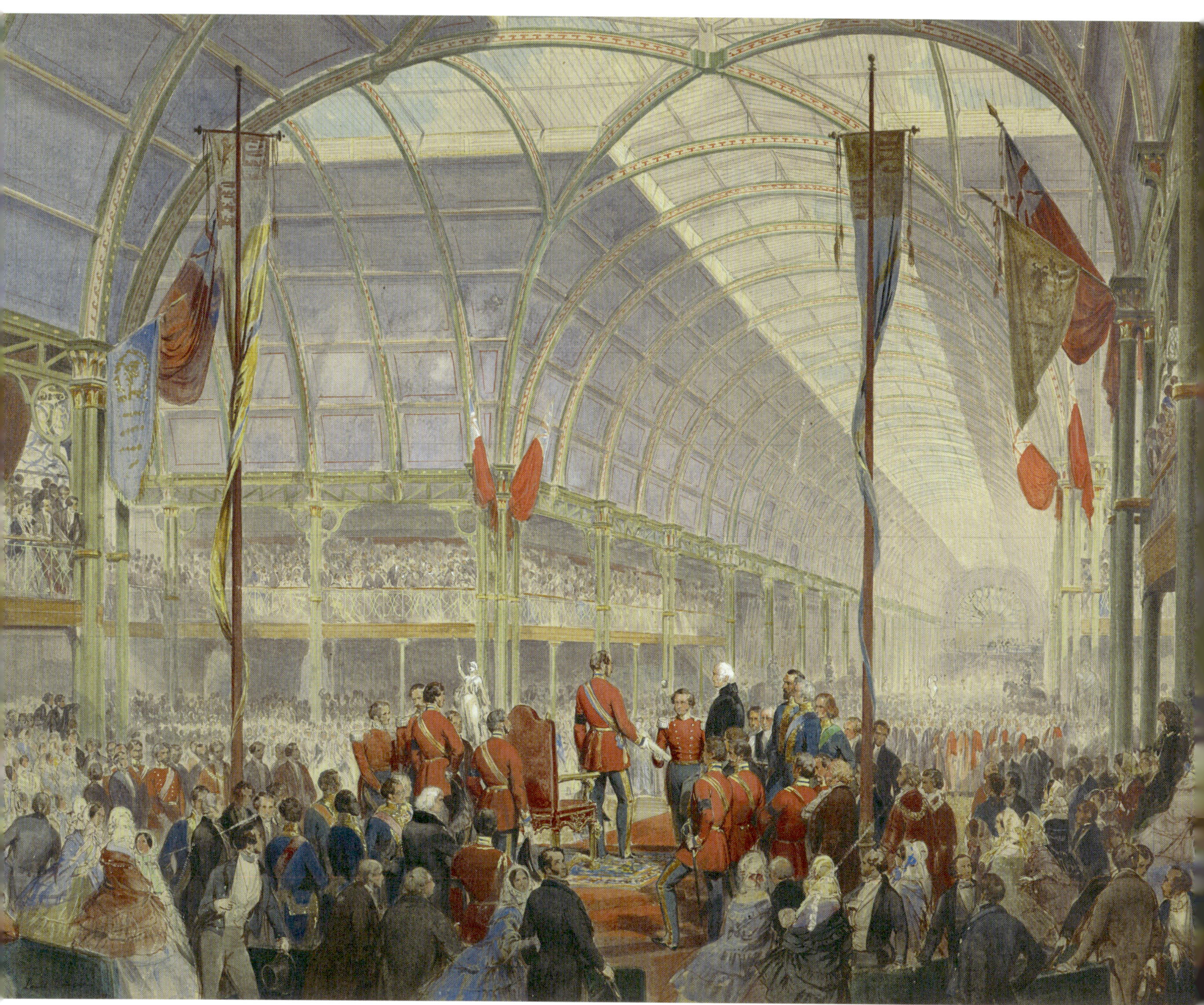

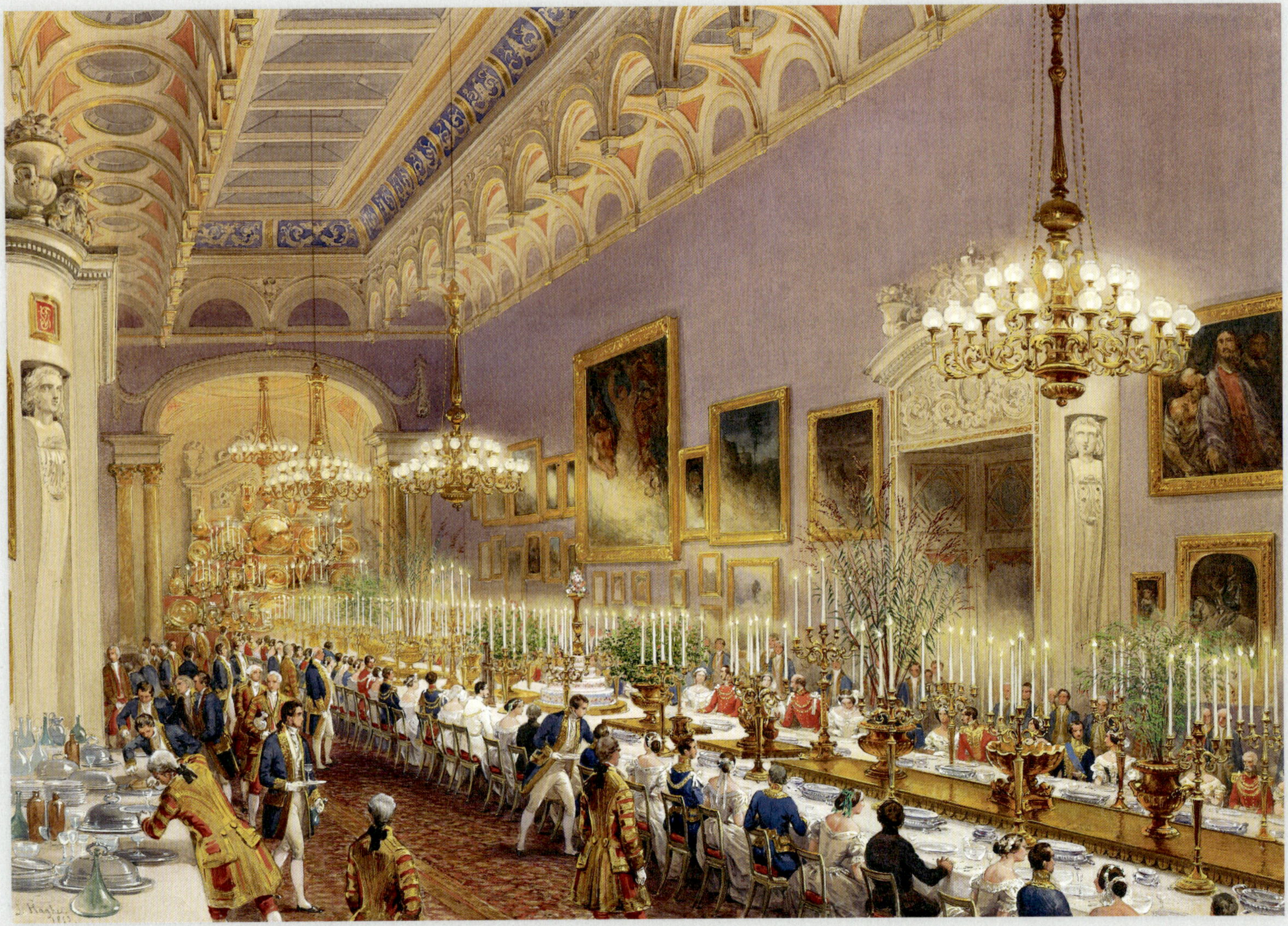

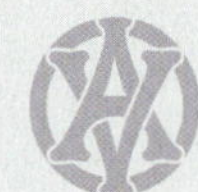

with hundreds of candles, flowers and silver, with a further grand display of silver at the far end of the Picture Gallery, is undoubtedly as important as the guests in the picture. The inclusion of a significant number of royal servants, and the attention paid to their splendid livery and assiduousness in carrying out their tasks, also contributes to the overall impression of the magnificence of the occasion. At both the christening banquet and the children's ball it is likely that the artists were designated a position from which to observe and sketch the action, which would have played a role in determining their compositions – though the finished watercolours presented to their patrons were not those made on the spot, but would have been worked up in the studio from a number of different sketches. Whether certain artistic choices were made by the artist or the patrons is in many cases unknown, but Victoria and Albert were certainly shown works in progress, giving them the opportunity to offer their opinions and propose alterations.[33]

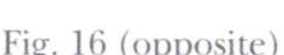

Fig. 16 (opposite)

LOUIS HAGHE

The banquet for Prince Leopold's christening, 1853

Pencil, watercolour and bodycolour, 33.0 × 47.4 cm

RCIN 919917

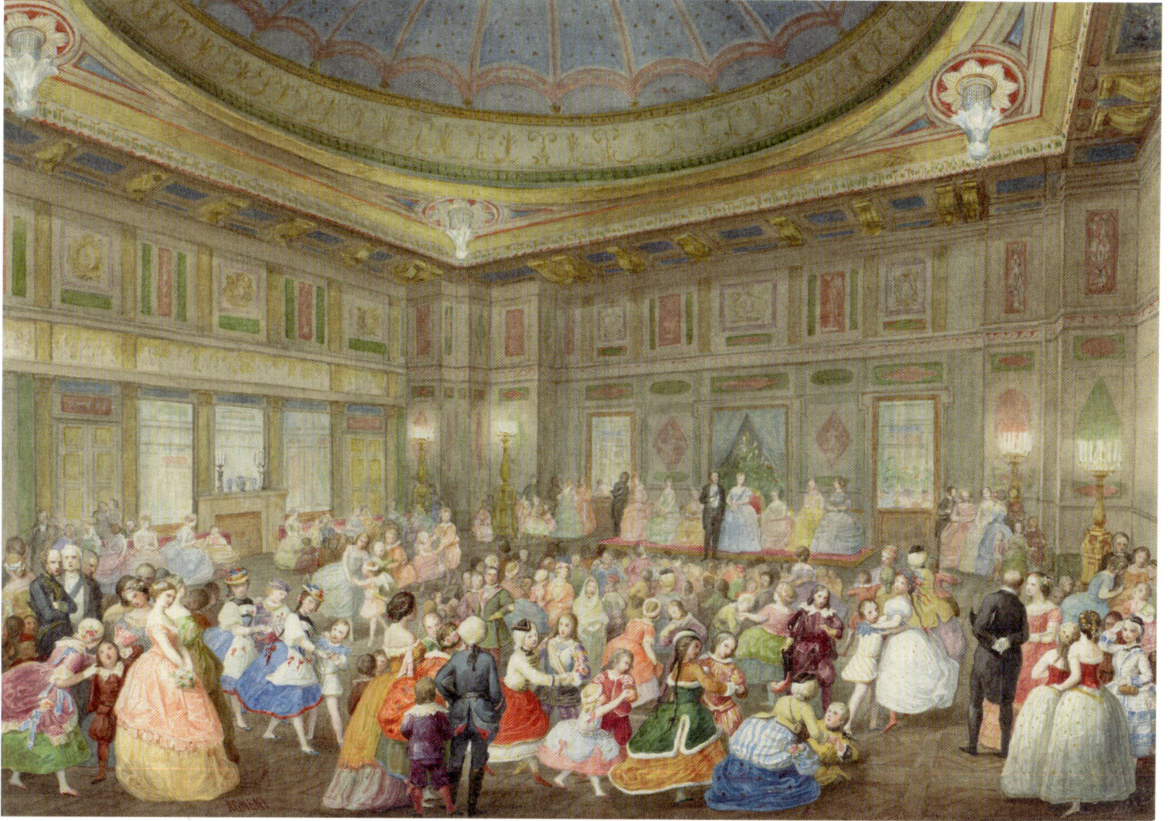

Fig. 17 (right)

EUGENIO AGNENI (1816–79)

The children's costume ball at Buckingham Palace, 1859

Pencil and watercolour, 31.0 × 45.0 cm

RCIN 919909

Although Haghe, like Nash and Roberts, was patronised extensively by Victoria and Albert, there were instances when an artist's services were engaged only once – as was the case with Eugenio Agneni. He presumably came to royal attention in 1858 through the mythological scenes he painted in the Queen's Room in the newly rebuilt opera house at Covent Garden, during a stay of a few years in England.[34] His watercolour of the juvenile ball held in 1859 in the Ball Supper Room at Buckingham Palace (fig. 17) to celebrate the sixth birthday of Leopold, the youngest prince, and also attended by four of his siblings (the Princesses Alice, Louise and Helena and Prince Arthur) as well as their parents, is lively and brightly coloured – an especially fitting record of a type of event which Agneni's patron Victoria enjoyed 'thoroughly … look[ing] as happy as any one of the children', according to Prince Arthur's tutor Major Howard Elphinstone (1829–90).[35] Additionally, as demonstrated by comparison with photographs taken of the royal children in their outfits a week or so after the ball (fig. 18), Agneni successfully captured the details of the costumes worn by the attendees.[36] Again, in this watercolour the royal children are not the central subjects of the composition – Louise and Helena (in dresses with blue skirts) dance with Arthur and Leopold over to the left. Victoria made no comment about either the watercolour or the artist in her journal, but one possible reason for Agneni not gaining any further commissions – especially given that he solicited more in a letter to Marianne Skerrett – may be the artist's connections with the revolutionary movement in Italy.[37] The first two decades of the Queen's reign were punctuated by revolutions against continental monarchies, to many of

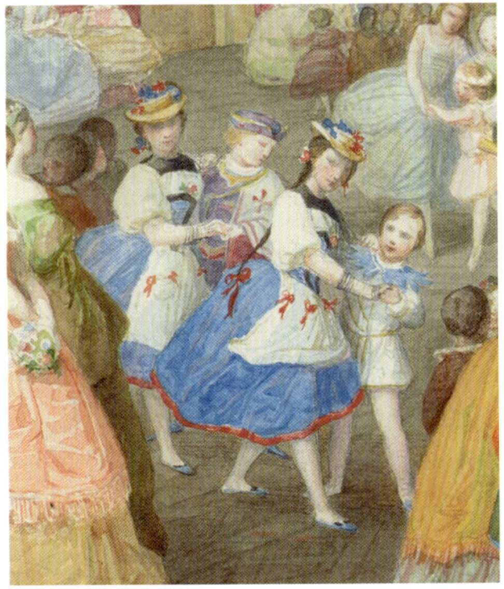

Fig. 17 (detail)

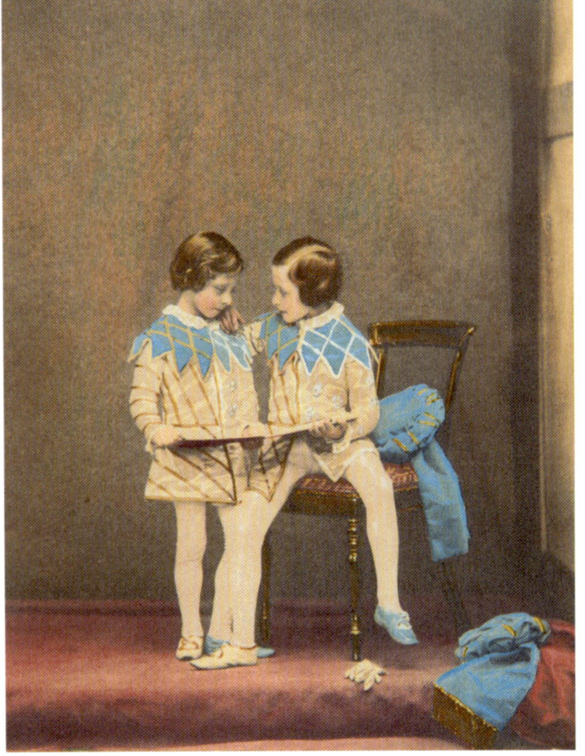

Fig. 18

LEONIDA CALDESI (1823–91)

Prince Leopold and Prince Arthur in the costume of the sons of King Henry IVth, 1859

Hand-coloured albumen print, 10.3 × 8.1 cm

RCIN 2914286

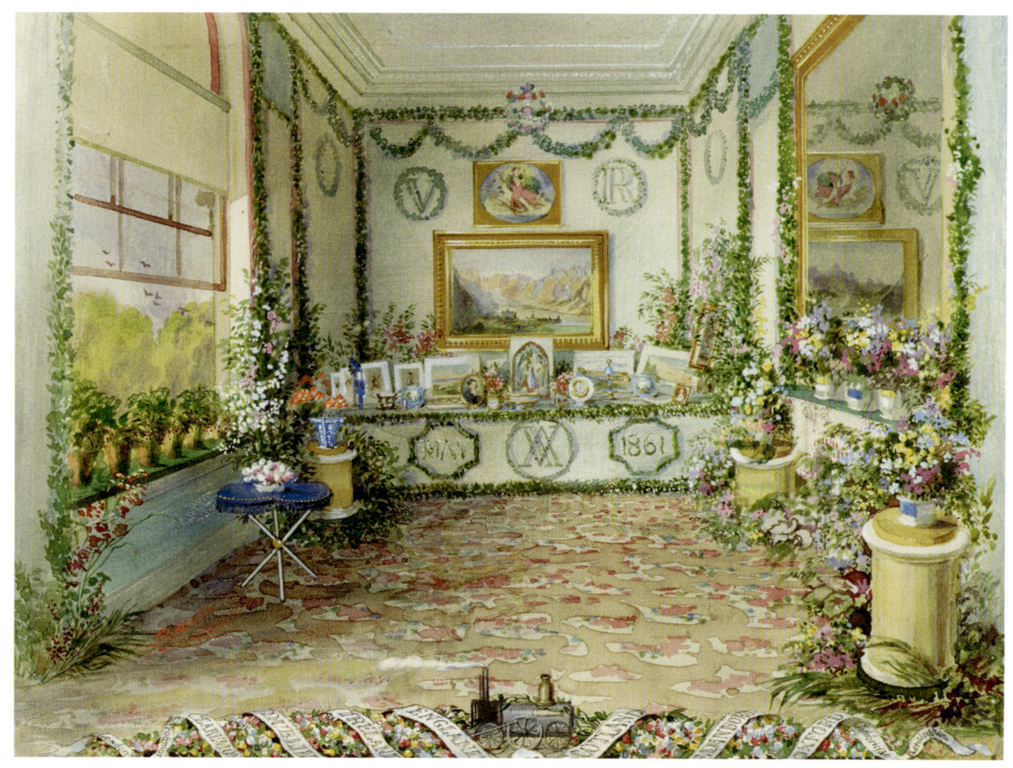

Fig. 19

JAMES ROBERTS

Queen Victoria's birthday table at Osborne House, 1861

Pencil, watercolour and bodycolour, 18.3 × 24.5 cm

RCIN 919874

which Victoria and Albert were connected by familial ties. Agneni himself admitted to a correspondent that he had inserted a political joke into his commission for the Queen; the two children in the right foreground who have taken a tumble to the floor are the son and daughter of the Austrian ambassador, Rudolf Graf Apponyi (1812–76), and it was the Austrian Empire, which ruled Northern Italy, that the Italian revolutionaries were fighting.[38]

Christmas and birthdays

From 1848 Queen Victoria spent almost every birthday (24 May) at Osborne House, where the royal family observed a tradition which had begun in her childhood. This was the birthday table, arranged with presents and flowers, which by the second decade of her married life incorporated more and more elaborate decorations. Although Agneni's watercolour of the juvenile ball was the only representation of a royal birthday party in the View Albums, six watercolours recording these temporary displays were included in them. James Roberts was commissioned to paint ten representations of these tables for the Queen from 1851 to 1861, the first seven of which she interleaved into the pages of her journal.[39] The birthday tables were only ever photographed, and never again painted, after Albert's death.[40]

The last watercolour that Roberts painted of Victoria's birthday table (fig. 19) includes a unique decorative feature – a frieze running along the bottom of the work, comprising a depiction of a small train surrounded by flowers garlanded with a ribbon, on which the names of cities, towns and royal residences are inscribed. The mood of the watercolour, with its bright colouring, the abundance of flowers and the window to the left opening out onto a sunny blue sky, is apparently spring-like and light-hearted.[41] However, Victoria felt strongly

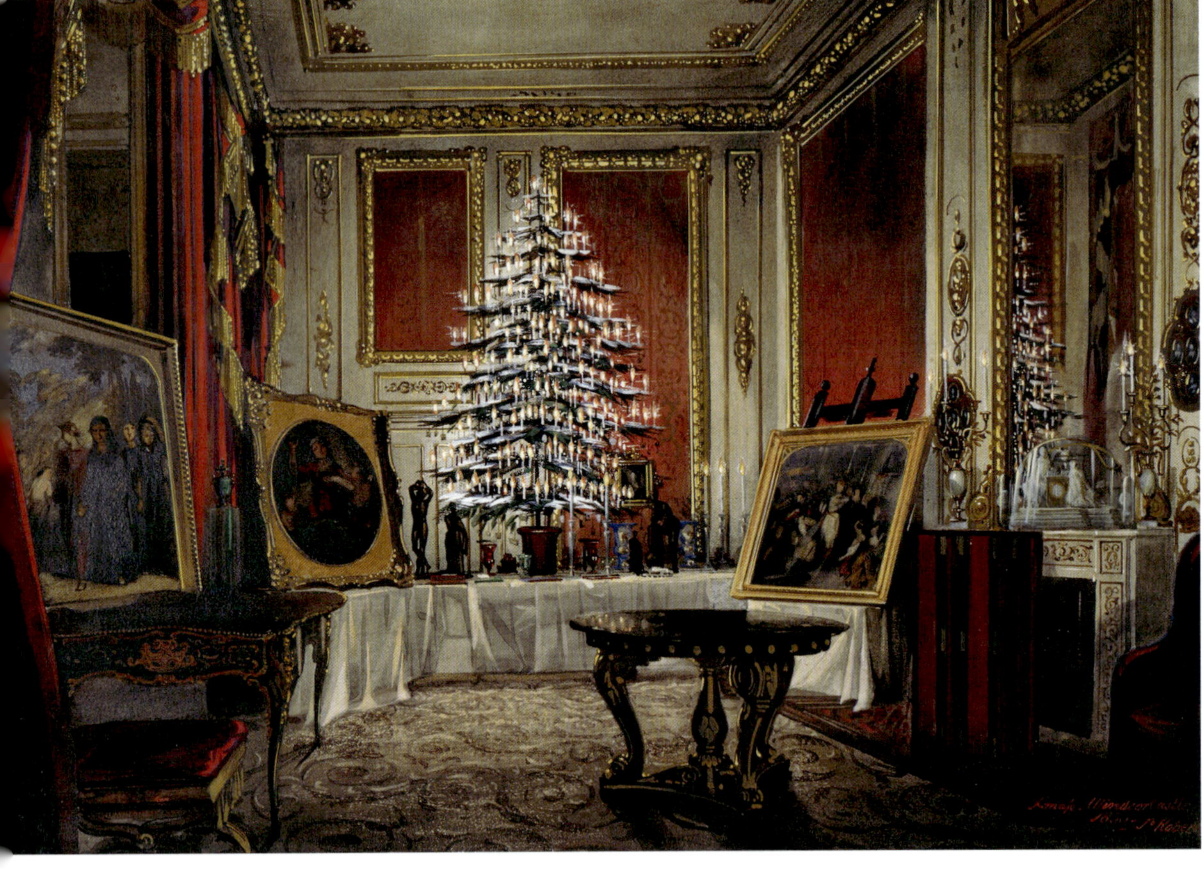

'Today I have two children of my own to give presents to, who, they know not why, are full of happy wonder at the German Christmas-tree and its radiant candles.'

– Prince Albert

Fig. 20

JAMES ROBERTS

Queen Victoria's Christmas tree at Windsor Castle, 1850

Watercolour and bodycolour, 26.5 × 38.6 cm

RCIN 919812

that her birthday was overshadowed by the recent loss of her mother, the Duchess of Kent, who was represented on the birthday table through gifts of two watercolours that she had commissioned before her death, and visually in a small copy of her portrait by Winterhalter, ordered by Prince Albert.[42] The three royal residences inscribed on the flower and ribbon garland all had particular associations with the Duchess, and perhaps, therefore, there is an element of memorialisation in the inclusion of this detail.[43]

Joseph Nash had painted some birthday table views in the 1840s, and it may have been for reasons of economy that the commission was shifted from Nash to Roberts, whose prices were around half those of his peer.[44] Perhaps for the same reason Roberts supplanted Nash in a commission to record the Christmas tables of the royal family in 1850, which Nash had previously painted in 1845.[45] Again, Victoria and Albert maintained a tradition from their own childhoods in preparing display tables of presents, each surmounted by a small Christmas tree. Prince Albert, writing somewhat wistfully to his father on Christmas Eve 1841, remembered his own childhood and noted, 'Today I have two children of my own to give presents to, who, they know not why, are full of happy wonder at the German Christmas-tree and its radiant candles.'[46] Some years later, a maid of honour remarked that she had never seen 'anything prettier than the whole arrangement' of the Christmas tree tables.[47] Presents were exchanged on Christmas Eve, and Victoria's journal entries for that day often refer to her and Albert arranging the tables. On Christmas Eve 1850 the Queen recorded that the family assembled 'a little after 6 … & my beloved Albert 1st took me to my tree & table, covered by such numberless gifts, really too much, too magnificent … The 7 Children were then taken to their tree, jumping & shouting with joy over their toys & other presents … Mama had her tree & table in the same room, & Albert his, in the 3rd last room.'[48] Roberts was paid for three watercolours – presumably showing the tables and trees in the three rooms – but only two survive, which illustrate Victoria's table (fig. 20) and those of her mother and children. As with the watercolours of the birthday tables, it is possible to distinguish the works of art given by Prince Albert to his wife on this occasion – including the particularly personal gift of a watercolour he commissioned from Edward Corbould illustrating Victoria's favourite scene from the opera *Le Prophète* (seen in the right foreground). Corbould's watercolour was framed and around three times the size of the works by Roberts commissioned for the View Albums, but it was also more than ten times the price.[49]

'The privacy of domestic life' – Osborne and Balmoral[50]

On 17 October 1844, Queen Victoria wrote to her uncle Leopold from Osborne House (which she and Prince Albert were then leasing), describing it as 'delightful, so private'. Five months later, she confided the news that they had purchased the estate: 'You will, I am sure, be pleased to hear that we have succeeded in purchasing Osborne in the Isle of Wight … It sounds so snug and nice to have a place of one's own, quiet and retired.'[51] Osborne was chosen for a family home in preference to Brighton Pavilion, which had been built for George IV. Though Victoria and Albert enjoyed staying at the Pavilion in the first few years of their marriage, the expanding size of Brighton had ramifications for their privacy; as the Queen noted in her journal at the beginning of 1845, the 'publicity' of the town was 'disagreeable'.[52] Osborne had all the benefits of Brighton – its clean air and proximity to the sea – but with the seclusion from the public that the royal family craved, as well as a greater separation from the political centre of London.

Although initially Victoria wrote of the improvements that Albert had planned for the existing Osborne House, by 15 May 1845 she was referring to the building of 'the new house' due to begin the next day. Prince Albert played a leading role in designing and superintending the construction of the new Italianate villa, which was completed in 1851.[53] It is not surprising, therefore, that the royal couple included two watercolours in the fourth View Album which documented stages of the building of their 'sweet seaside home', as Victoria called it. Her maid of honour, Eleanor Stanley, wrote to her father from Osborne in 1852 that she could well understand Victoria and Albert's love of the house 'so entirely of their own creation'.[54]

The Queen's watercolour tutor, William Leighton Leitch, painted many views of Osborne. Leitch's name occurs frequently in Victoria's journal and, as was usual for nineteenth-century landscape artists, he travelled on command both to teach and to execute commissions – a lifestyle illustrated by the character of Walter Hartright in *The Woman in White*, the 1859 novel by Wilkie Collins (1824–89). The frequency of his visits to Osborne afforded Leitch the opportunity to observe the building of the new home closely. Of the two watercolours documenting the evolution of Osborne House that were pasted into the View Album, one shows work in progress on the main wing and the terraces (fig. 21), while the other, probably slightly later, depicts the view from the terrace (fig. 22), then in the process of being laid. The picturesquely arranged stone building slabs, presumably soon to be utilised to complete the unfinished part of the terrace in the right foreground, are the focal point of the latter composition. The presence of these slabs dates the view to a specific point in the building of Osborne, but also alludes to the dominance of man over nature in a scene that is otherwise suffused with a timeless quality. This watercolour is attributed jointly to Leitch and another of his pupils, the Queen's

Fig. 21

WILLIAM LEIGHTON LEITCH

Osborne House under construction, *c*.1847

Pencil, watercolour and bodycolour, 10.6 × 21.4 cm

RCIN 919842

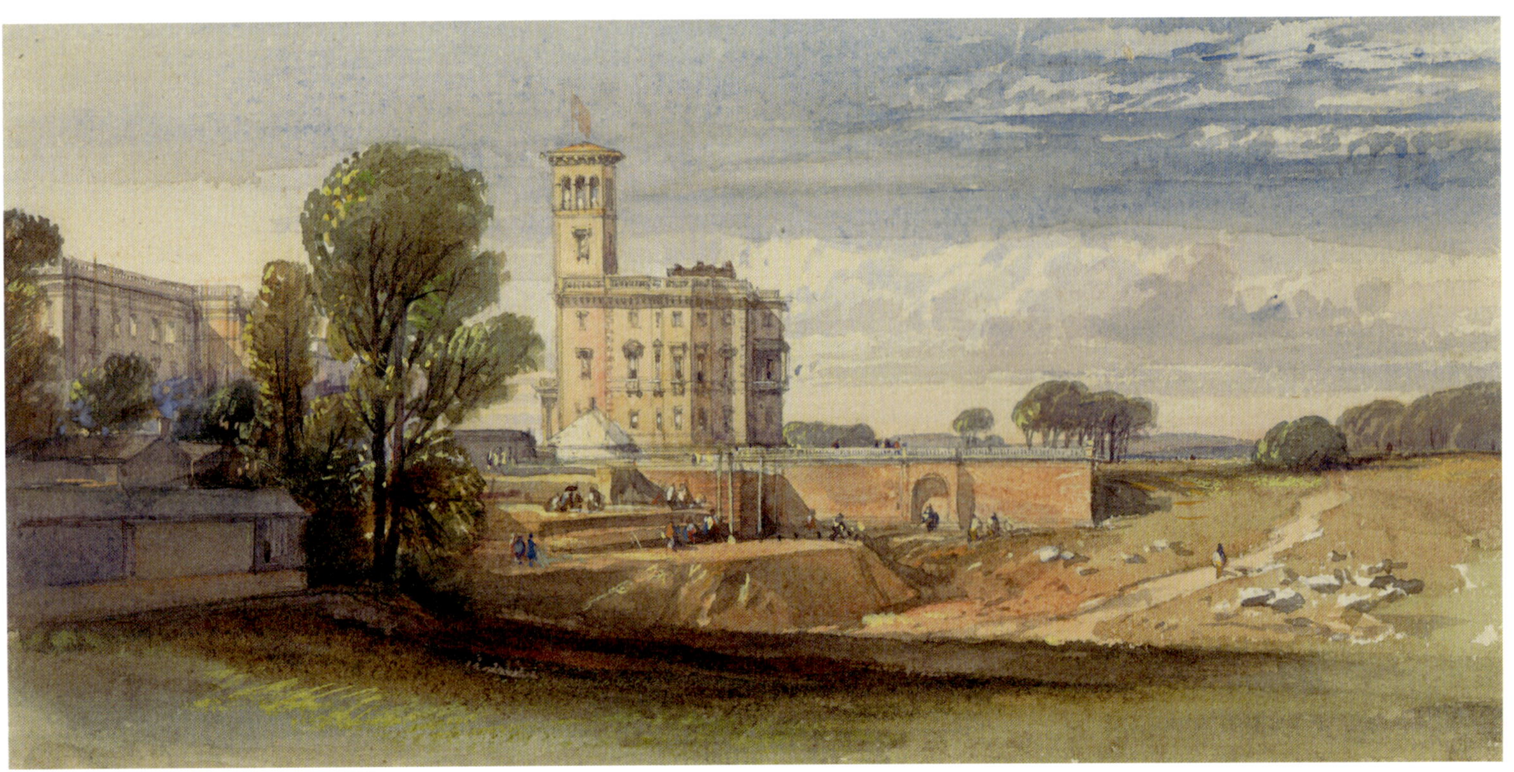

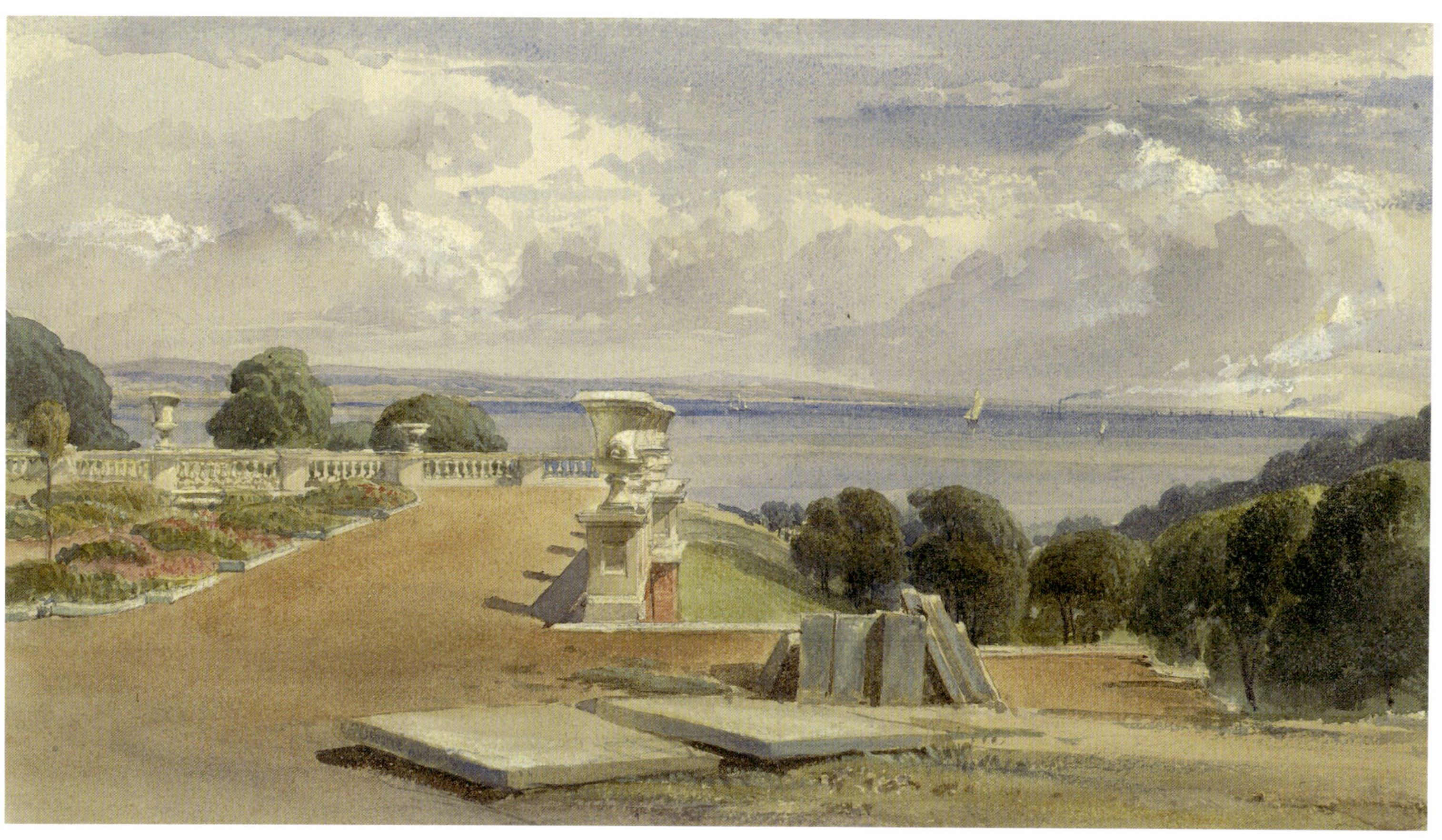

Fig. 22

WILLIAM LEIGHTON LEITCH
and CHARLOTTE CANNING (1817–61)

*The view from the unfinished terrace, Osborne House, c.*1848

Pencil, watercolour and bodycolour, 18.9 × 34.4 cm

RCIN 919848

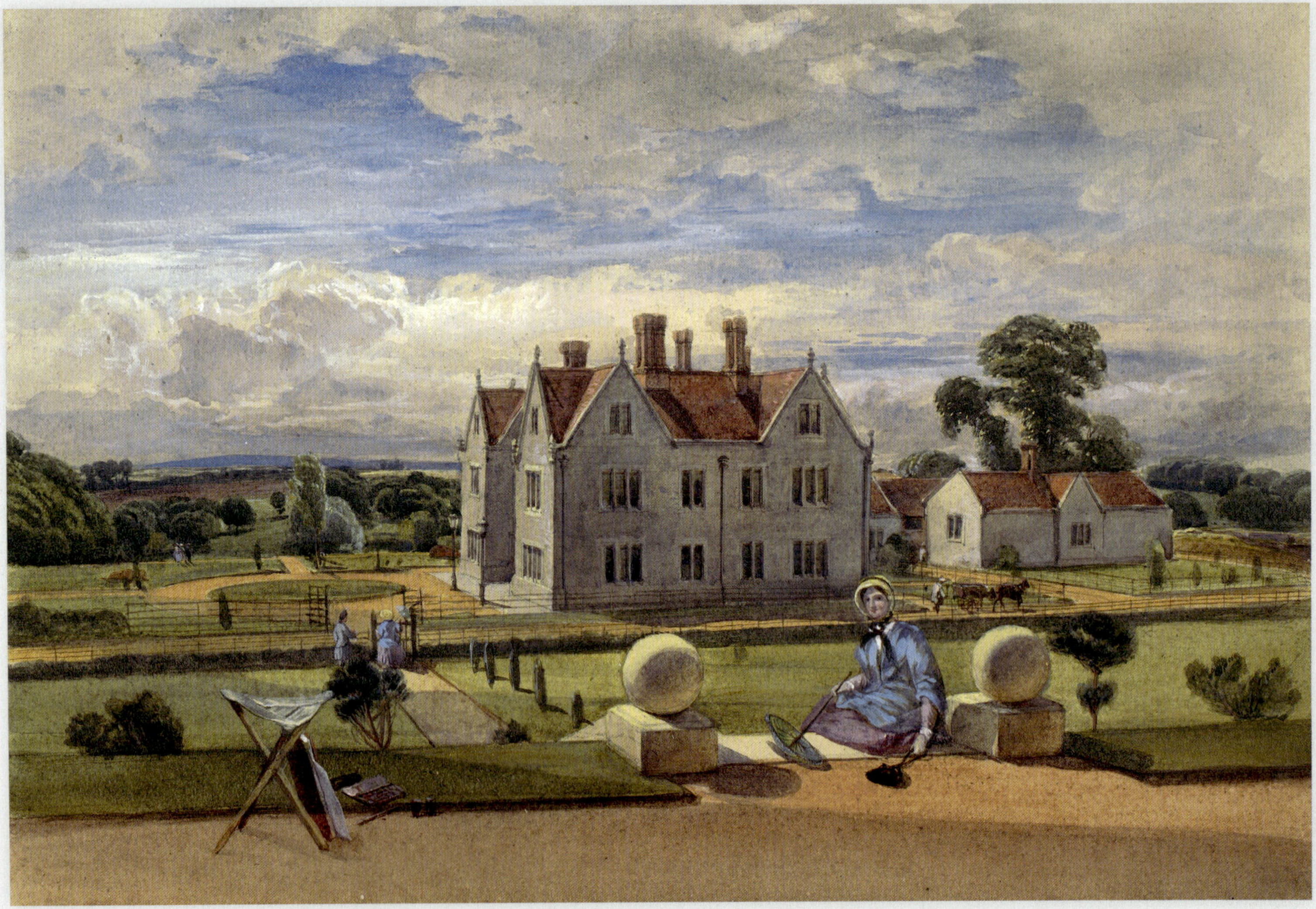

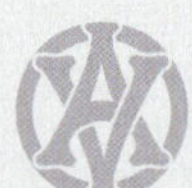

Fig. 23

WILLIAM LEIGHTON LEITCH

Barton Farm, Osborne, *c.*1850

Pencil, watercolour and bodycolour, 30.8 × 46.0 cm

RCIN 919878

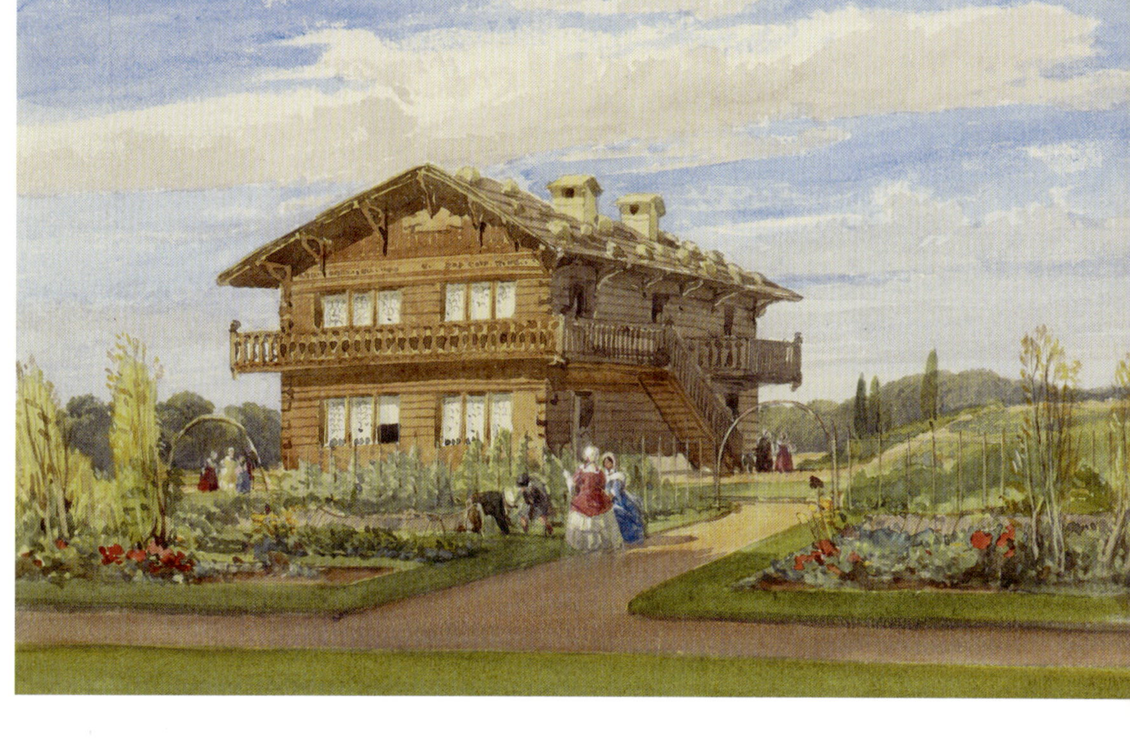

Fig. 24

WILLIAM LEIGHTON LEITCH

The Swiss Cottage, Osborne, 1855

Pencil, watercolour and bodycolour, 19.7 × 27.8 cm

RCIN 919867

lady-in-waiting Charlotte Canning. It was therefore probably made during a lesson, Leitch assisting with elements of the composition – the perspective, perhaps – and colouring. Many of Lady Canning's very accomplished watercolours were commissioned or requested by Victoria for her View Albums (see pp. 50 and 98).

A later view made at Osborne by Leitch explicitly refers to the purpose of his visits there. It depicts a scene at Barton Farm on the estate and was probably worked up from a sketch captured while he was giving the Queen a lesson (fig. 23). In the left foreground are painting materials at the foot of an abandoned stool being watched over by a lady-in-waiting; in the distance, Victoria, in a bonnet and holding a parasol, is being escorted towards the farm building by a man in Highland dress. This watercolour, mounted in the fifth View Album, alludes to the informal nature of the royal family's sojourns on the Isle of Wight, as does another work by Leitch from a later album of the Swiss Cottage (fig. 24), a wooden chalet built for – and partially by – the royal children. In 1848 Eleanor Stanley recorded a domestic scene she witnessed at Osborne House: 'yesterday evening, [the children], assisted by their august Papa, and sanctioned by the presence of their royal Mama, who was looking on, washed a basketful of potatoes, and shelled a ditto of peas, which they are to cook for themselves today if they are good.'[55] With the creation of the Swiss Cottage a few years later, the princes and princesses were given their own space to play, experience aspects of adult life and learn useful skills – for example, they grew their own vegetables, learned to cook and sew and developed their own museum. In Leitch's view, one of the princes is shown working in the garden alongside (presumably) a gardener, and the bright blue sky common to all of his representations of scenes of Osborne reflects the accounts of the Queen and her ladies of the pleasant weather there.

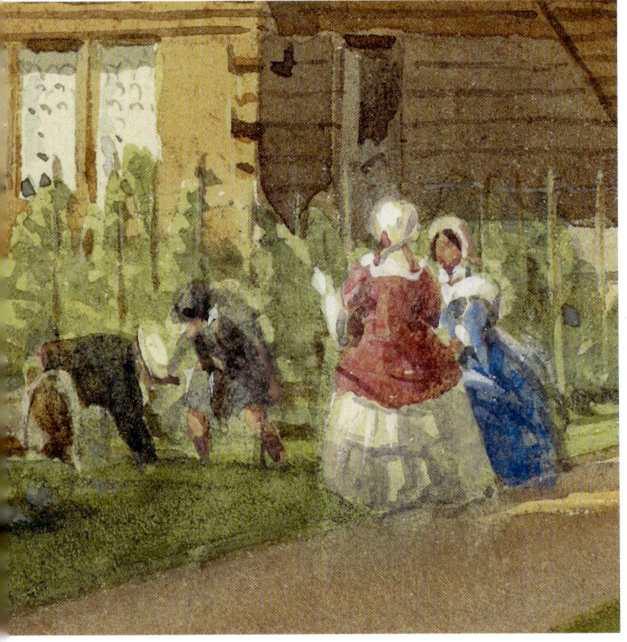

Fig. 24 (detail)

Less clement weather did not prevent Balmoral Castle, the other private residence Victoria and Albert built, becoming equally – if not more – beloved by its two primary inhabitants, though many members of the court and government did not share their appreciation: Lord Salisbury (1830–1903), the Queen's last prime minister, nicknamed Balmoral 'Siberia'.[56] Having visited Scotland several times in the 1840s, Albert purchased the lease to the estate of Balmoral in Aberdeenshire in 1848 purely based on watercolours by James Giles (1801–70), a Scottish landscape artist whose work Victoria and Albert came to admire greatly. As with Osborne, the Queen and Prince decided to replace the existing house with something larger and, after buying the estate outright in 1852, had a castle erected in the Scottish Baronial style.[57] On their last day in the Highlands that year (11 October), a ceremony was held to mark royal possession of Balmoral – the building of a cairn on Craigowan. Present on this occasion was William Wyld, a British-born but French-based artist. Victoria and Albert knew his work well by the autumn of 1852; Wyld had worked for their aunt and close friend Louise, Queen of the Belgians (1812–50), in the 1840s, but more pertinently had painted and been paid for two watercolours commissioned for the View Albums in April 1852.[58] The duration of Wyld's invitation to Balmoral does not appear to have been fixed from the outset, according to Wyld himself, who wrote to a correspondent on 25 September, twelve days after his arrival, that he saw 'no chance of my getting away – I hardly expect I shall leave before the Court leaves.'[59] As the two watercolours he painted of the ceremony of the cairn attest, he did remain there till the end of the royal stay.

> *'Yesterday evening, [the children], assisted by their august Papa, and sanctioned by the presence of their royal Mama, who was looking on, washed a basketful of potatoes, and shelled a ditto of peas, which they are to cook for themselves today if they are good.'*
>
> – Eleanor Stanley

Queen Victoria wrote a detailed description of the building of the cairn in her journal, which her tenants and servants attended:

> *I placed a stone first, then Albert, the children each according to their ages, the Ladies & Gentlemen, & then every body present came with a stone in their hand, which they placed. McKay played [the bagpipes] & whiskey was served round to all … It was a gay pretty sight … At the last, when the cairn, which I should say was 7 or 8 ft. high, was completed, Albert climbed up to the top of it & placed the last stones, after which 3 cheers were given.*[60]

Wyld's first watercolour (fig. 25) shows the Queen, dressed in a Highland-inspired outfit of a checked skirt and plaid shawl, being handed the first stone to place on the spot, with Prince Albert, and some of the princes (in kilts) and princesses looking on. The second watercolour (fig. 26) captures the scene after Albert added the final stone, with those present celebrating the completion of the cairn. Wyld inscribed this watercolour 'One Cheer more!'

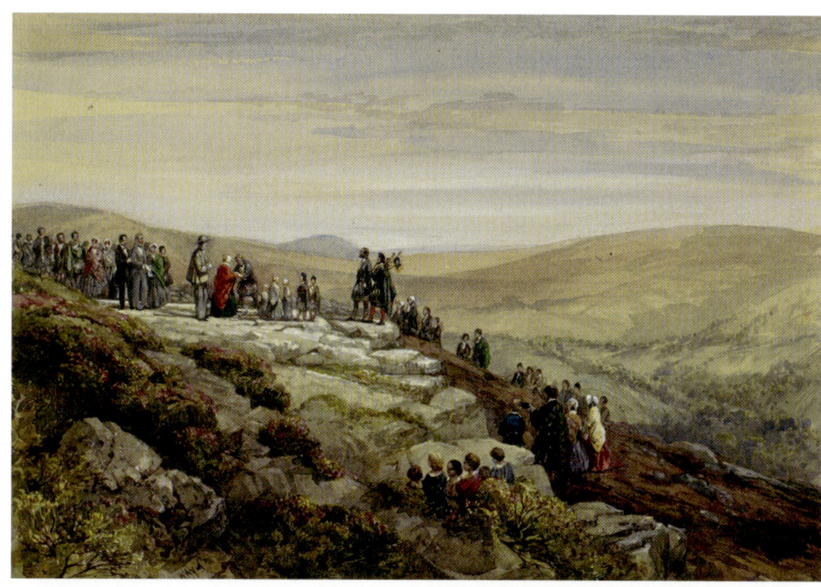

Fig. 25 (above right)

WILLIAM WYLD (1806–89)

The placing of the first stone of the cairn on Craigowan, 1852

Pencil, watercolour and bodycolour, 22.8 × 35.0 cm

RCIN 919482

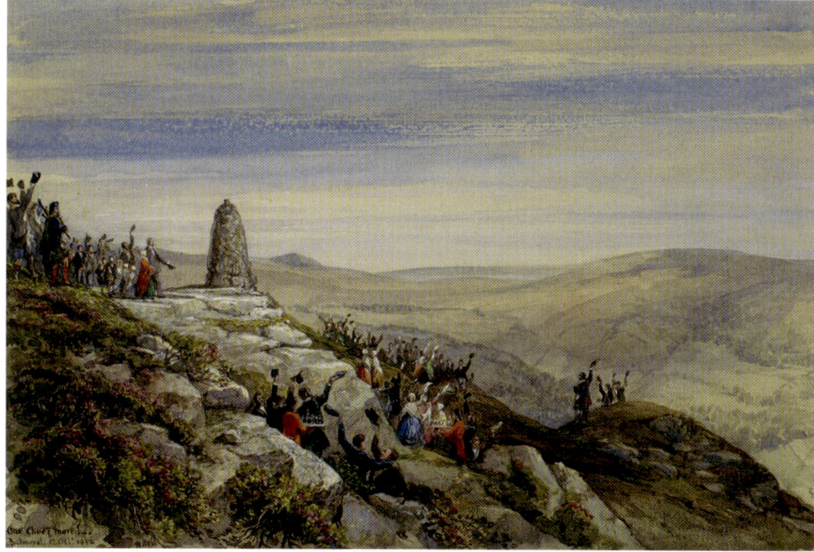

Fig. 26 (right)

WILLIAM WYLD

The completion of the cairn on Craigowan, 12 October 1852

Pencil, watercolour and bodycolour, 22.0 × 35.0 cm

RCIN 919483

While at Balmoral Wyld worked particularly hard (twelve hours a day by his own account), 'wishing to give the Queen satisfaction'. Though he intimated to his correspondent that Victoria was a demanding patron, wanting 'something fresh every day', he characterised his contact with her as surprisingly informal and friendly: 'I am getting on very well with Her Majesty, who altho' a Queen is one of the most amiable women I ever spoke to.'[61]

Another artist who spent time at Balmoral, the Swedish watercolourist Egron Sellif Lundgren, similarly found Victoria, whom he saw frequently during his three-week visit in 1859, extremely amenable, describing her as 'always most Charmingly gracious.'[62] During his stay, Lundgren witnessed a Highland fête held at Balmoral (fig. 27). The eighth View Album included a sequence of his sketches of various games. These watercolours are striking for their limited tonal range and their sometimes unfinished nature, where the lightly sketched background figures emphasise the strength and corporeality of the men engaged in sport. Victoria described the race depicted by Lundgren (fig. 28) as 'a pretty wild sight', and thought the men looked 'cold with their bare legs & nothing on but their shirts & kilts'.[63]

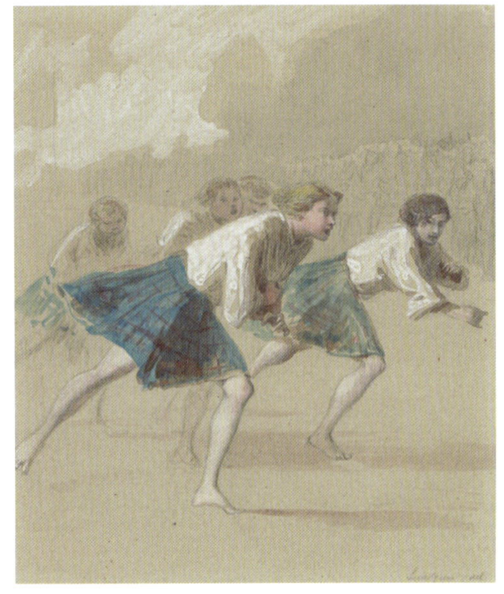

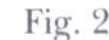

Fig. 28

EGRON SELLIF LUNDGREN (1815–75)

The race, 1859

Pencil, watercolour and bodycolour, 24.3 × 20.7 cm

RCIN 919488

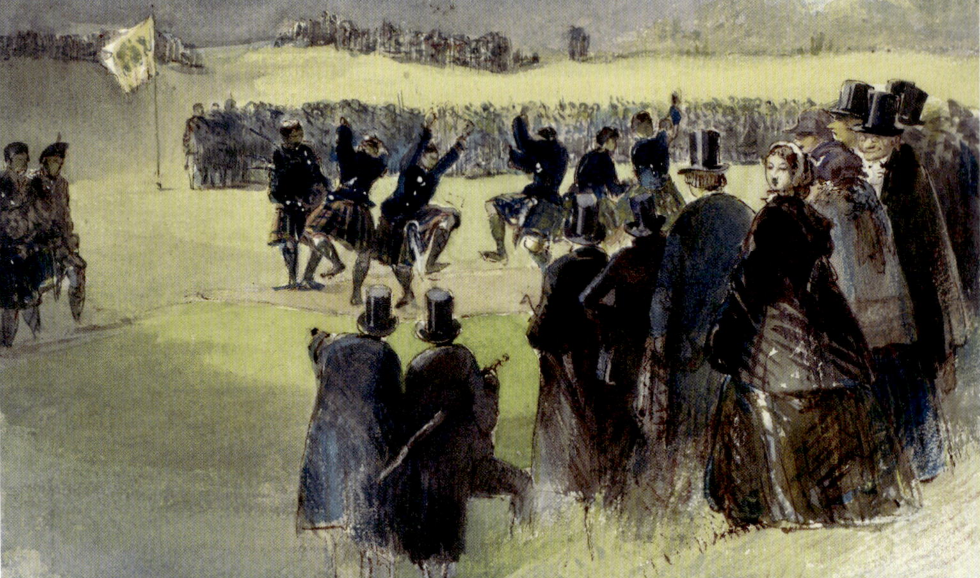

Fig. 27

EGRON SELLIF LUNDGREN

The Highland Fête at Balmoral, *c.*1859

Pencil, watercolour and bodycolour, 17.5 × 30.0 cm

RCIN 919485

There are repeated references in the letters and accounts of Victoria and Albert's household to the royal couple's increasing love of the Highlands and life at Balmoral. In the monarch's own writings, her descriptions of the scenery, the activities she and her family engaged in and her feelings about Scotland were dramatically visceral. This perhaps accounts for the substantially greater number of watercolours in the View Albums relating to life at Balmoral than those of Osborne; while Victoria loved the air, views and privacy afforded by Osborne, Balmoral offered the same qualities but on a greater scale. It was more remote, certainly much wilder, and with historic and romantic associations to which she was especially alive given her love of the novels of Sir Walter Scott (1771–1832), which were set in an idealised version of Scotland. Additionally, Victoria and Albert decorated many of their interior spaces at Osborne House with scenes from their life in the Highlands, as 'reminders of the life [they] enjoyed at the opposite end of the kingdom', such as two large watercolours (see pp. 38–9) by the German artist Carl Haag, who became a favourite.[64] After the Prince's death he was commissioned by the Queen to paint 'some pictures of dear Memories' – again Scottish scenes which were hung at Osborne.[65]

Haag was another artist whose work was introduced to Victoria and Albert through their relatives. In this instance, it was Victoria's half-brother Charles, Prince of Leiningen (1804–56), and Albert's brother Ernest, Duke of Saxe-Coburg and Gotha (1818–93), who commissioned Haag to paint a double portrait of them set in a mountainous landscape as a Christmas present for the Queen in 1852.[66] The watercolour was enthusiastically received, and depictions of the royal family and their retainers or acquaintances in an outdoor setting – such as a charming portrait of Lizzie Stewart and Mary Symons (fig. 29), daughters of the Queen's forester and a local merchant respectively, who later both went into royal service – became the template of Haag's work for the British monarch.

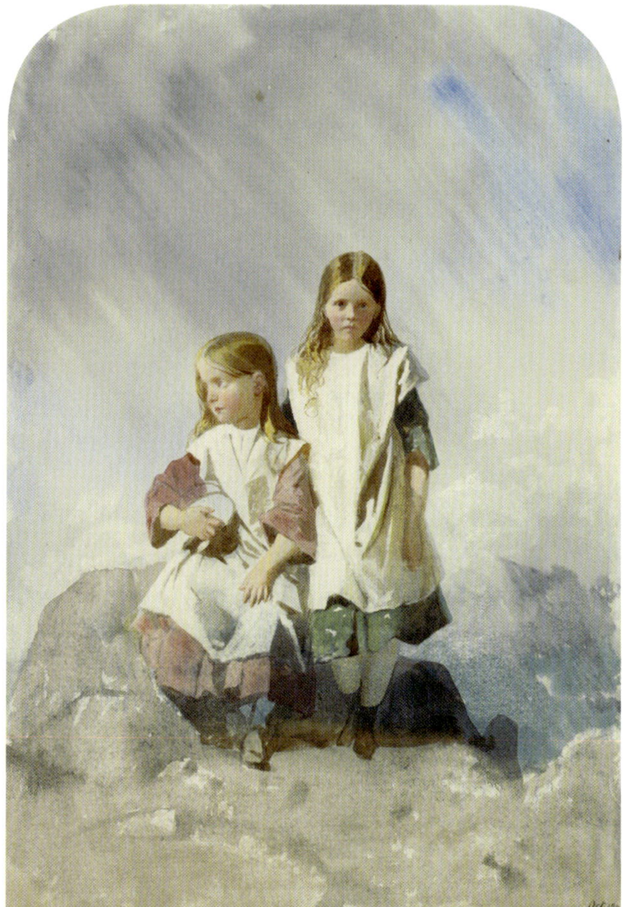

Fig. 29

CARL HAAG (1820–1915)

Lizzie Stewart and Mary Symons, October 1853

Pencil and watercolour, 50.5 × 35.0 cm

RCIN 920747

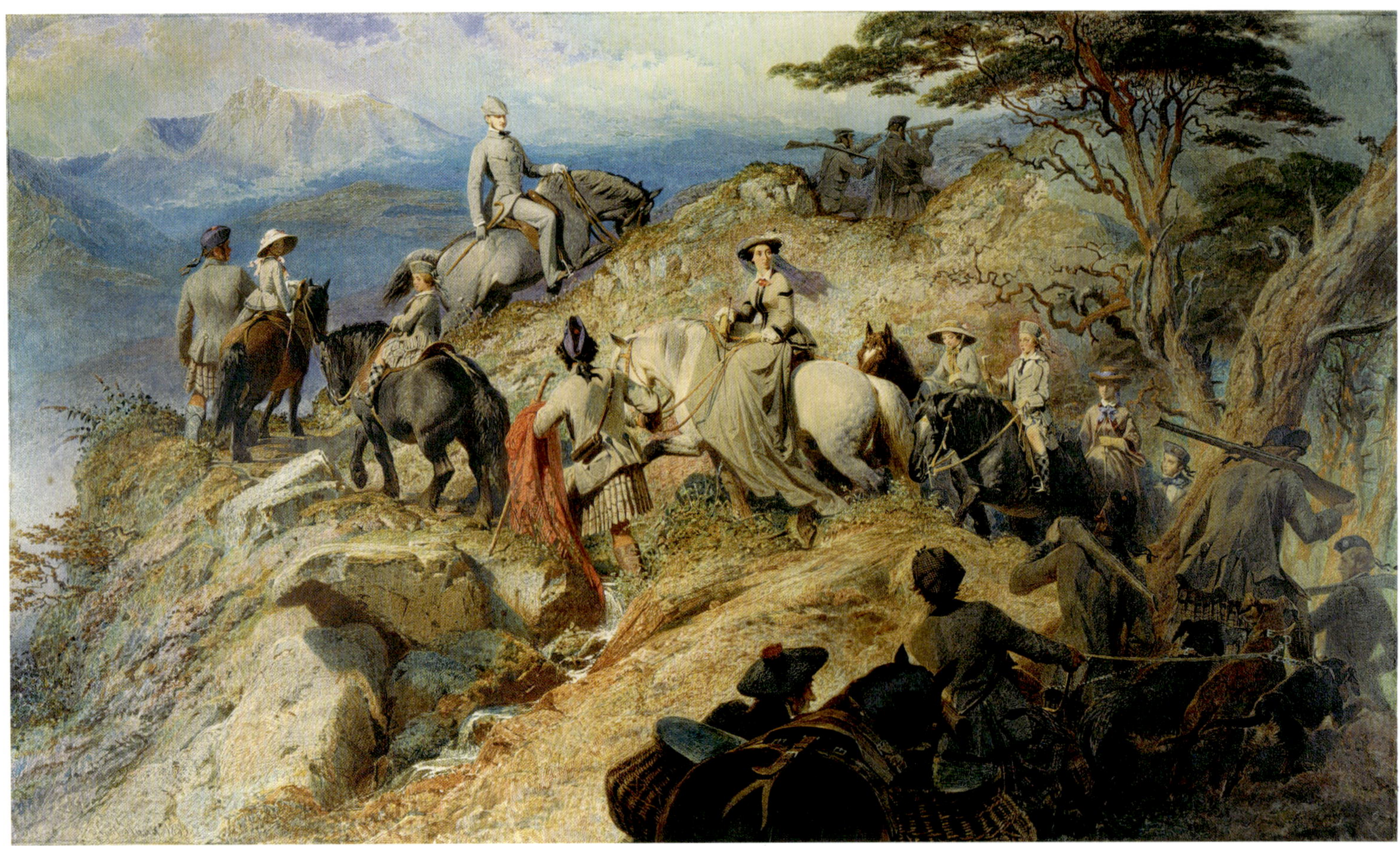

Fig. 30

CARL HAAG

Morning in the Highlands: the Royal Family ascending Lochnagar, 1853

Watercolour and bodycolour with scraping out, 77.0 × 133.6 cm

RCIN 451257

Morning in the Highlands: the Royal Family ascending Lochnagar (fig. 30) and *Evening at Balmoral Castle: the stags brought home* (fig. 31), the two large-scale watercolours hung at Osborne House, were a somewhat unusual commission for Haag. The first was ordered by Albert as a gift for his wife for Christmas 1853, and the second by Victoria for her husband's birthday the following August – though the two patrons were each aware of the other's commission, as Haag discussed his work with both of them.[67] Haag made extensive preparatory studies for each painting in which the arrangements of figures and objects were no doubt very carefully worked out, but his skill was such that they have a fluidity and on-the-spot quality.[68] In a study for *Evening*, the heavily textured paper used by Haag, along with his broad brushstrokes, contributes to the tactile depiction of the coats of both

Fig. 31

CARL HAAG

Evening at Balmoral Castle: the stags brought home, 1854

Watercolour and bodycolour with scraping out,
76.5 × 133.3 cm

RCIN 451255

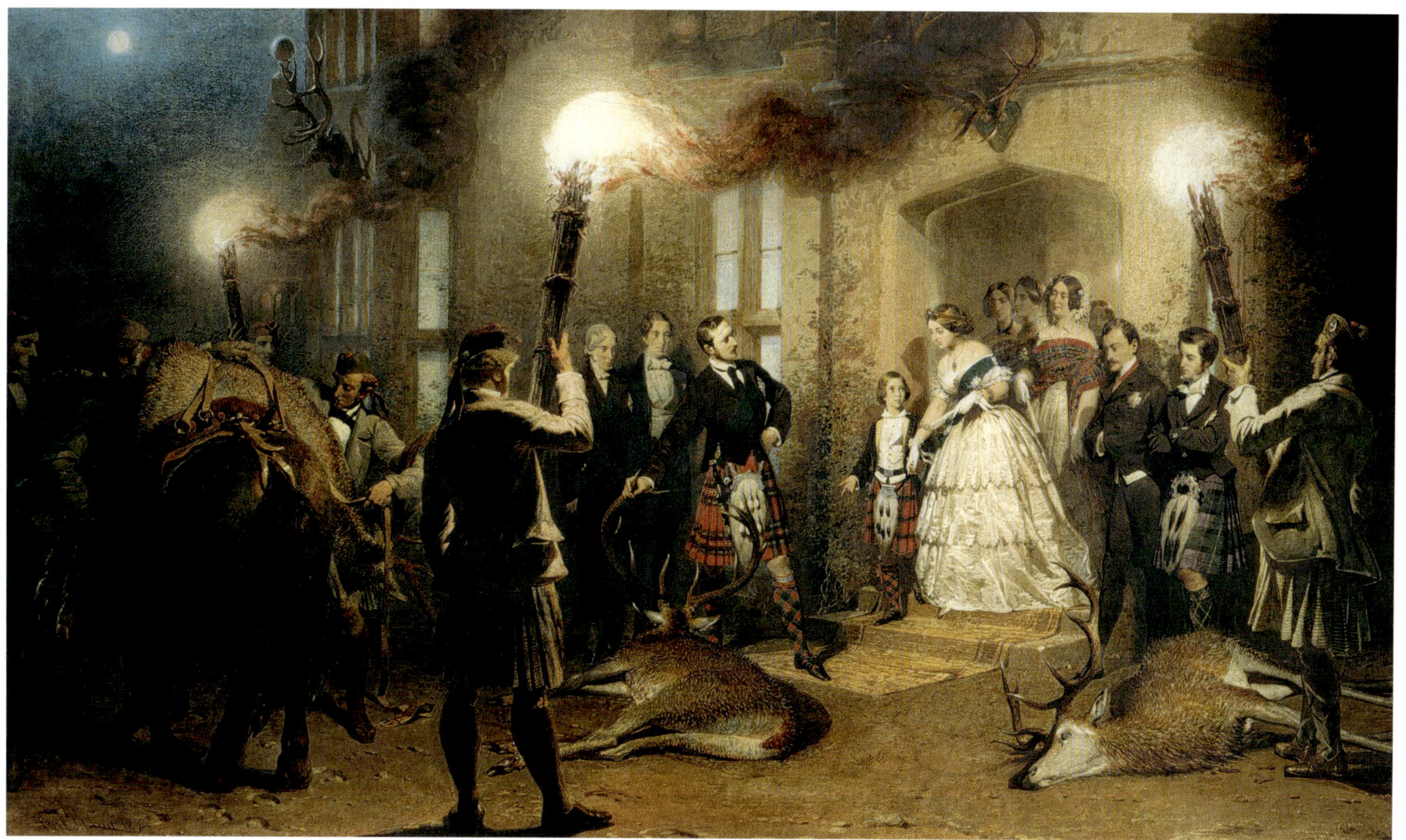

the pony and the stag, and the fleeting way the protagonist John Mackenzie meets the viewer's eyes reinforces the overall naturalistic impression of the scene (fig. 32).

Haag's idiosyncratic watercolour technique was recognised – though not always approved of – by his contemporaries.[69] He never used opaque white bodycolour for his highlights, for example. In the study for *Evening*, the highlights (the tips of the stag's antlers, and the white collar worn by Mackenzie) are created through the careful cutting of shapes out of the painted surface to reveal the white paper below. A similar method is apparent in another sketch Haag made for his first commission from Victoria (fig. 33), where

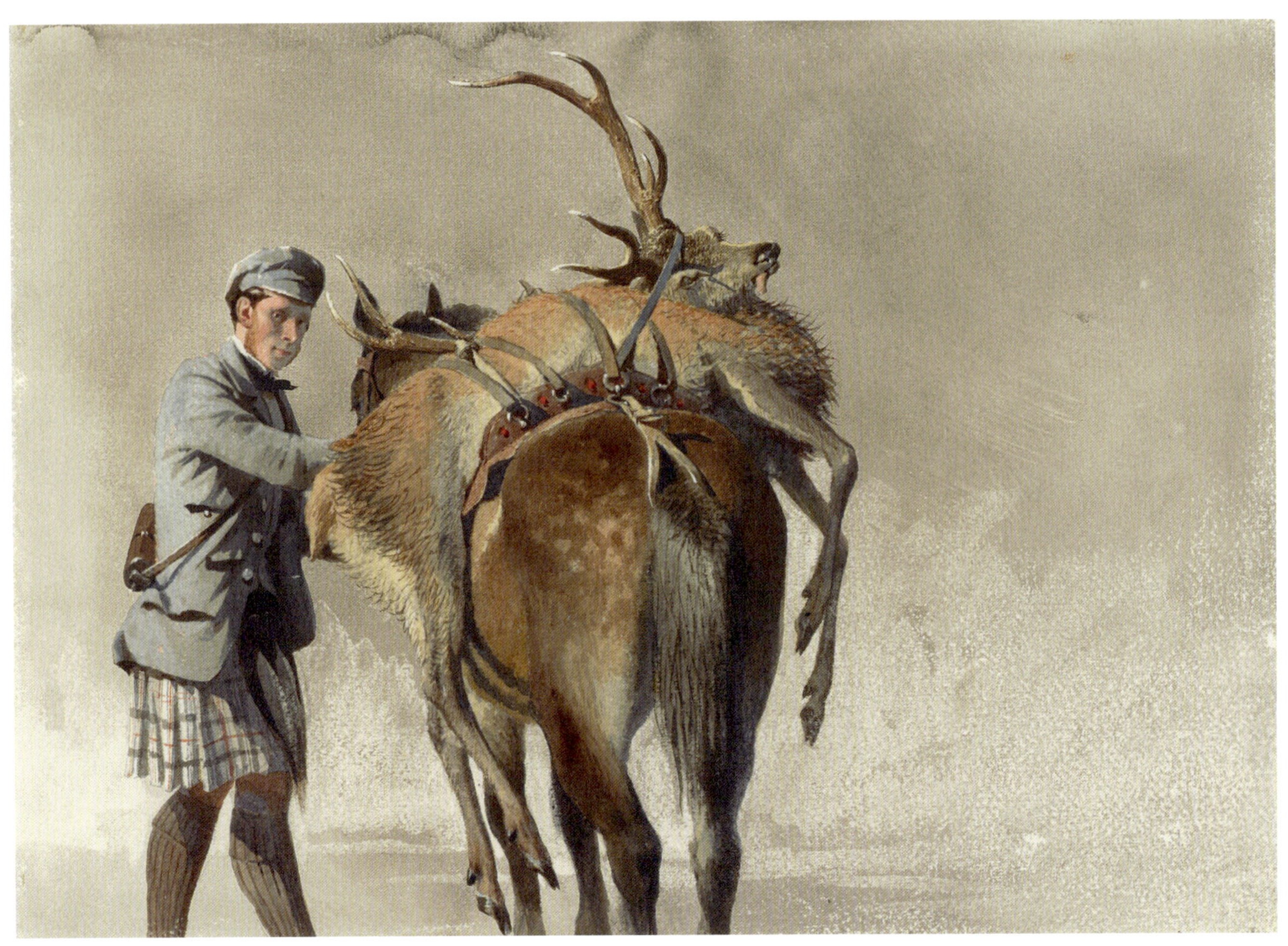

Fig. 32

CARL HAAG

John Mackenzie with a dead stag on a pony, 1853

Watercolour and bodycolour with excising, 35.2 × 50.4 cm

RCIN 920750

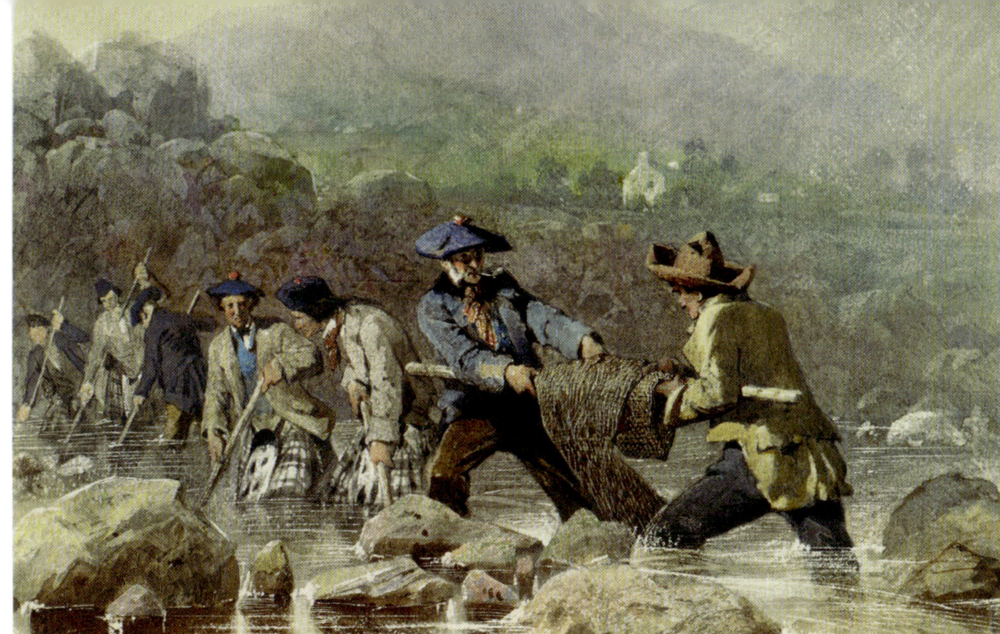

Fig. 33

CARL HAAG

Salmon leistering in the River Dee, 1853

Watercolour and bodycolour with scraping out, 27.2 × 39.2 cm

RCIN 920762

the artist has scraped off the top layer of paper – sometimes quite robustly over large areas – in order to create the highlights in the water surrounding the fishermen and the white patches on their kilts. Having joined the royal party to watch and sketch salmon fishing in the River Dee on his first visit to Balmoral in September 1853, Haag was soon commissioned by the Queen to produce a finished watercolour of the scene as a surprise birthday present for Prince Albert for the following year. The sketch illustrated here is for a group of figures in the background of this work. It also highlights another element of Haag's characteristic technique, which was to build up strong layers of watercolour to create a richness of colouring described by one reviewer as giving his works 'the husky air of a crayon-drawing'.[70]

Interest in Haag's technique was not just confined to his artistic contemporaries and critics. Haag was another artist who gave the Queen lessons; he was an 'admirable Master' who taught her 'more about the anatomy of the figure than anyone ever did before', and she copied several of his works.[71] Haag must also have discussed with Albert his innovative method for fixing his watercolours, for a note in the archives of the artists' suppliers Winsor & Newton, against a transcription of Haag's recipe for his 'preparation for fixing & preserving watercolour drawings', states that 'this is used by Mr Haag & HRH Prince Albert advised him to get us to prepare it for general sale'.[72]

❀ ❀ ❀

In 1873 Queen Victoria mourned the loss of Franz Xaver Winterhalter and Edwin Landseer, who died three months apart, describing them as her 'personal attached friends of more than 30 years standing'.[73] The death of William Leighton Leitch a decade later also provoked memories of the happy years of her marriage. Victoria described him in her journal as 'my kind old Drawing Master, such an excellent artist … connected with happy & sad times', and was anxious to acquire more of his watercolours at the sale of his studio contents; she also read his 'very interesting' biography the year it was published.[74] Long hours spent sitting for portraits, watching their children being painted or being taught to paint themselves generated conversation, familiarity and sometimes friendship between patrons and artists. Victoria and Albert developed close relationships with some of those artists they entrusted with the task of recording the most important people and places in their lives.

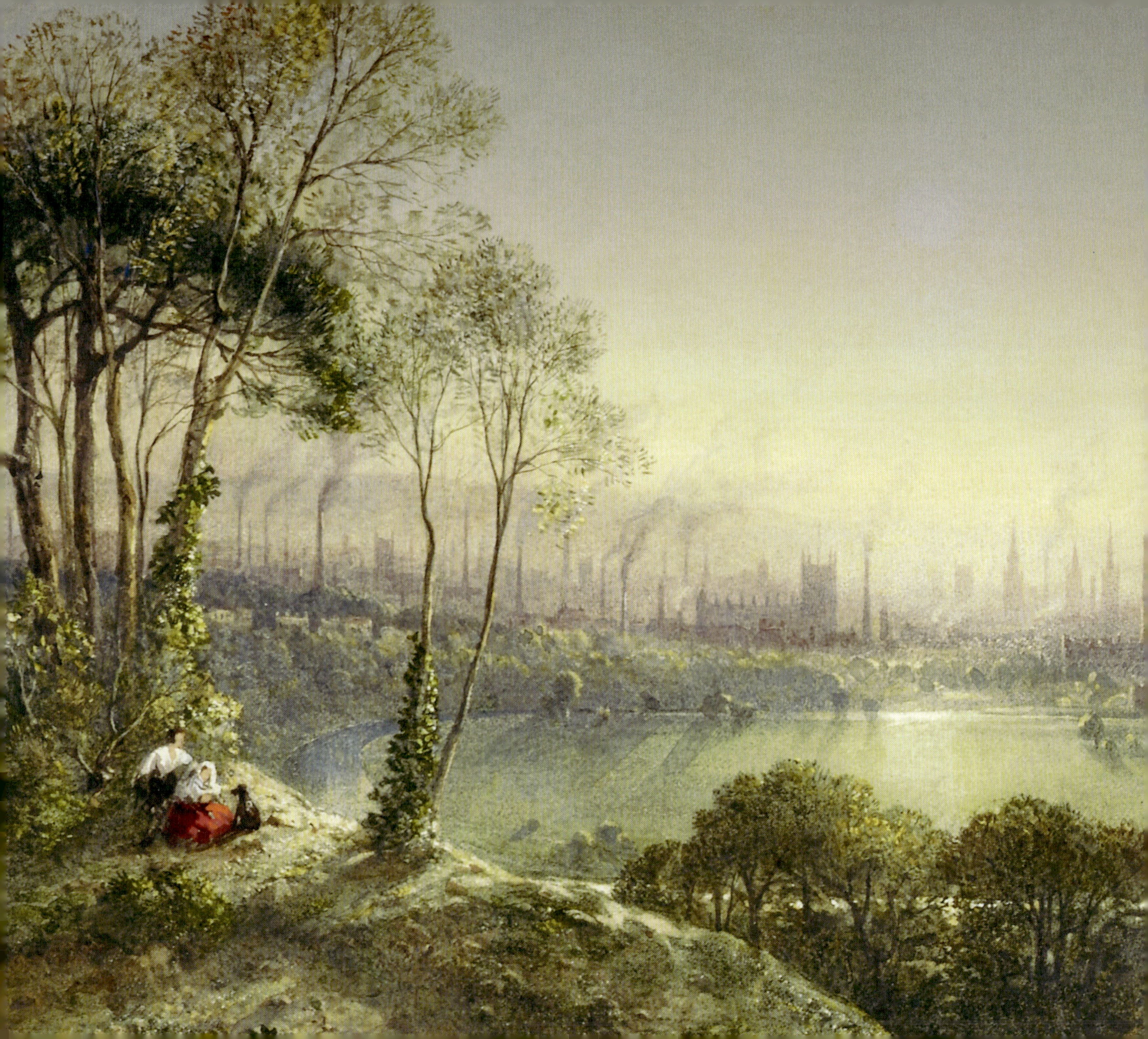

CHAPTER 2

TRAVELLING THE KINGDOM

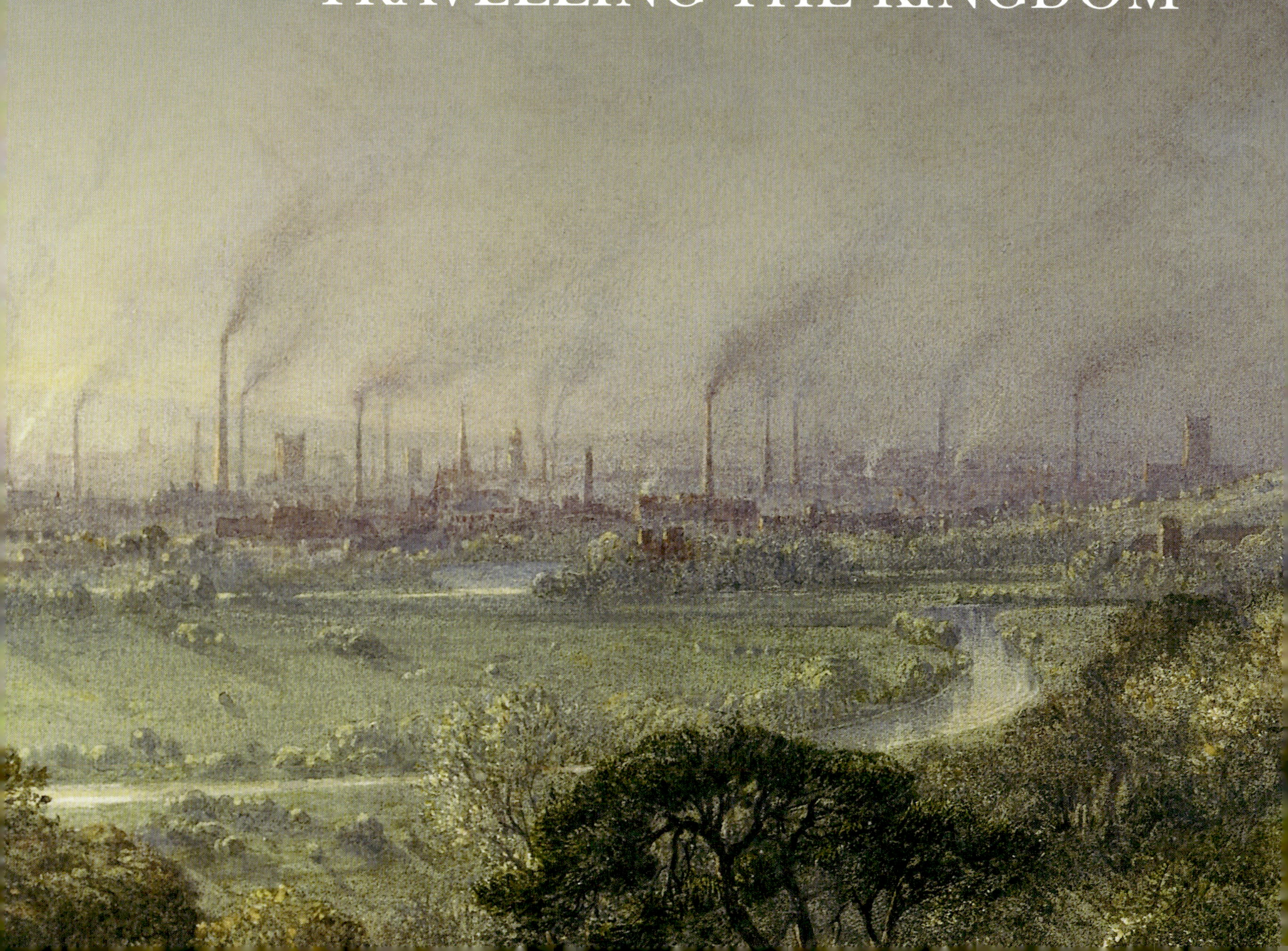

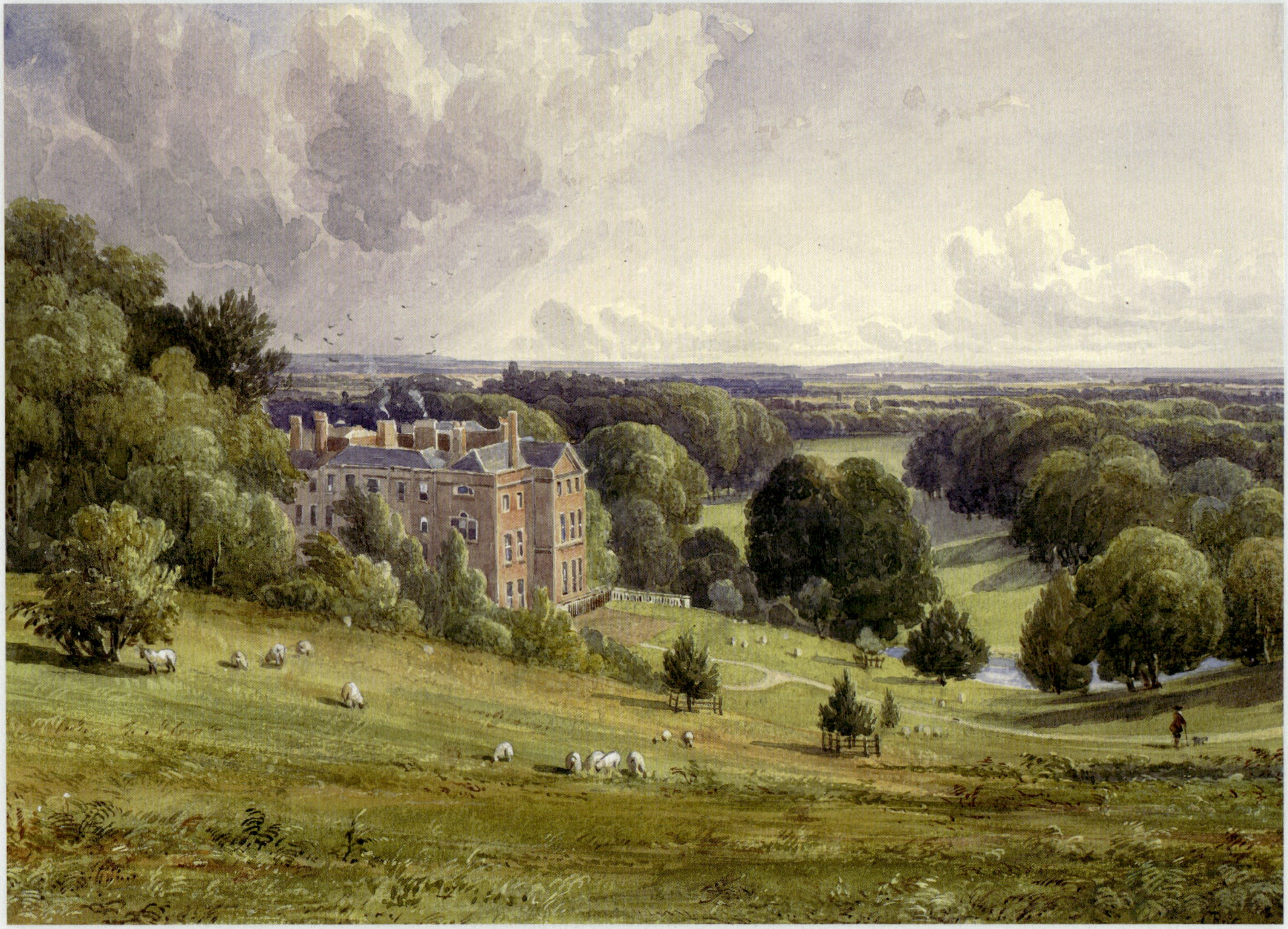

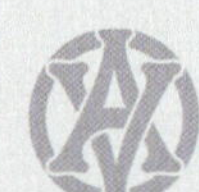

CHAPTER 2

Travelling the kingdom

'Our little tour was most successful, and we enjoyed it of all things; nothing could be more enthusiastic or affectionate than our reception everywhere, and I am happy to hear that our presence has left a favourable impression, which I think will be of great use.'[1]

– Queen Victoria

Fig. 34

CALEB ROBERT STANLEY

Brocket Hall, 1841

Pencil, watercolour and bodycolour, 21.7 × 32.5 cm

RCIN 920153

Writing to her uncle Leopold a few days after she and Albert returned to Windsor from a six-day tour of Bedfordshire and Hertfordshire in July 1841, Queen Victoria displayed an awareness of the requirement for her visibility as the monarch, the nation's figurehead. This stress on the public nature of her role, as well as the reciprocal relationship between Victoria and her subjects – to be seen, and to witness, respectively – had already been expressed by Prince Albert in a letter the previous summer, recounting a shocking assassination attempt on the Queen's life. Albert noted that the royal couple took a short public drive in their carriage immediately after the event, 'partly to give Victoria a little air, partly also to show the public that we had not, on account of what had happened, lost all confidence in them'.[2]

By 1844, following several domestic and international tours, the *Illustrated London News* prophesied that 'the reign of Victoria will present to the historian as many Royal progresses as that of Elizabeth.'[3] The impetus to travel more widely may have come from the Prince; writing in her journal on the night of their return from Hertfordshire, Victoria recorded that it had 'interested Albert so much seeing so many places'.[4] This was their second trip away from home, as in June 1841 they had spent two nights at Nuneham House in Oxfordshire, a seat of Edward Vernon-Harcourt, Archbishop of York (1757–1847), to facilitate Albert's presence in Oxford for the annual Commemoration of the University's benefactors. Victoria and Albert's frequent and wide-ranging travels around the British Isles during their marriage, and the opportunity this afforded the wider public to see the royal family in person, were extensively reported in the press. Significantly, the couple were themselves also active consumers of the coverage they generated – Victoria recorded their joint creation of what they called the 'Journey albums': '6 in number, begun in [18]42 – into which we placed all the prints, woodcuts [from illustrated newspapers] & photographs we c[oul]d get of all the places we visited, went thro', & events wh[ich] took place – and it was such an amusement to collect all these on our journeys.'[5] As newspaper artists criss-crossed the country to provide illustrations to accompany press reports on the royal family throughout the 1840s and 1850s, so too did Victoria and Albert commission artists to provide depictions of the towns and cities they visited, the places at which they stayed and the sights they saw, which they integrated into their View Albums.

Visits to country houses

The trip to Oxfordshire and the short tour of Bedfordshire and Herfordshire in 1841 were both represented in the first View Album. Eight watercolours, all exterior views of the houses and grounds in which Victoria and Albert stayed, were mounted consecutively in the volume, two relating to the first trip and six to the second. The latter were all painted by Caleb Robert Stanley, and thus presumably done at the behest of the Queen rather than as a gift from the owners of the houses she visited.[6] Stanley's watercolours do not reflect the public dimension of this first royal tour, as reported both in *The Times* and by Victoria herself in her journal. There are no depictions of the massed crowds and the decorations staged to welcome the royal procession as it travelled through towns such as Chesham, Dunstable, St Albans and Rickmansworth – passing through Welwyn, Victoria recorded that a band preceded their carriages, as did women 'strewing flowers' – nor of the other stage-managed opportunities for the public to see their queen, such as on their arrival and promenade on the lawn at the Prime Minister Lord Melbourne's seat, Brocket Hall, which they visited for lunch on the last day of their tour.[7] As *The Times* reported, the estate grounds had been 'opened to the public, [and] a great number of spectators had assembled, who greeted Her Majesty and the Prince in the most loyal and enthusiastic manner, which Her Majesty and His Royal Highness acknowledged most frequently'.[8]

Rather than being records of the tour itself, then, the watercolours by Stanley are souvenirs of the houses visited by Victoria and Albert. This meant that they aligned well – in subject, and choice of artist (see p. 15) – with the other works mounted in the first View Album, which were primarily views of royal residences. Of the Hertfordshire and Bedfordshire watercolours, the two depictions of Brocket Hall were perhaps the most important for Victoria because of her affection for Lord Melbourne (1779–1848), who was her principal adviser and a constant dependable presence in the early years of her reign. Stanley's view of the house and grounds from above (fig. 34) presents it in a picturesque and idyllic light, surrounded by a rolling green landscape on which sheep graze and which dips down to the lake in the middle distance, with an uninterrupted view across the Hertfordshire countryside bathed in sunlight. Victoria and Albert were charmed with the hall's situation, according to the Queen herself: 'We were … much pleased with Brocket, the grounds of wh[ich] are beautiful, & w[hi]ch I had so long wished to see.'[9]

Fig. 35
JOSEPH NASH
The State Drawing-Room, Stowe, 1845
Pencil, watercolour and bodycolour, 31.7 × 44.5 cm
RCIN 920174

A few years later Victoria and Albert commissioned Joseph Nash to follow in their footsteps to record a visit to another grand country house. On being appointed to the Order of the Garter in 1842, Richard, 2nd Duke of Buckingham and Chandos (1797–1861), told the Queen 'he would esteem it an immense honour, if we could ever visit him at Stowe.'[10] She and Albert did so in January 1845, staying for three nights. Three years later, the Duke was declared bankrupt and a sale of Stowe's entire contents – which had been much admired by the royal guests – was held from August to October 1848. Of the two watercolours painted by Nash, the interior view of the State Drawing Room (fig. 35) is the only

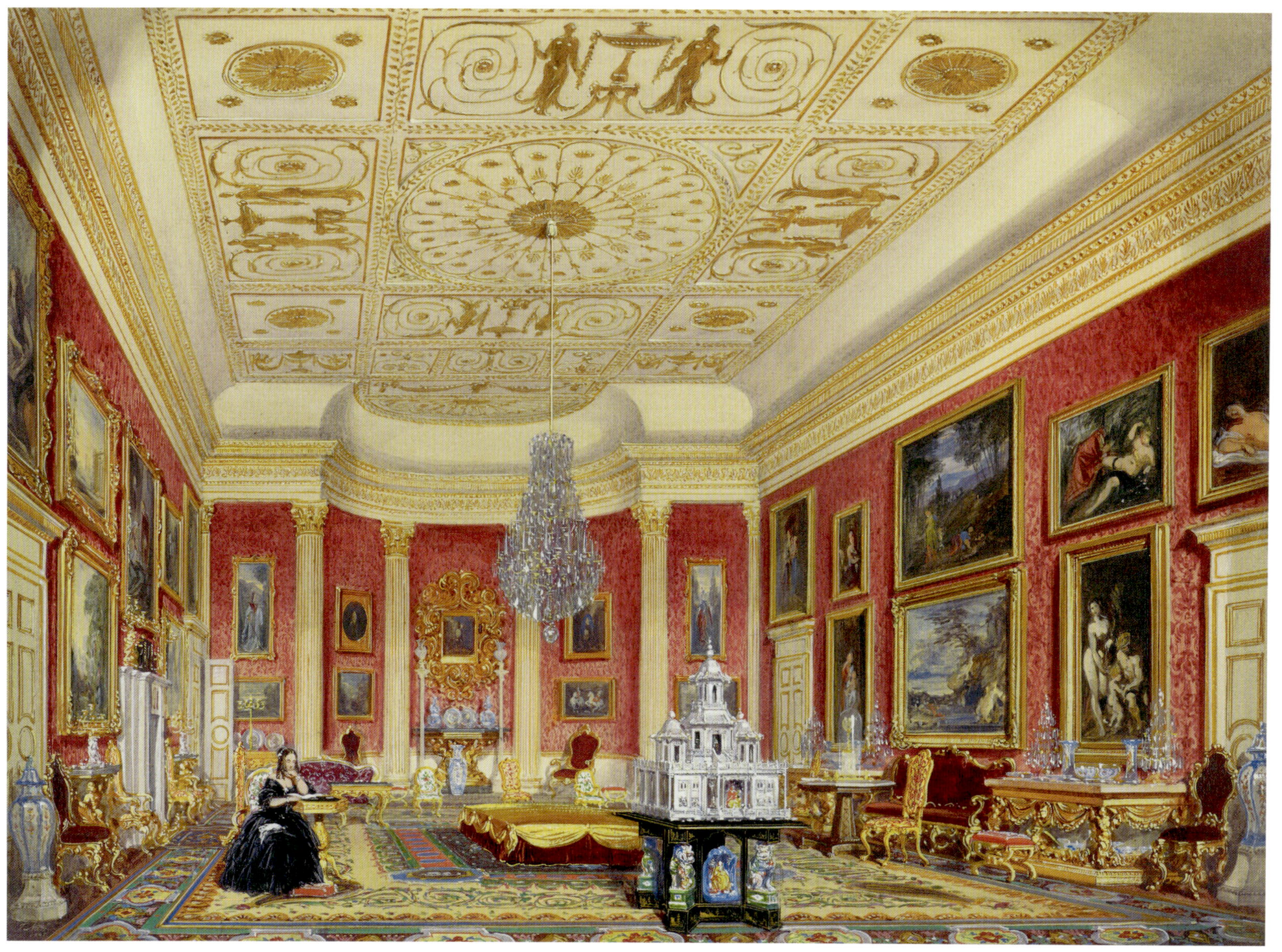

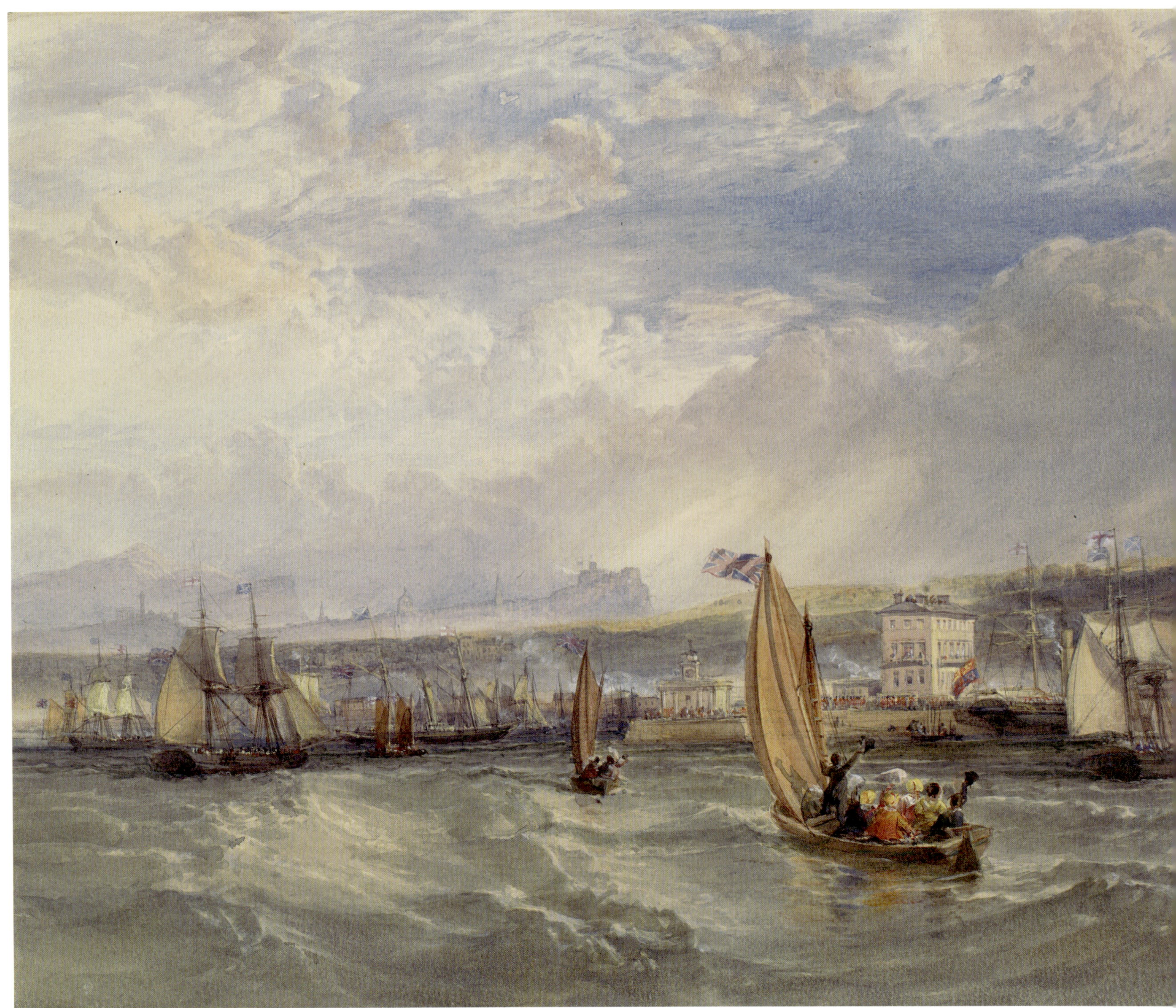

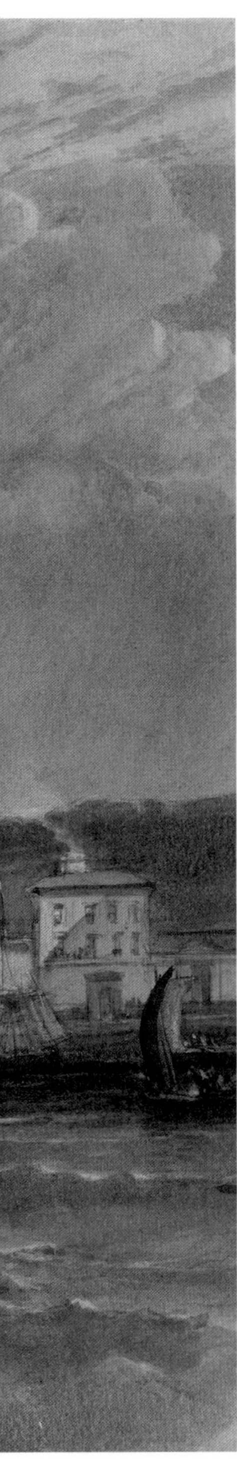

record of the appearance of the room at this period.[11] The figure in a black dress, the sole occupant of the room, may represent Victoria herself; she described spending part of the first morning at Stowe reading and writing while Albert went out shooting. Whether the Queen asked to feature in the view or Nash himself decided to include her is unknown.

The early tours in Scotland

In September 1842 Victoria and Albert made, in the Prince's words, a 'delightful, exciting tour through Scotland' lasting two weeks.[12] The tour, largely arranged by Walter, 5th Duke of Buccleuch (1806–84), and his wife Charlotte (1811–95), was primarily private, but as the sovereign's first visit to Scotland it had to incorporate at least a few public appearances.[13] The royal couple first went to Edinburgh: as the Queen recorded in her journal, it 'made a great impression on us; it is quite beautiful and totally unlike anything *I* have seen', later confiding to Lord Melbourne that Albert, too, 'who has seen so much, says it is the finest town he ever saw'.[14] They then visited Dalkeith House, Scone Palace and Taymouth Castle in the Highlands and Drummond Castle in Perthshire. Two years later, the Duke of Buccleuch commissioned a series of ten watercolours from William Leighton Leitch (who, at the time, was teaching the Duchess watercolour painting) to present to the Queen and Prince as a souvenir of their first visit to the country.

The first of these watercolours shows the arrival of the royal yacht at Granton Pier in Edinburgh (fig. 36). Leitch's watercolour highlights the warm welcome enjoyed by Victoria and Albert, with figures massed on the quay and the men amongst the people depicted in the vessels surrounding the royal yacht (identified by the royal standard waving in the breeze) lifting their hats in salute. Leitch may have taken his cue from press reports as well as the numerous accounts published after the tour's end – including one written at Victoria's command – which sought to put a positive spin on what was termed by one commentator 'a singular combination of *the sublime and the ridiculous*'.[15] In contrast to the orderly arrival depicted by Leitch, the royal yacht was in fact considerably delayed by bad weather and the carefully planned welcoming ceremony

Fig. 36

WILLIAM LEIGHTON LEITCH

Queen Victoria landing at Granton Pier, 1844

Pencil, watercolour and bodycolour,
25.0 × 36.0 cm

RCIN 919577

> *[Edinburgh] made quite an impression on us; it is quite beautiful and totally unlike anything I had ever seen.'*
>
> – Queen Victoria

fell into disarray. While the *Illustrated London News* did give some sense of the confusion, its correspondent glossed over the facts with a poetic description of Victoria's setting foot on Scottish soil, when 'a brilliant sun burst at the moment, lighting up the scene'.[16] Neither the Queen nor the authors of other accounts referred to this auspicious weather event relieving what was otherwise a wet and misty day, but there is a strong suggestion of sunshine in Leitch's watercolour, with patches of blue sky.[17]

Such was the love that Victoria and Albert developed for the Highlands during their first visit to Scotland that they returned two years later, spending three weeks at Blair Castle in Perthshire, lent to them by Lord and Lady Glenlyon. While away, Prince Albert reported to his stepmother that he, the Queen and the three-year-old Princess Vicky, who had accompanied them, were 'all well, and liv[ing] a somewhat primitive, yet romantic, mountain life'.[18] Fifteen watercolours relating to this second visit were mounted into the second View Album – the largest group in the volume. Six were by Charlotte Canning, who was kept busy, in Victoria's words, 'making numbers of pretty little sketches of the scenery about here, for me', and seven by Leitch, whose services Lady Canning probably suggested to Victoria and Albert (perhaps to relieve the pressure on herself).[19] The other three were painted by Charles Landseer, brother of the famed animal painter Edwin who had already enjoyed much royal patronage.[20] The majority of the watercolours by Leitch and Canning in the album are views of the landscape surrounding Blair Castle, with the addition of two depictions by Leitch of unnamed figures from the Atholl Highlanders (who formed the Queen's guard during her visit to the castle, sleeping outside in tents). Landseer painted two portrait studies of servants of the Duke of Atholl, as well as a scene capturing some of the activity outside the castle. Leitch's posed figures (fig. 37) function as representatives of the many Highland military figures surrounding the royal family during their visit – they stand in front of architectural elements of the castle, wearing full Highland dress and

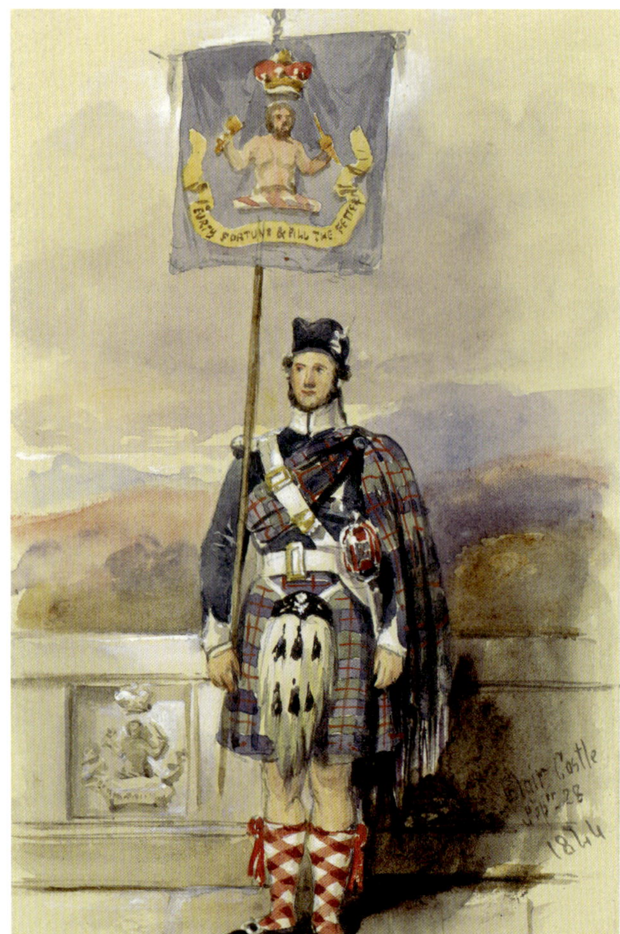

Fig. 37

WILLIAM LEIGHTON LEITCH

A standard-bearer to the Duke of Atholl's Guard, 28 September 1844

Pencil, watercolour and bodycolour, 21.4 × 13.5 cm

RCIN 919544

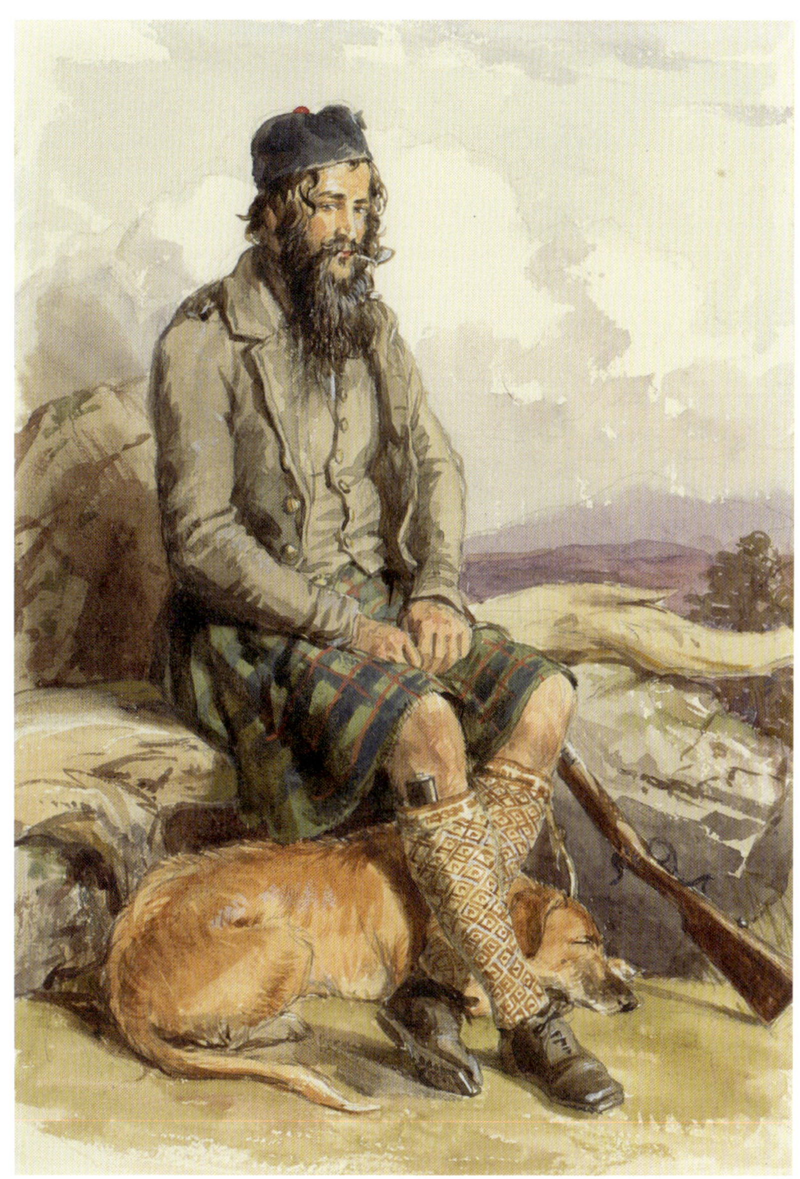

Fig. 38

CHARLES LANDSEER (1799–1879)

Billy Duff, 1844

Pencil, watercolour and bodycolour, 25.2 × 17.6 cm

RCIN 920774

armed with accoutrements distinguishing their position. Landseer's depiction of Billy Duff (fig. 38), another of the Atholl Highlanders, is entirely different in character, portraying a more natural moment where the resting soldier smoking a pipe appears to regard us frankly, as his dog sleeps at his feet. Victoria and Albert visited Scotland again in August 1847, which was the last time before the acquisition of Balmoral. They toured the west coast of the country and commissioned twenty watercolours of its sights for the View Albums.

Wales

On the way to Scotland in the summer of 1847, the royal yacht sailed up the west coast of England and Wales. The Queen, Prince, their two eldest children and Charles, Prince of Leiningen admired the Welsh scenery, including the ruins of Caernarvon Castle, before they sailed through the Menai Straits to allow Albert and Charles to inspect the Menai Bridge and visit Penrhyn Castle. Victoria, who had visited both Caernarvon and Penrhyn castles as a thirteen-year-old princess with her mother, did not set foot on Welsh soil, which appears to have been counter to the expectations of the local authorities and public.[21] However, the Queen was aware that the people were 'anxious to see us' and a published account of the visit

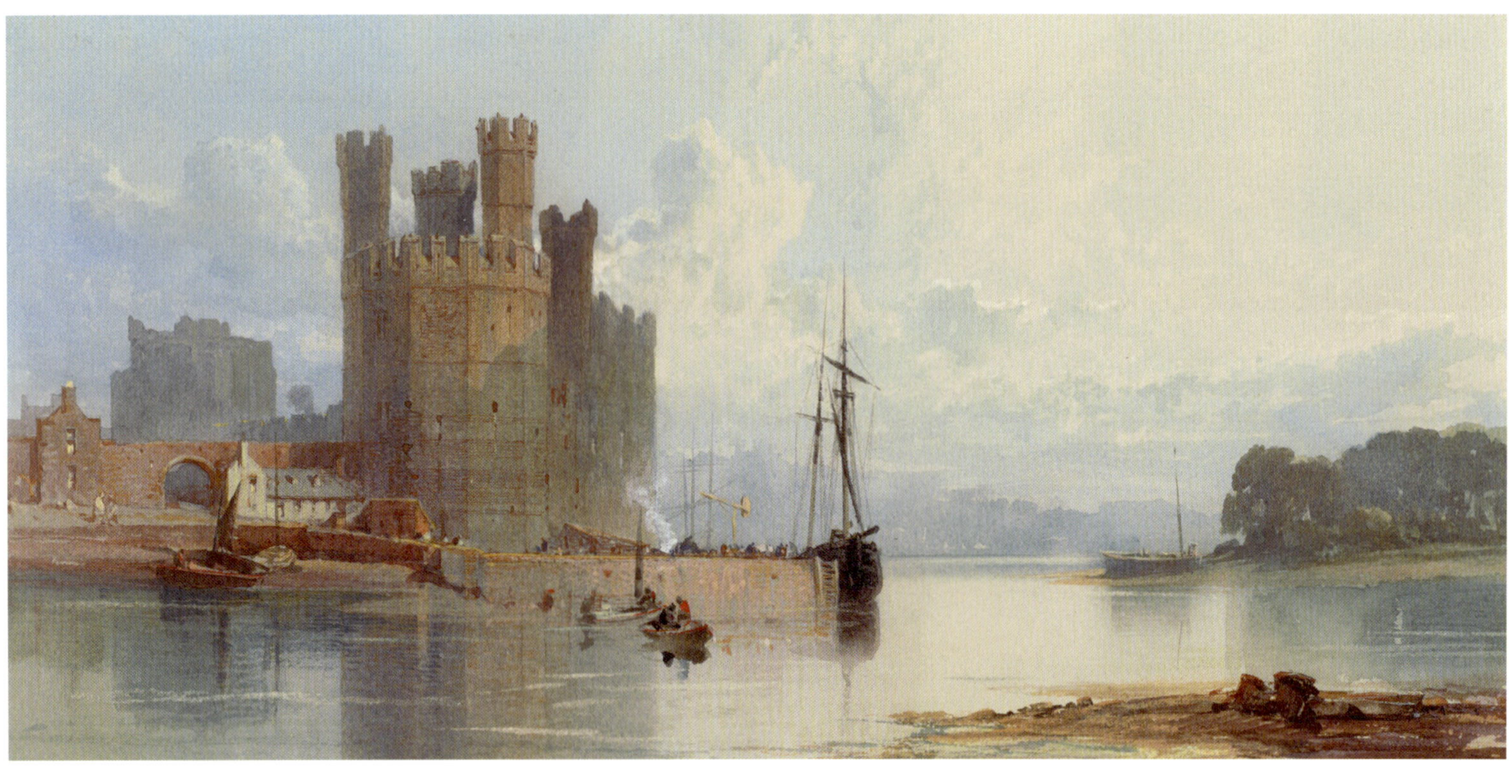

(dedicated with permission to her) described her vessel, anchored by the Menai Bridge, being 'surrounded by boats, all of which were suffered to approach close to the royal yacht, and thousands of loyal hearts were gratified with a very good view of our Most Gracious Sovereign, who was seated to the rear of the pavilion, sketching, and occasionally playing with the Princess Royal and the Prince of Wales. Her Majesty now and then acknowledged by a smile or friendly nod the loyal cheers of her subjects.'[22]

An undated view of Caernarvon Castle (fig. 39) was included in the fourth View Album. Painted by Thomas Miles Richardson, it displays qualities associated with his best work – the 'bright contrasts of colour, and a deftness of handling' and his frequent 'extend[ing of] the field of vision laterally by the use of paper of widely oblong

Fig. 39

THOMAS MILES RICHARDSON (1813–90)

Caernarvon Castle, *c.*1847

Watercolour and bodycolour with scraping out, 23.5 × 46.3 cm

RCIN 913681

proportions' – as described in a posthumous assessment of his career.[23] Richardson was born in Newcastle and spent much of his early career there as a pupil of his father (of the same name). Victoria and Albert do not appear to have been patrons of Richardson Senior, but they owned five watercolours by his son, whose name occurs with approbation in two of the Queen's accounts of visits to the Old Watercolour Society – in 1854 she thought his landscapes 'beautiful', and a year later remarked on 'splendid paintings' by Richardson and Carl Haag.[24]

Another view of the same area mounted into a later View Album is very different in character. In 1847 Victoria recorded seeing 'the works being made for the tube for the railways' as the royal yacht sailed through the Menai Straits, by which she meant the tubular railway bridge then under construction, designed by the engineer Robert Stephenson (1803–59). Inaugurated in March 1850, the bridge was widely recognised as innovative in design as well as being an important link between Anglesey and North Wales, and indeed between England and Ireland.[25] Victoria and Albert broke their journey back from Scotland in the autumn of 1852 in order to carry out, as was reported by the *Illustrated London News*, a 'special visit and a minute inspection' of the bridge, accompanied by Stephenson.[26] The Queen wrote a detailed account of the experience in her journal, revealing her interest in both the structure's appearance and engineering, which she described as 'stupendous' when she saw it from the older Menai Bridge.[27] A watercolour view of the bridge by Frank Dillon conveys its scale, with tiny figures dotted around the composition emphasising its monumentality (fig. 40). It may be that the watercolour was presented to the royal couple to commemorate their visit, as there is no record of its commission or of payment being made for it.[28] Indeed the watercolour has been trimmed (losing the last digit of the date), suggesting that it was originally larger than watercolours mounted in the View Albums.

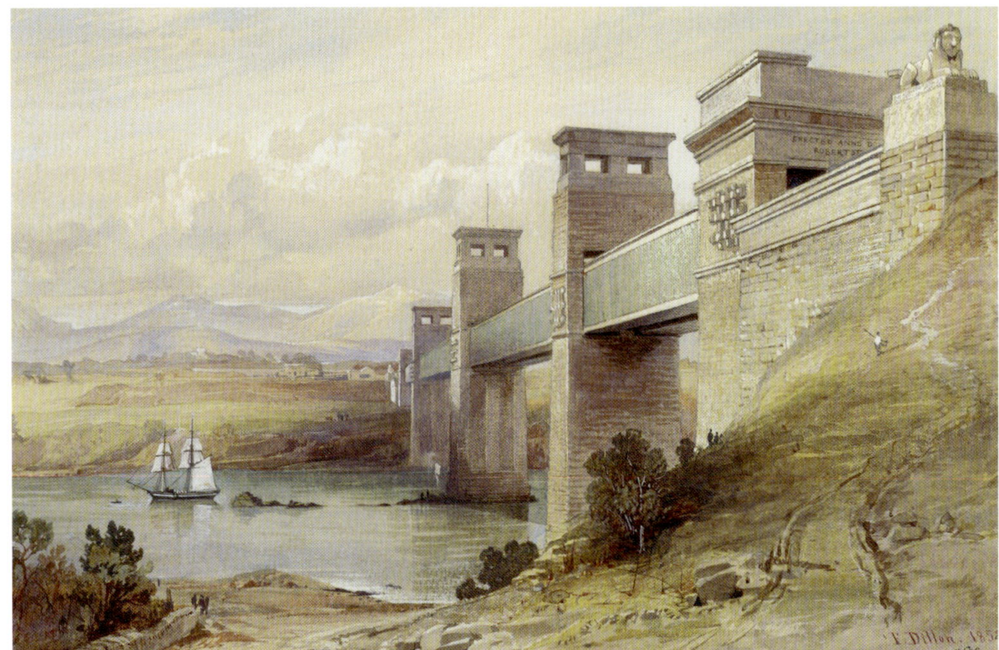

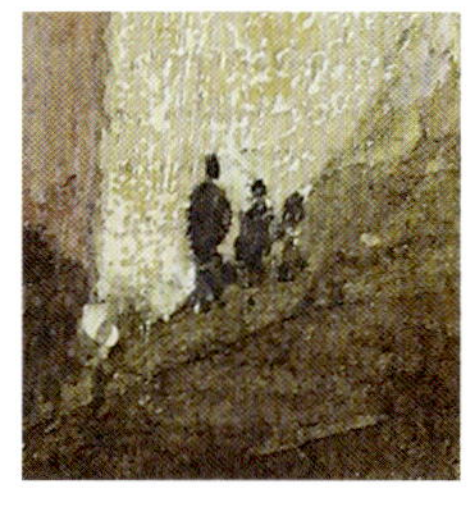

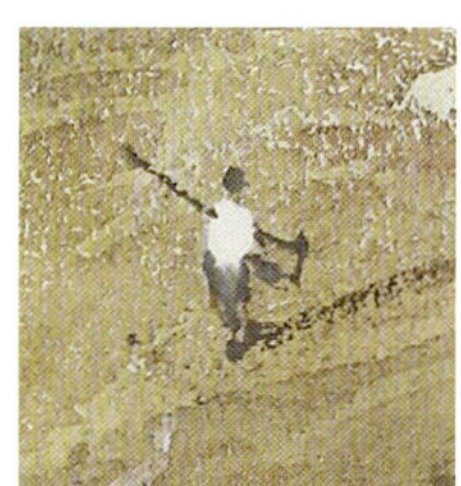

Fig. 40

FRANK DILLON (1823–1909)

The Britannia tubular bridge over the Menai Straits, 1852

Pencil, watercolour and bodycolour, 25.8 × 39.8 cm

RCIN 920228

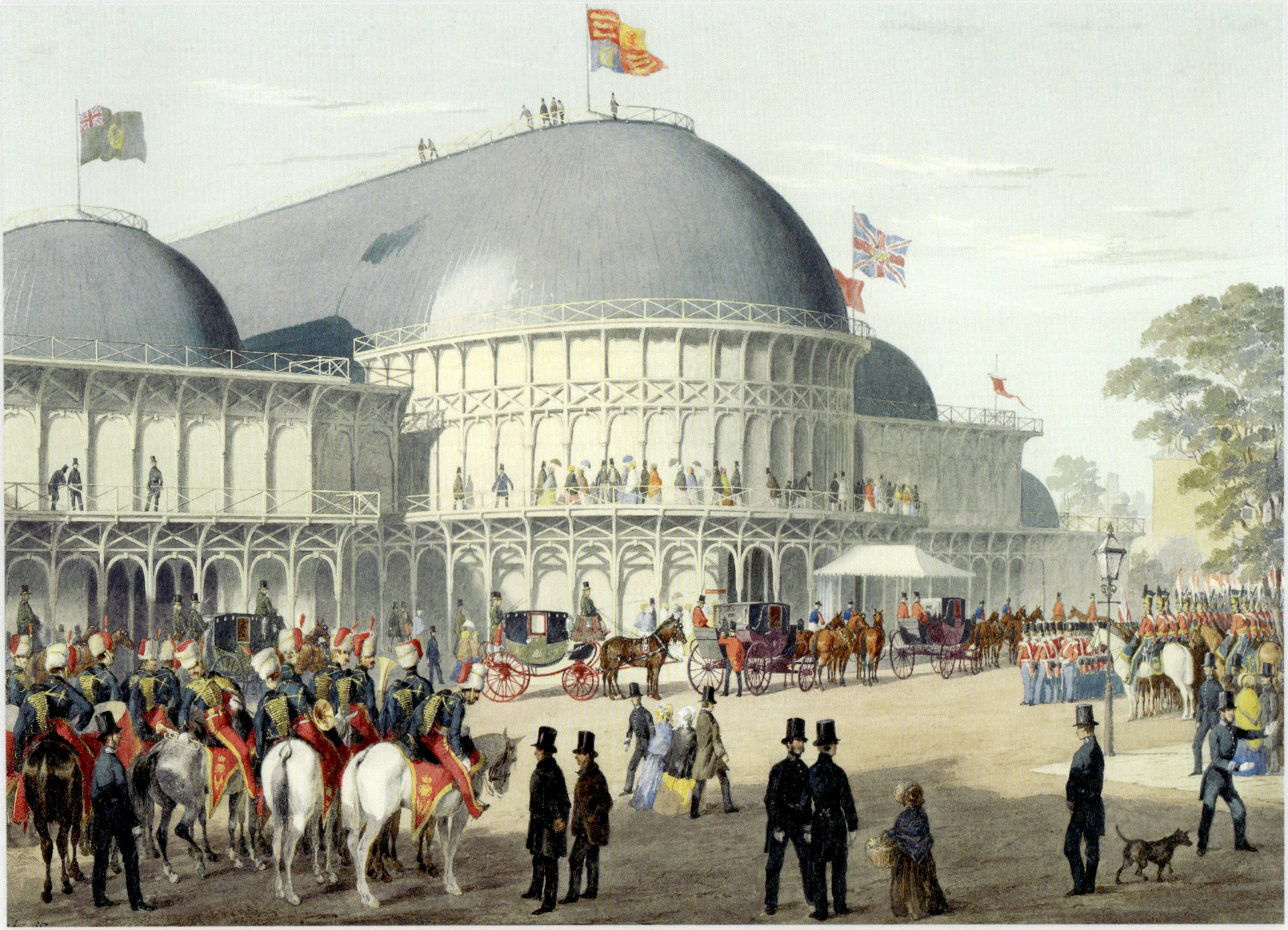

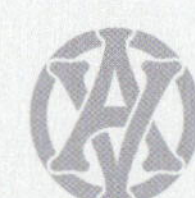

Ireland

In 1853 Victoria and Albert made their second visit to Ireland to see the Great Industrial Exhibition in Dublin, to which they loaned several fine and decorative works of art.[29] After their first state visit to the exhibition on 30 August, when they were received by the Executive Committee and took part in a short ceremony before touring the building, Victoria and Albert visited another three times and purchased some of the goods on display.

The Queen appears to have held contradictory impressions of the exhibition building which, like the Crystal Palace in London, had been specially constructed for the event – on one occasion she described herself as 'quite delighted' with it,[30] but to her journal she confided that she thought the structure 'ugly on the outside, but very fine in the interior'.[31] However, she did commission a 'picture of the Exhibition building in Dublin' (fig. 41) from Michael Angelo Hayes, a local artist who was Military Painter-in-Ordinary to the Lord Lieutenant of Ireland: this was Edward Eliot, 3rd Earl of St Germans (1798–1877), who facilitated the payment from the privy purse to Hayes and therefore presumably recommended him for the commission. Hayes's evocation of the somewhat stolid building seems to chime with Victoria's less than enthusiastic response to it; by comparison, a series of watercolours by James Mahony in the National Gallery of Ireland, which depict interior views of the royal visit, are romantic in sensibility, emphasising the light that bathed the interior from the partially glazed roof (fig. 42). While the building is a commanding backdrop to Hayes's scene, his focus is the activity outside, where a variety of soldiers, police officers and members of the public appear to be waiting for the appearance of the royal party, presumably about to leave the exhibition for the empty carriages drawn up at the entrance to the pavilion.

Fig. 41

MICHAEL ANGELO HAYES (1820–77)

Queen Victoria and Prince Albert visiting the Irish Industrial Exhibition, Dublin, 30 August 1853

Pencil, watercolour and bodycolour with gum arabic, 32.5 × 46.0 cm

RCIN 920229

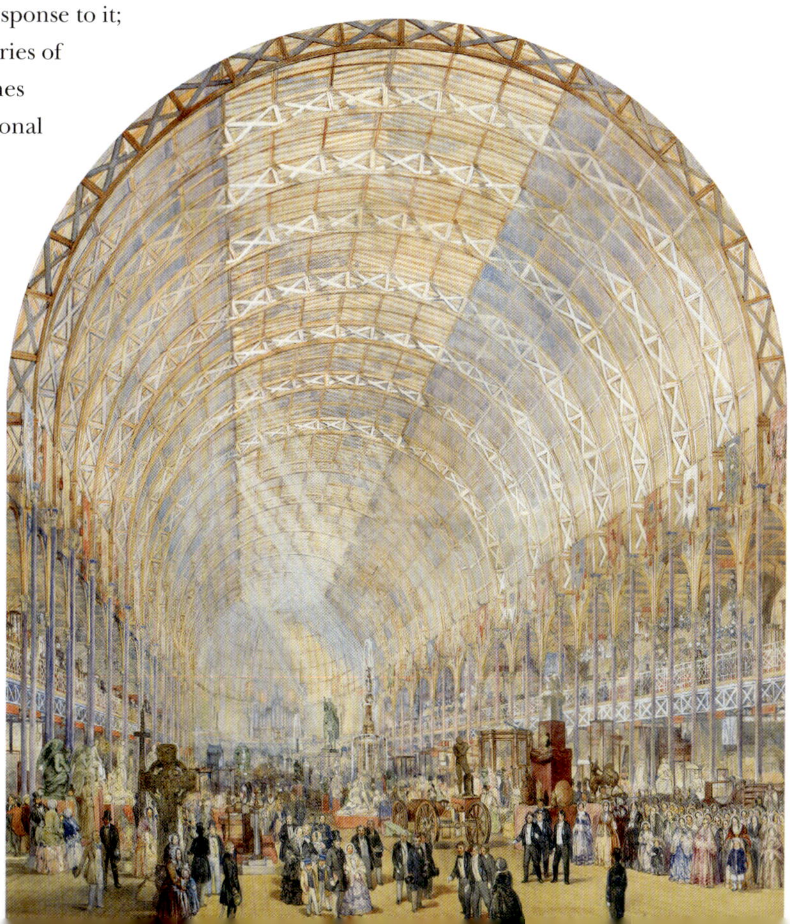

Fig. 42

JAMES MAHONY (*c.*1816–59)

The fourth visit by Queen Victoria and Prince Albert to the Irish Industrial Exhibition, Dublin, *c.*1854

Pencil, watercolour and bodycolour, 72.8 × 65.6 cm

National Gallery of Ireland, NGI.2452

Two watercolours inserted into the last of the View Albums which relate to a visit Victoria and Albert made to Ireland with some of their older children in the summer of 1861 are testament to their eagerness for tourist experiences. Their party travelled to Killarney in County Kerry, which had gained popularity as a tourist destination in the nineteenth century; the first report on the tour in *The Times* began 'Her Majesty has at last visited the loveliest spot in all her wide dominions.'[32] The royal family stayed first with Valentine Browne, Lord Castlerosse (1825–1903), at Killarney House before spending two nights at Muckross Abbey with Henry Herbert, Lord Lieutenant of the County of Kerry (1815–66), and his wife Mary. After a drive around the lake on her first full day there, Victoria declared herself 'enchanted with the extreme beauty of the scenery … It is one of the finest drives I have ever taken'; later that evening, after dinner, she recorded that their local hosts were 'so pleased at Killarney having been duly admired'.[33]

Mary Herbert was an accomplished watercolour artist – *The Times* claimed that 'among water-colour artists Mrs Herbert is held to be the most gifted amateur in the kingdom' – and the Queen noted that the walls of the rooms in which they stayed at Muckross were 'hung with beautiful watercolours by Mrs Herbert – chiefly views of Killarney'.[34] Victoria may have already been aware of Herbert's work, as her lady-in-waiting Charlotte Canning had met the Herberts in Rome in 1846 and admired Mary's art, writing to her sister that Mary's drawings were 'most beautiful, and make me very envious'.[35] With no evidence in either the Queen's journal or payment records, one can only speculate as to whether Victoria asked her hostess for examples of her work, or Mary Herbert chose to present Victoria with two of her watercolour views of the lake (fig. 43) as a souvenir of the visit. The sizes of the watercolours accord with many others known by Herbert in Muckross House and the National Library of Ireland, which may lend credence to the idea that Mary offered them to her guest.[36]

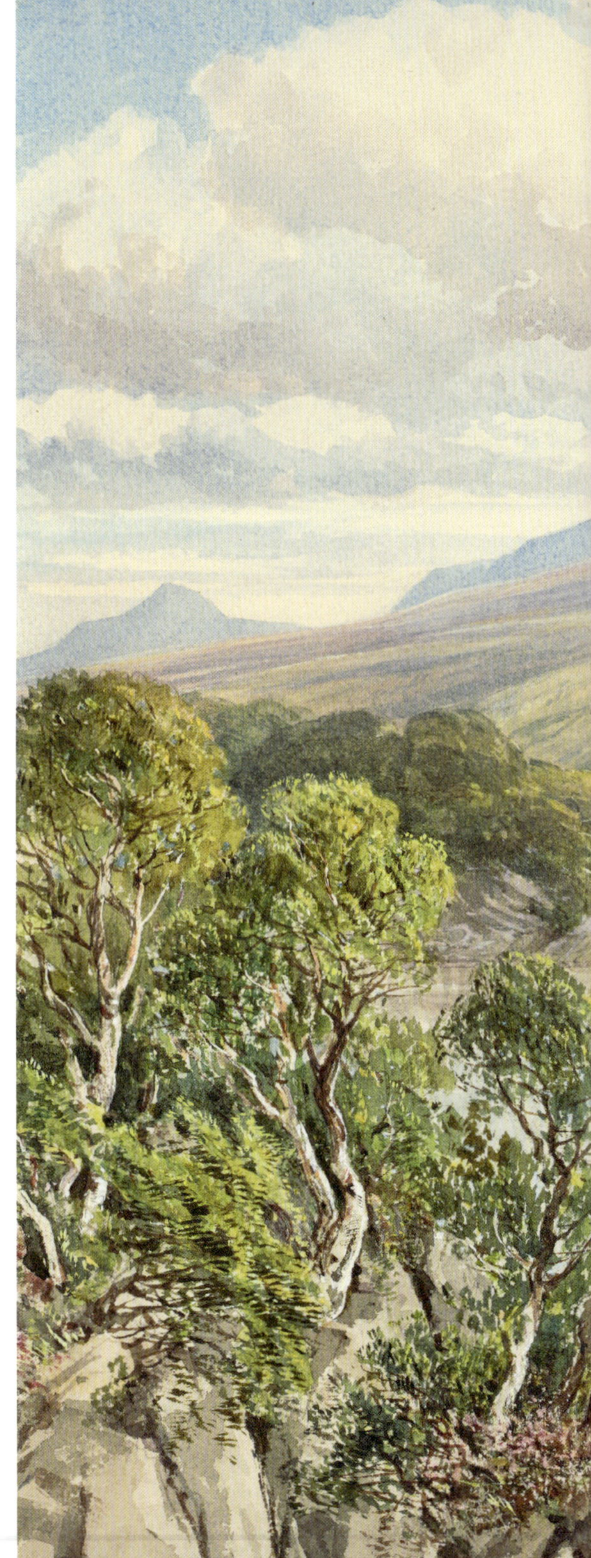

Fig. 43

MARY HERBERT (1817–93)

*Killarney Middle Lake from Copper Mine Bay, c.*1845–61

Pencil, watercolour and bodycolour, 29.7 × 45.0 cm

RCIN 920254

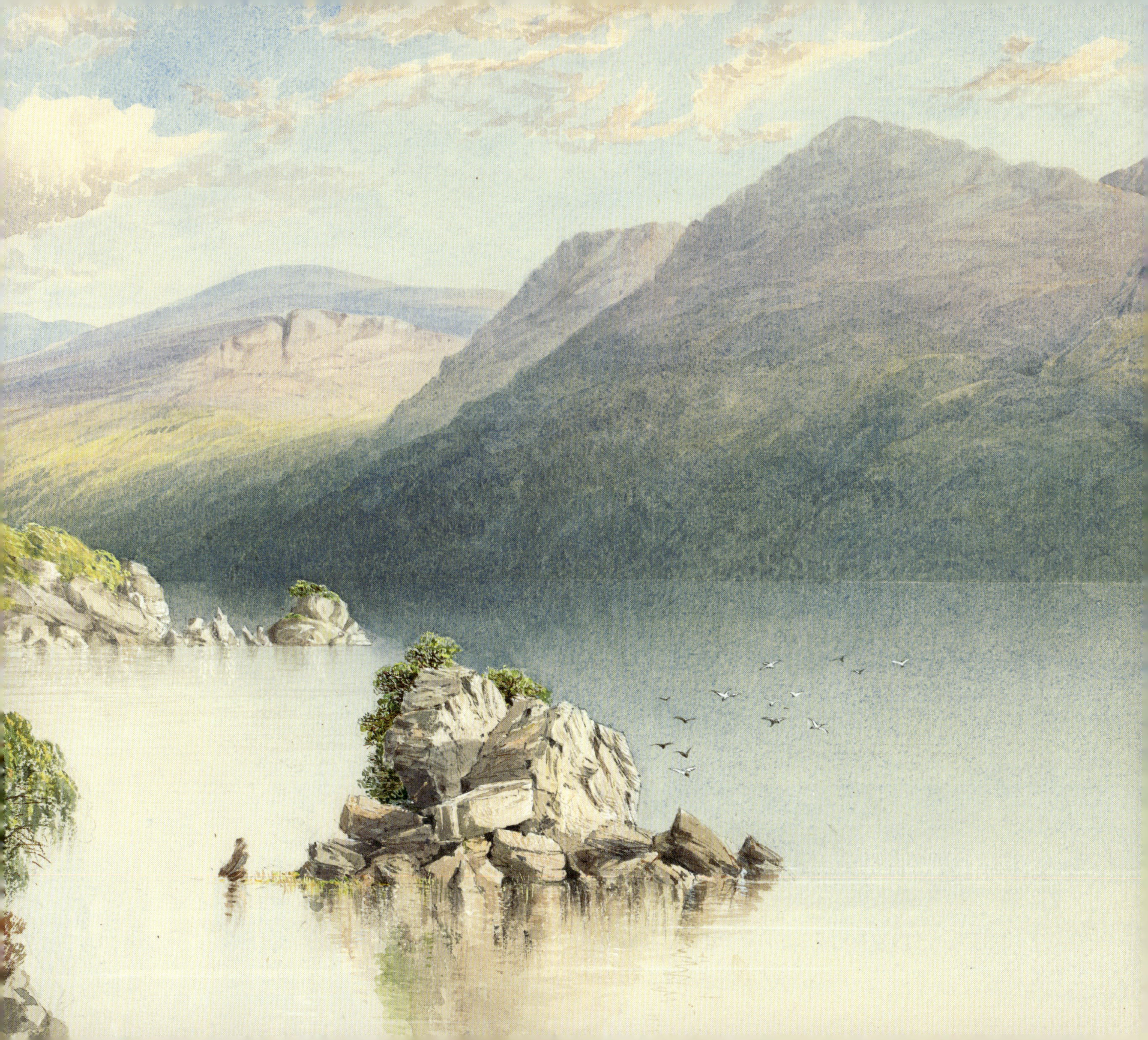

The Queen made two watercolours and two drawings at Muckross, one of which – a slight pencil sketch of a boat – she annotated: 'From a drawing by Mrs Herbert in my sitting room at Muckross Aug: 28. 1861'.[37] Immediately after the two watercolours by Mary Herbert in the ninth View Album were two further views of the lake, copies made by Richard Principal Leitch after works by Mary, which must have been commissioned soon after the royal family's return from Ireland.[38]

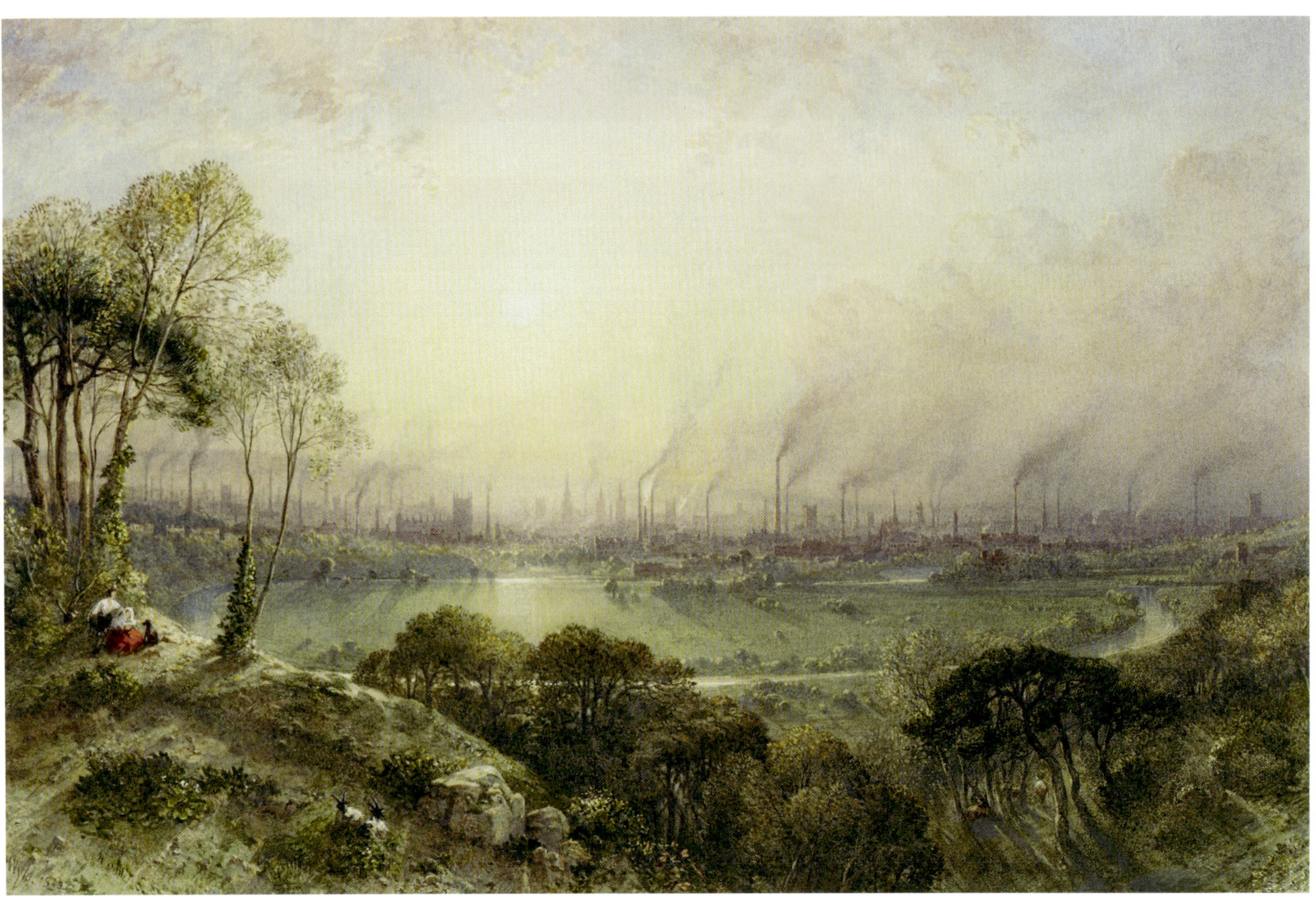

> ‘[*the view from Worsley Hall was*] *very extensive but very flat, & endless chimneys & factories rise around, in the direction of Manchester.*’
>
> – Queen Victoria

The North and the Midlands

Prince Albert’s interest in industry, manufacturing and civic development was sustained throughout his married life. Victoria’s journals are full of references to Albert taking advantage of their tours around the country to visit towns and cities, inspect factories, meet engineers, scientists, mechanics and other figures of industry, lay foundation stones and open buildings and industrial works.[39] During a visit to Drayton Manor, the seat of Prime Minister Robert Peel (1788–1850), in November 1843, for example, Albert seized the opportunity to go to Birmingham to ‘see its manufactures’.[40] Victoria shared her husband’s interest in modernisation, but her responses to the industrial areas she travelled through often emphasised its aesthetic and human impacts.[41]

The industrial focus of William Wyld’s watercolour of Manchester (fig. 44) correlates with Victoria’s own account of the visit she and Albert made to the city in October 1851, which Wyld’s view commemorates. Writing of the view from Worsley Hall in Salford, where the royal party stayed for two nights and which was approximately six miles west of Kersal Moor, the Queen recorded that it was ‘very extensive but very flat, & endless chimneys & factories rise around, in the direction of Manchester’.[42] In her own sketch of the vista (fig. 45), there

Fig. 44 (opposite)

WILLIAM WYLD

Manchester from Kersal Moor, 1852

Watercolour and bodycolour with gum arabic and scraping out, 31.9 × 49.1 cm

RCIN 920223

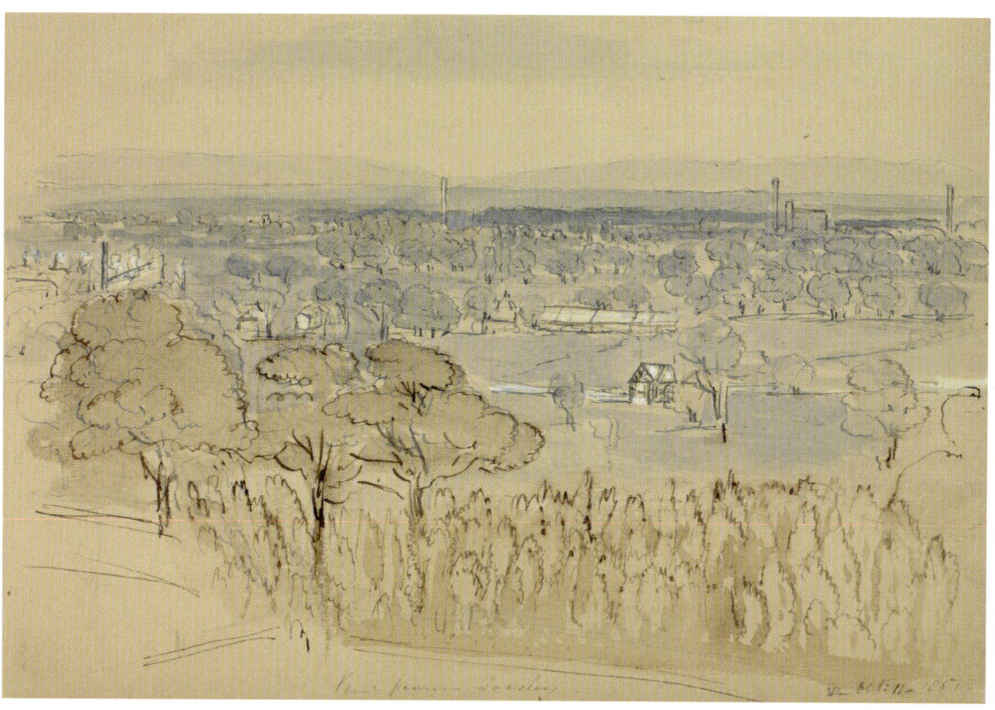

Fig. 45 (right)

QUEEN VICTORIA

A view from Worsley Hall, 11 October 1851

Pencil, pen and ink, watercolour and bodycolour, 17.7 × 25.4 cm

RCIN 981313.am

are far fewer industrial buildings than in Wyld's view, which depicts a long line of smoking chimneys on the horizon; these, however, are romanticised by the golden light of the setting sun and the inclusion of a pastoral foreground. Wyld's watercolour was reproduced, with Victoria and Albert's permission, in the *Art-Journal* of 1 July 1857, where it followed an account of the Manchester Art Treasures exhibition held that year. The accompanying text gave a brief history of Manchester with a focus on its recent manufacturing progress, and judged Wyld's work 'most agreeable'.[43]

In the Manchester view, church towers and spires are seen among the factory chimneys, reminding the viewer of the co-existence of the ancient and the modern. This was a theme which had come to the fore on the royal party's visit to Liverpool during the same trip, when the Queen, Albert and Vicky all greatly admired the new neo-Grecian St George's Hall, the interior of which was then unfinished. Victoria wrote in her journal that it was 'one of the finest modern buildings imaginable, quite worthy of ancient Athens ... Albert, whose great mind is always so ready to admire & approve all that is vast, great, & grand, was delighted.'[44] Wyld painted a watercolour of St George's Hall (fig. 46) in addition to his view of Manchester, and the fact that these two images from the short tour in the north-west, quite different in subject and treatment, match references in the Queen's journal suggests that they are likely to have been selected by Victoria and Albert themselves to be included in the fifth View Album.

The Queen visited Leeds seven years later to open its Town Hall, of which she wrote appreciatively in her journal: 'The Town Hall is a really magnificent building of very fine proportions – in the style of St George's Hall, at Liverpool.'[45] She also commissioned a view of this impressive civic monument for her album from Joseph Nash Junior (1835–1922), son of the Joseph Nash who had worked frequently for Victoria and Albert in the

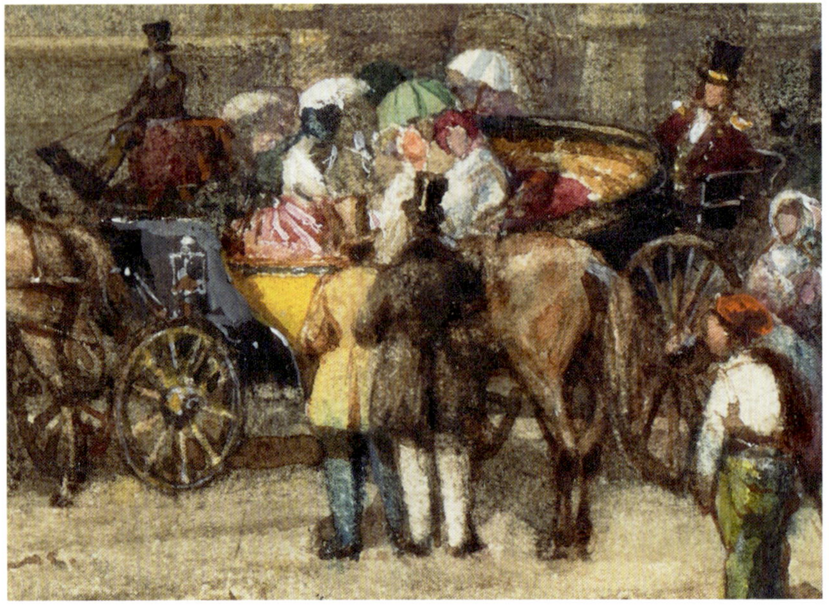

Fig. 46

WILLIAM WYLD

St George's Hall, Liverpool, 1852

Pencil, watercolour and bodycolour with gum arabic, 32.2 × 48.3 cm

RCIN 920219

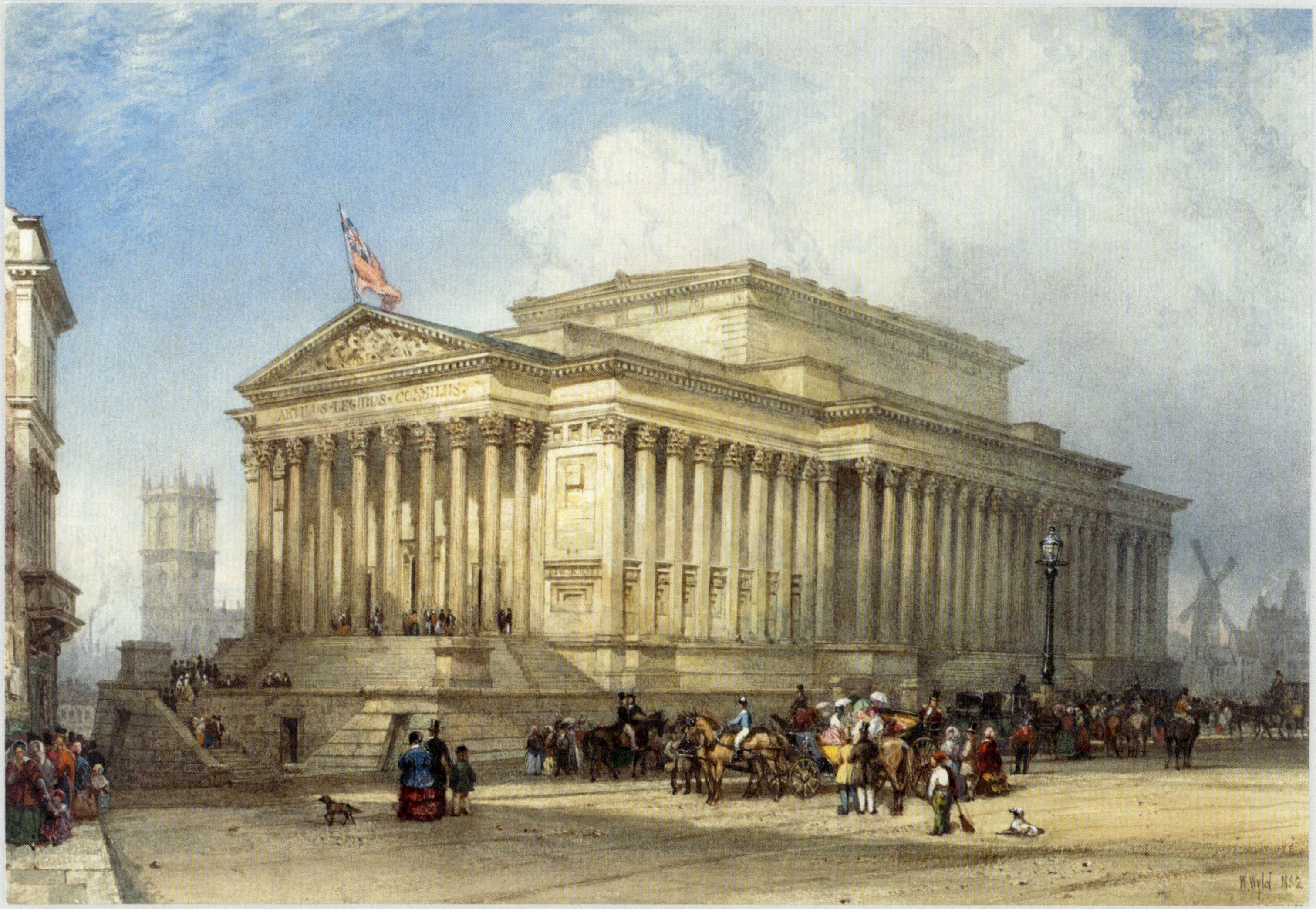

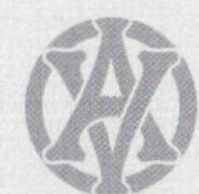

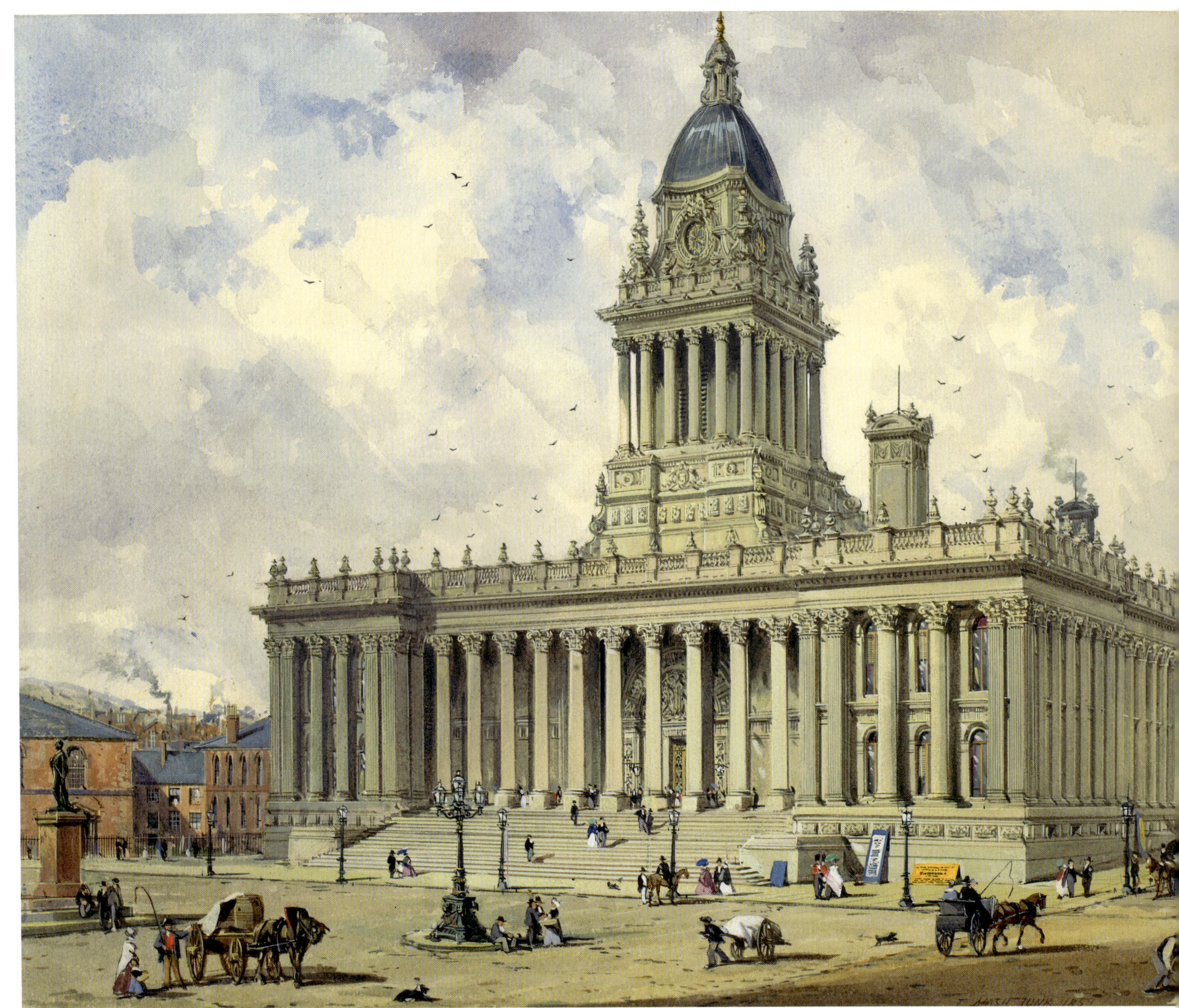

Fig. 47

JOSEPH NASH JUNIOR
(1835–1922)

The Town Hall, Leeds, 1859

Pencil, watercolour and bodycolour,
30.7 × 44.5 cm

RCIN 920246

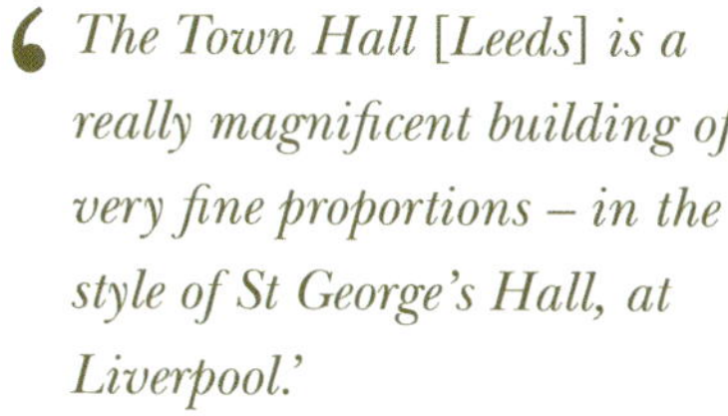

‘*The Town Hall [Leeds] is a really magnificent building of very fine proportions – in the style of St George’s Hall, at Liverpool.*’

– Queen Victoria

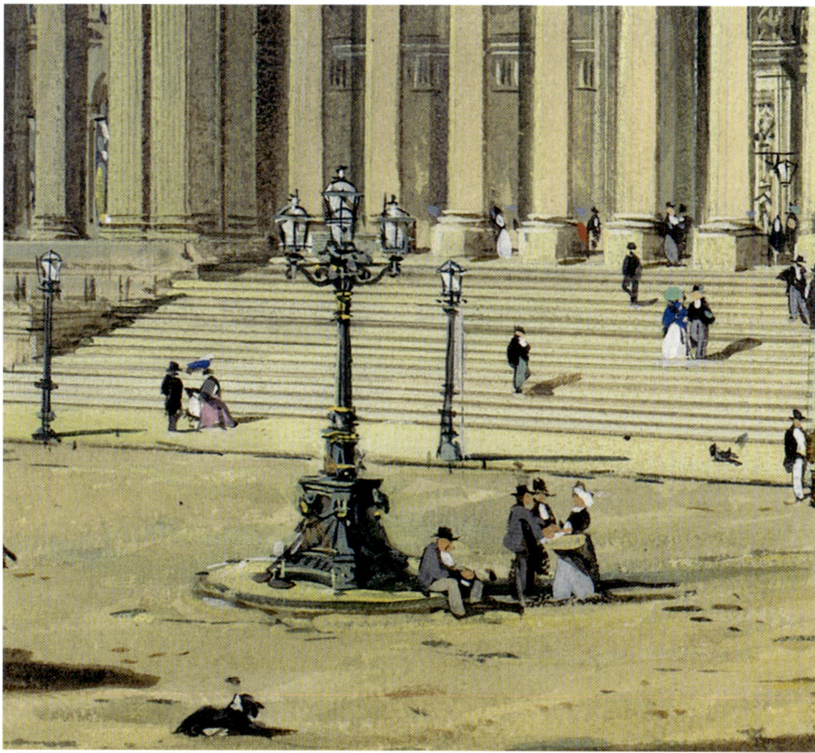

1840s and 1850s (see pp. 16, 28 and 110). Nash was paid for this watercolour (fig. 47) and his travel expenses at the beginning of November 1859. The commission could have been given to a local artist, which might have been cheaper, and there were illustrations of the Town Hall already available for Nash to base his work on; to do so would not have been unusual. But in sending Nash to the city to paint the building, the royal couple were demonstrating a concern for fidelity and a desire for (and willingness to pay for) an authentic, eye-witness view, including local detail. It may be that his employment was a gesture of support from Victoria and Albert, as Nash Senior had become unwell in the mid-1850s and was unable to continue painting.[46] His son’s work presumably found favour with the royal patrons, as he received another commission from them a few years later.

The son of another of Victoria and Albert's favoured artists, William Leighton Leitch, was also given a commission at around the same time, which again celebrated civic pride and achievement. Richard Principal Leitch painted a view of Aston Hall in Birmingham (fig. 48) following Victoria and Albert's visit there in June 1858 to open its grounds as a public park. Leitch's view of the hall and grounds speaks to the purpose of the royal visit, in that it shows members of the public enjoying the new park, including a small girl to the right rolling her hoop. He also alludes to his own profession through the inclusion of a stool and artist's portfolio in the immediate foreground. The fluidly painted figures combine with the carefully delineated but not highly finished appearance of the building (across the left-hand side of which strong shadows stretch) to suggest the capturing of a fleeting moment in time.

Tours of the South Coast on the royal yacht

On their travels around the country during their marriage, for both duty and pleasure, Victoria and Albert were pragmatic about the arrangements. When unfavourable winds or general bad weather caused difficulties and delays, their response was to reserve rooms in the nearest hotel, such as when they stayed at the George Inn at Perth and then the Station Inn at Crewe on consecutive nights on their way back from Scotland in September 1848, much to the surprise of the townspeople and indeed the hotel proprietors.[47] They also embraced modernity, travelling long distances by train from as early as the first Scottish tour in 1842. Unfortunately, no depictions of these aspects of their travels appear to have been commissioned. More conventionally, the albums did contain idyllic scenes of the coastal landscapes the royal family encountered while aboard one of their favoured modes of transport – the royal yacht, which they used to make regular cruises around the British coast and across to Ireland. With the purchase of Osborne in 1845, the south coast became a favoured cruising location, and provided the subjects for a number of watercolours mounted in the View Albums.[48]

On seeing the royal family towards the end of September 1846 after a few months absence, the Queen's maid of honour Eleanor Stanley described them as being 'browned with the sun'.[49] During the preceding months Victoria, Albert and their two eldest children, Vicky and Bertie, had made a number of excursions on the royal yacht, using Osborne as their base – visiting the largest of the Channel Islands, Guernsey and Jersey, and making stops along the south

Fig. 48

RICHARD PRINCIPAL LEITCH (1826–82)

Aston Hall, Birmingham, 1859

Pencil, watercolour and bodycolour, 23.0 × 33.4 cm

RCIN 920244

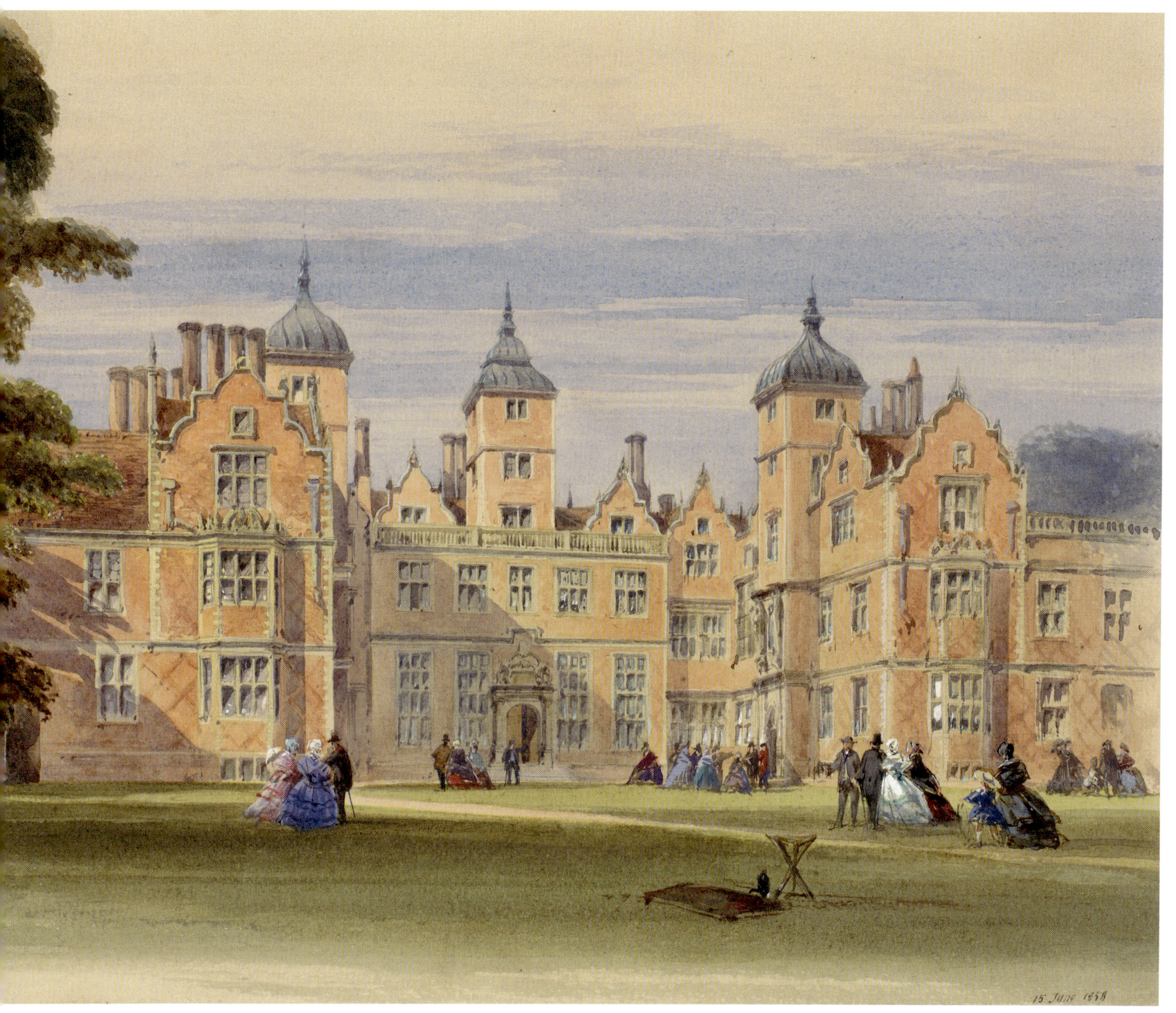
15 June 1858

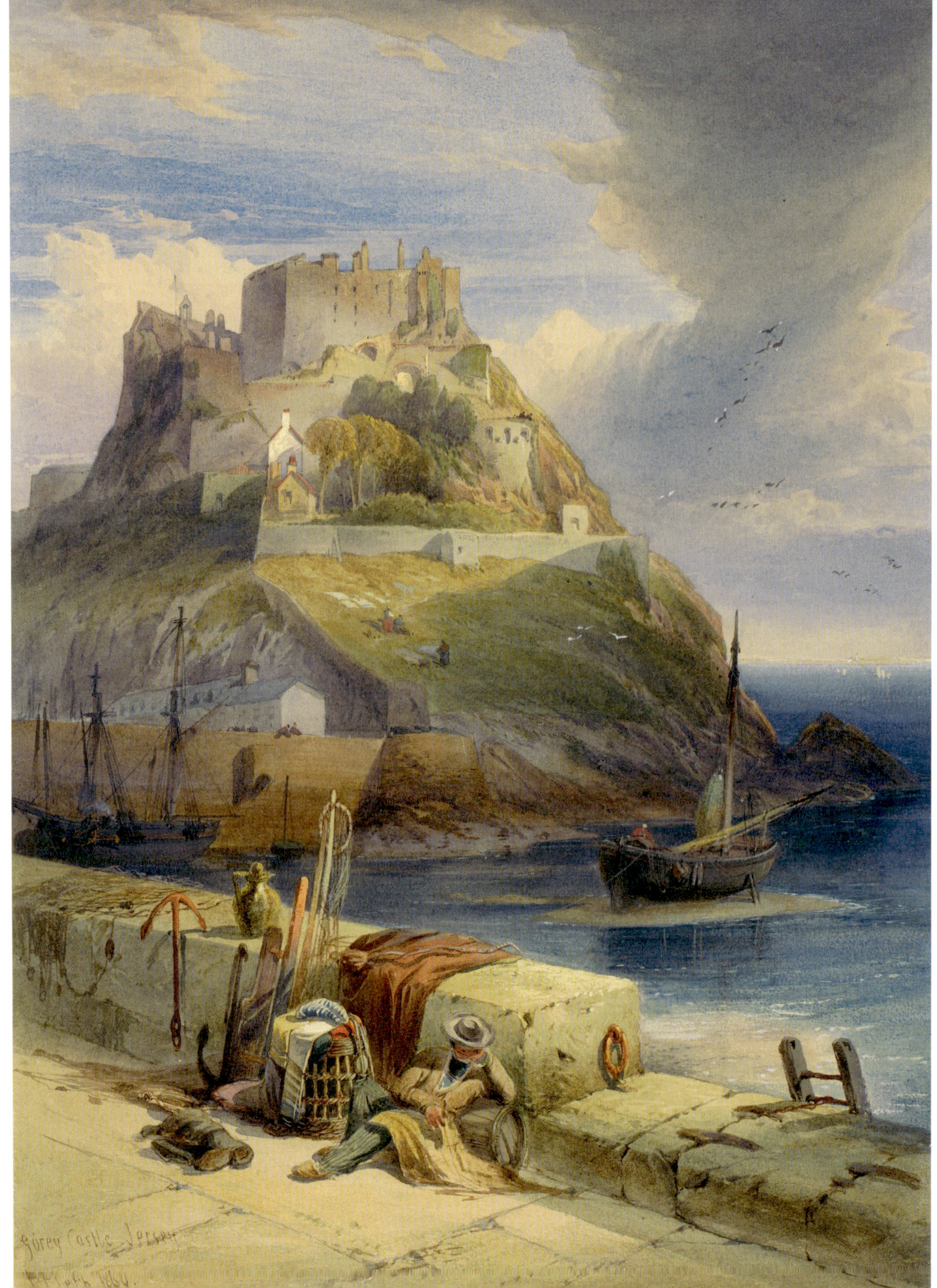
Gorey Castle Jersey

Fig. 49

RICHARD PRINCIPAL LEITCH

Gorey Castle, Jersey, 1860

Pencil, watercolour and bodycolour, 46.2 × 32.5 cm

RCIN 920248

coast on their way to Cornwall, the duchy of the Prince of Wales. The Queen wrote to her uncle Leopold from the yacht during one such trip, delighted with the reception they had received as well as the scenery; Jersey, she said, was 'beautiful, and like an orchard'.[50] While there, Victoria and Albert visited Gorey Castle (Mont Orgueil), on the east coast of the island. Thirteen years later, in August 1859, the royal yacht anchored off the same coast for a night, and the following year a view of the castle by Richard Principal Leitch was incorporated into the eighth View Album (fig. 49). The watercolour perhaps bears more relation to Victoria and Albert's first view of the castle in 1846 than their later one, as it is a romanticised daytime scene, where the eye is led upwards from the fisherman asleep on the jetty in the bottom foreground, via his boat moored in the bay behind, to the castle above on its rocky promontory. It is one of three Jersey views painted by Leitch in 1860 'according to the Queen's requests', as the entry in Victoria's private account book stipulates.[51]

A watercolour mounted in the fourth View Album which depicts the landing of the royal couple on Guernsey during the 1846 voyage (fig. 50) was painted by a local artist. Paul Jacob Naftel, a Guernsey-born landscape painter and drawing master, was then at the beginning of his career.[52] According to the *Illustrated London News,* which published a reproduction of his depiction of the scene (fig. 51), Naftel was present at Victoria and Albert's arrival at the town of St Pierre (St Peter Port) on 24 August:

> *[F]rom the extreme interest which it has excited among all the classes of her Majesty's loyal subjects at Guernsey, we have been induced to commemorate the Royal Visit, graphically; and this we are enabled to do with considerable effect, by the skill of an Artist who witnessed the animated spectacle of the Queen's Debarkation at the Harbour of the "privileged island;" – and has commemorated the most striking point in a very spirited sketch.*[53]

Two months later, the same newspaper reported, 'We understand that her Majesty was much pleased with Mr Naftel's picture of the Queen's landing at Guernsey. The artist has received a letter with this gratifying announcement, and stating that the keeper of the Privy Purse would forward 25 guineas to him.'[54]

As has been noted, Victoria and Albert kept abreast of press reports on their activities – the Queen recorded that the couple spent the evening of 9 September, the day they returned to Osborne from their cruise to Jersey and Cornwall, 'arrang[ing] prints of our journey' – and perhaps they saw the reproduction

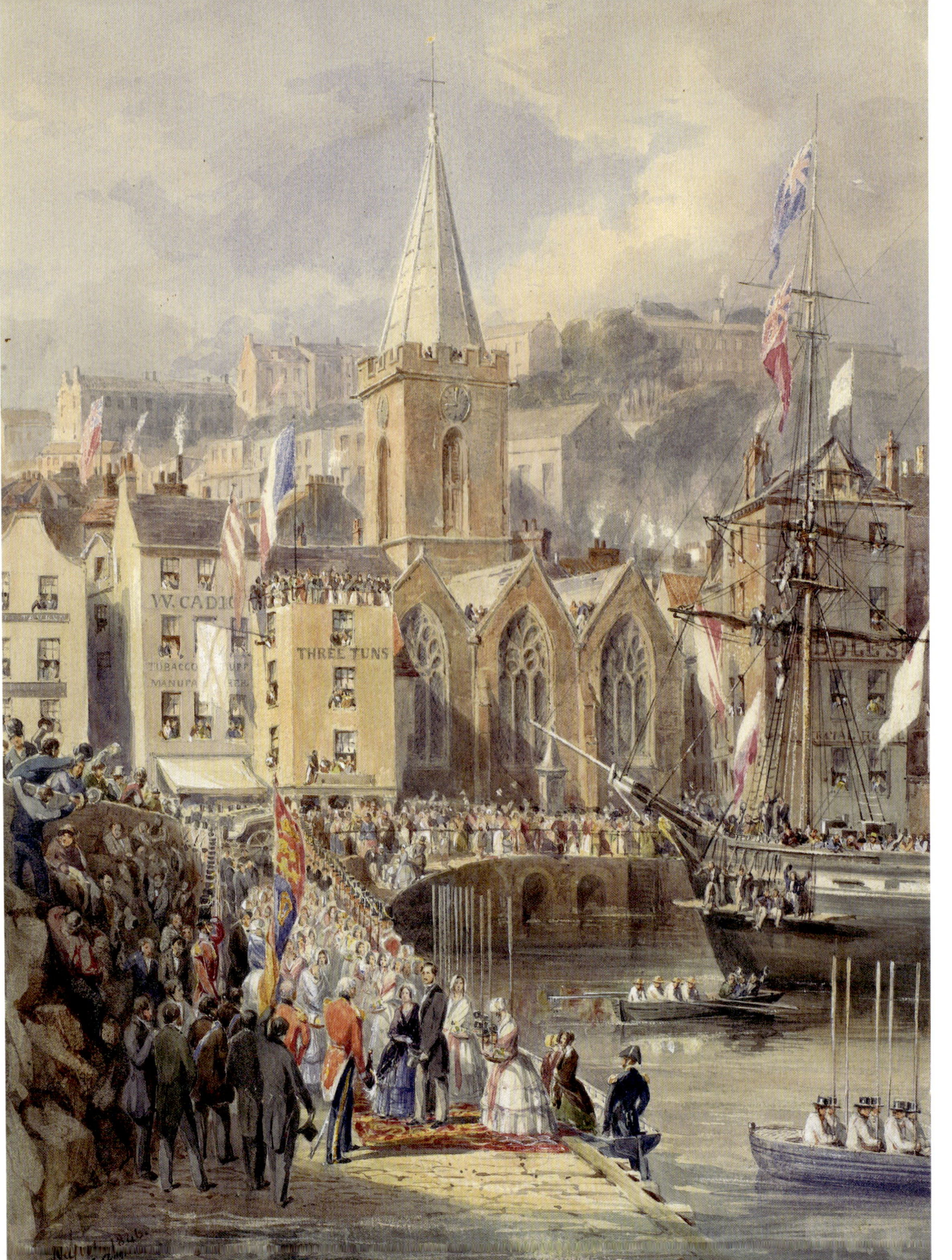

Fig. 50

PAUL JACOB NAFTEL (1817–91)

Queen Victoria and Prince Albert landing at St Pierre, Guernsey, 1846

Pencil, watercolour and bodycolour, 32.8 × 23.7 cm

RCIN 920182

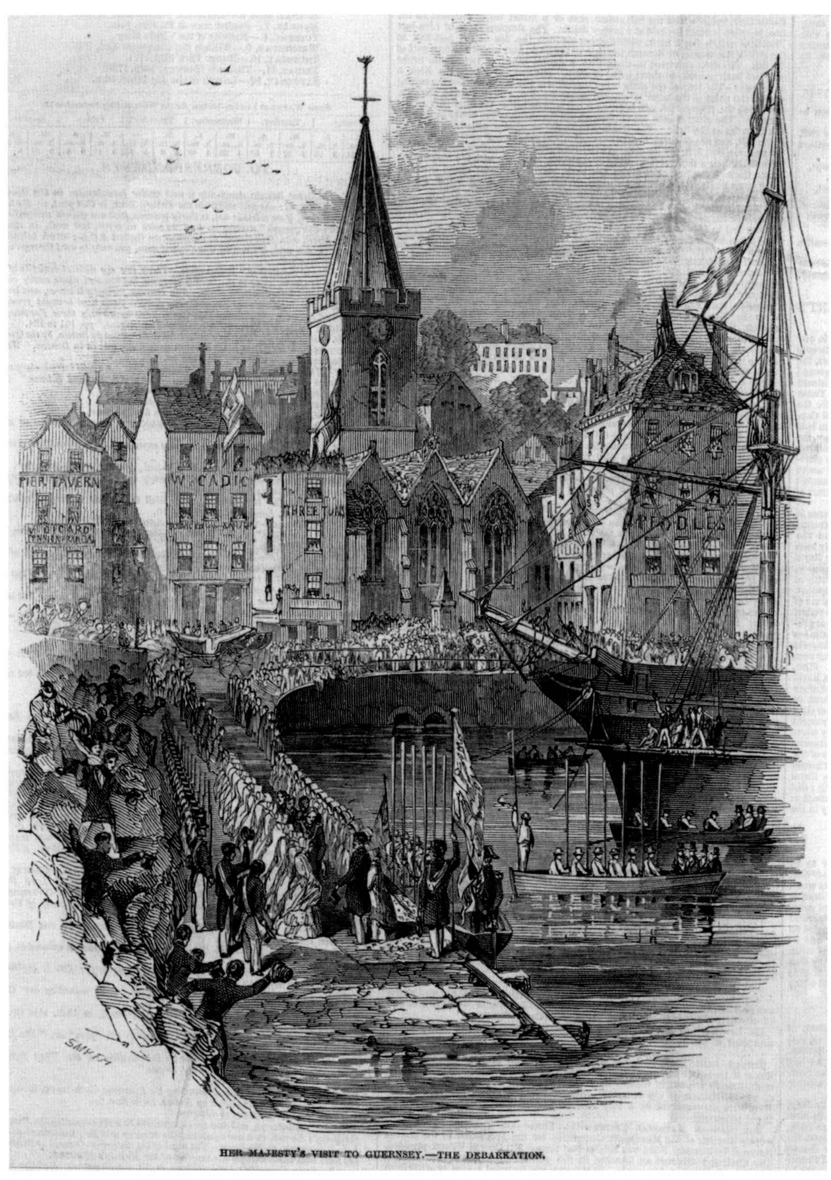

of Naftel's sketch in the *Illustrated London News* and enquired about the identity of the artist. There is a significant discrepancy between the newspaper illustration and the watercolour, which may suggest that the royal patrons requested a compositional alteration. In the former, the Queen and Prince have just stepped on to the quay and, seen from behind, turn towards an approaching figure in military dress – presumably General William Napier, Lieutenant Governor of Guernsey (1785–1860), who welcomed them to the island.[55] In the watercolour, however, it is Napier, with his hat doffed, who is pictured from behind, and Victoria and Albert face him and therefore the viewer. It is perhaps unsurprising that this illustration of a moment from their tours appealed so much to Victoria, who wrote of her delight when it was decided to visit Guernsey as she had for 'so long wished to see it'.[56]

❀ ❀ ❀

> *'We understand that her Majesty was much pleased with Mr Naftel's picture of the Queen's landing at Guernsey.'*
>
> – *Illustrated London News*

Fig. 51

After PAUL JACOB NAFTEL

Her Majesty's visit to Guernsey

Illustrated London News, 5 September 1846, p. 149

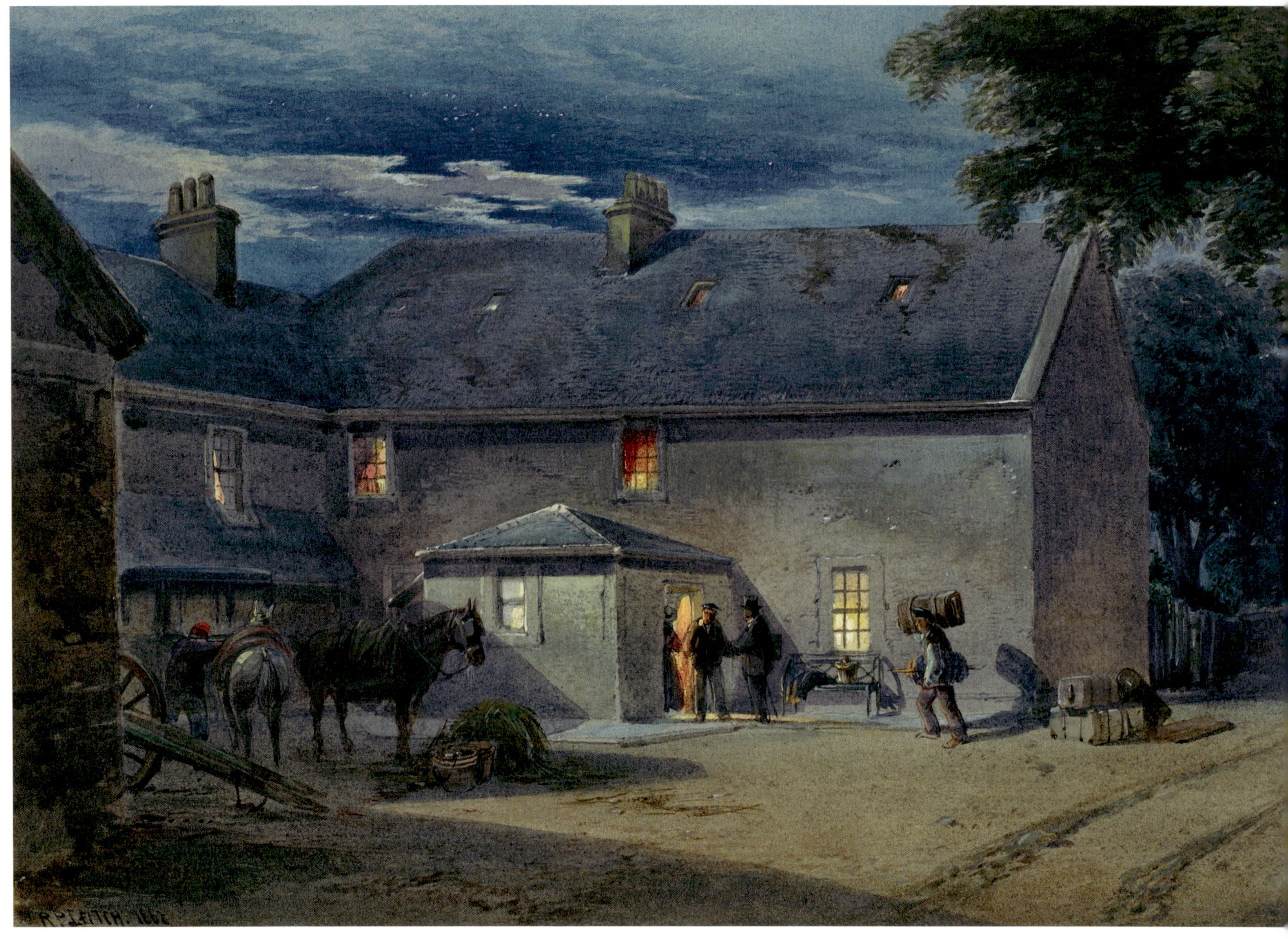

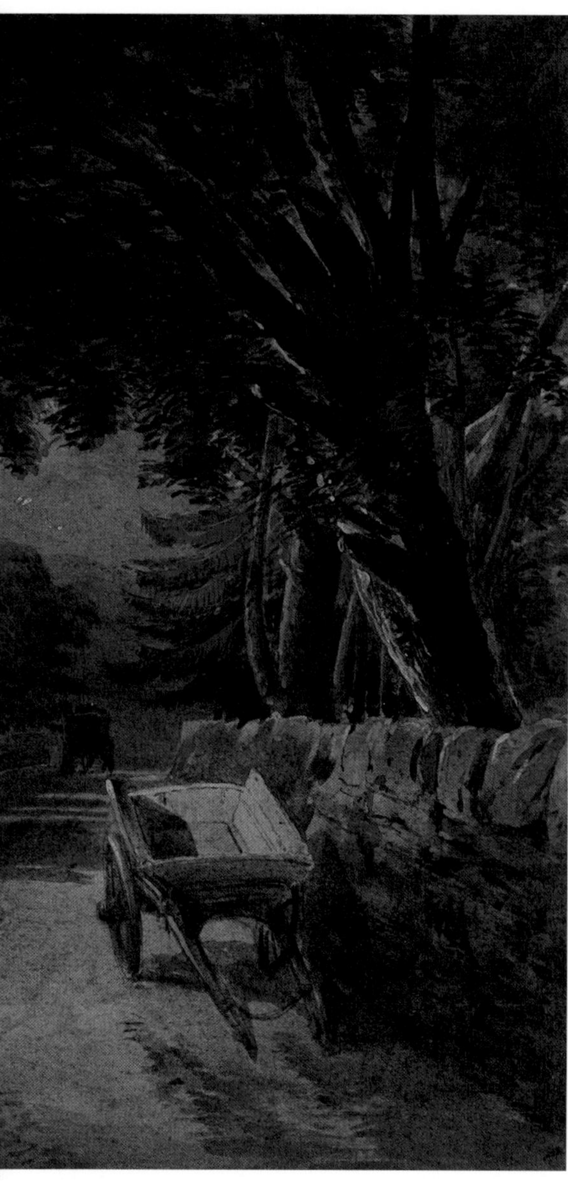

Fig. 52

RICHARD PRINCIPAL LEITCH

The farm at Dalwhinnie, 1862

Pencil, watercolour and bodycolour,
20.6 × 41.0 cm

RCIN 919656

> '*This was the pleasantest & most enjoyable expedition I ever took & the recollection of which will ever be most agreeable & increase my wish to make more.*'
>
> – Queen Victoria

In the last year or so of Albert's life, he and Victoria made four 'Great Expeditions' in the Highlands.[57] During these they would travel incognito and with a small suite for a few days, staying at local inns – on the first expedition (4–5 September 1860), Victoria recorded in her journal that they called themselves 'L[or]d & L[ad]y Churchill & party'.[58] After Albert's death the Queen commissioned a group of watercolours from Richard Principal Leitch relating to these trips. The fidelity of the views was important to her; photographs taken by George Washington Wilson of Highland scenery were deemed unsatisfactory, and so Leitch was sent instead.[59] Two of Leitch's watercolours were views of inns in which the royal party had stayed, including an atmospheric night scene at Dalwhinnie showing the royal luggage being carried in (fig. 52) from the third expedition in October 1861. Though Victoria was not especially impressed with the accommodation or food offered there, she did feel that 'this was the pleasantest & most enjoyable expedition I ever took & the recollection of which will ever be most agreeable & increase my wish to make more'.[60] She and Albert were to undertake only one further tour, however, and the incorporation of Leitch's scenes in the last two View Albums made for a poignant coda to these precious volumes.

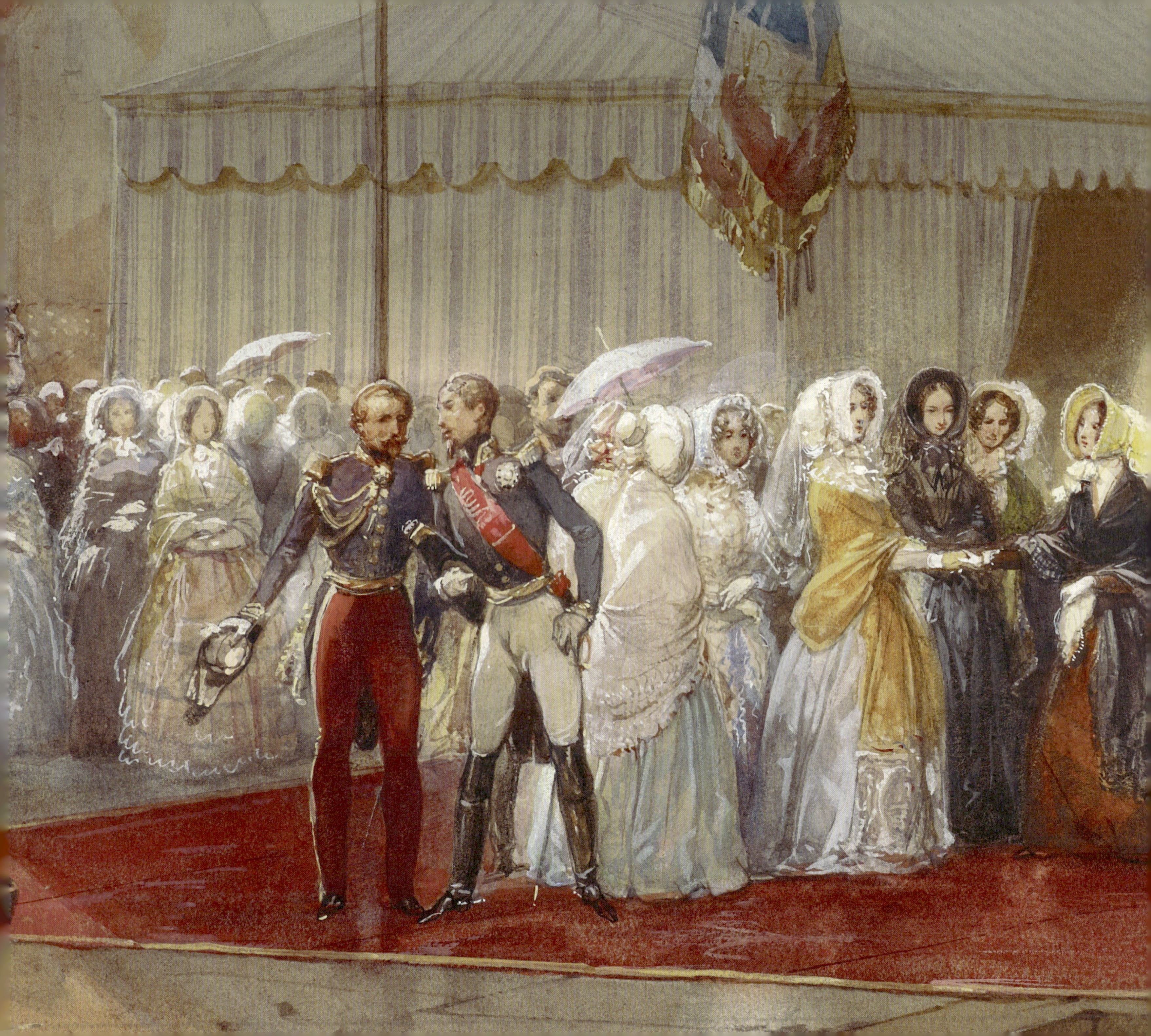

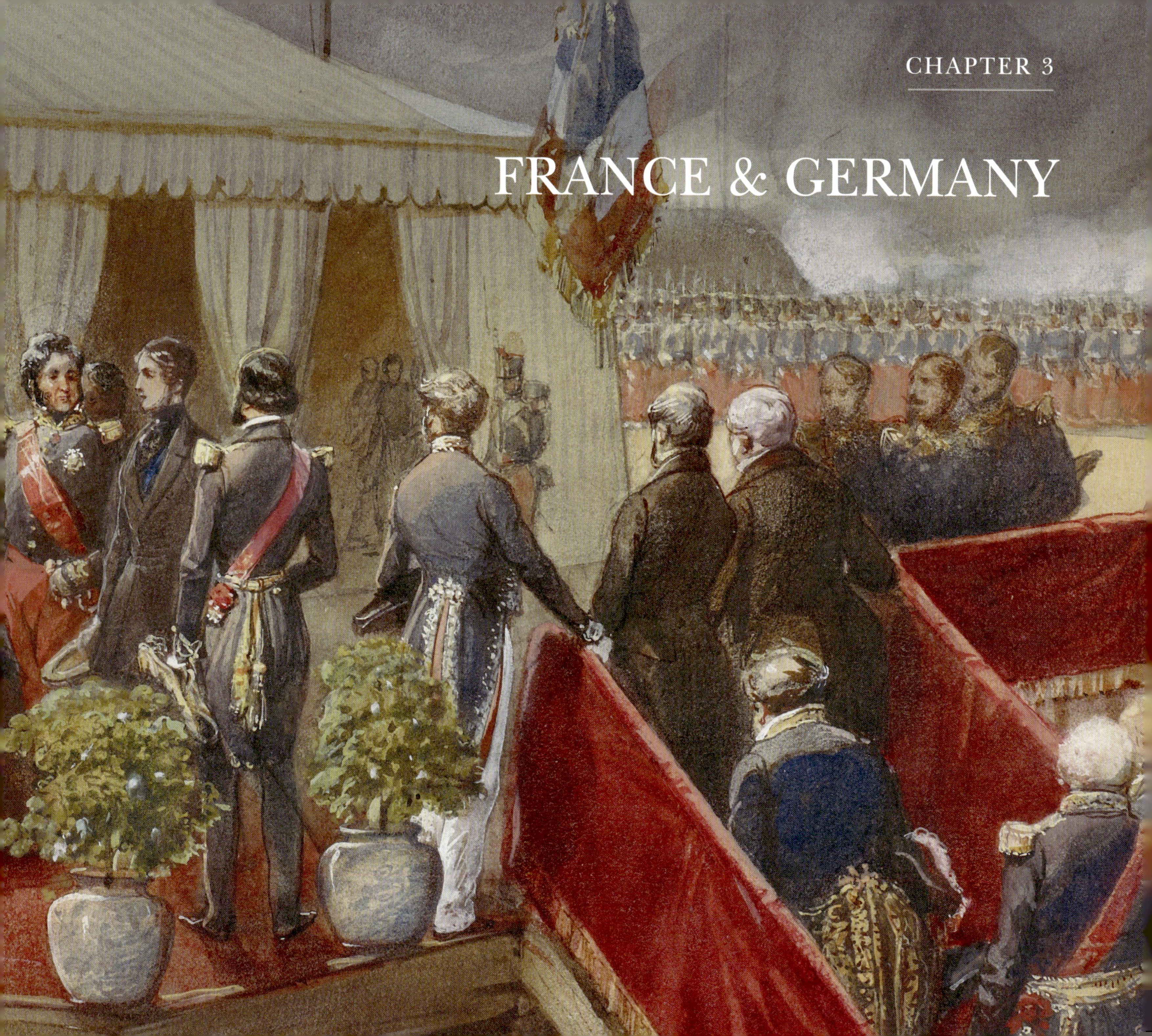

CHAPTER 3

FRANCE & GERMANY

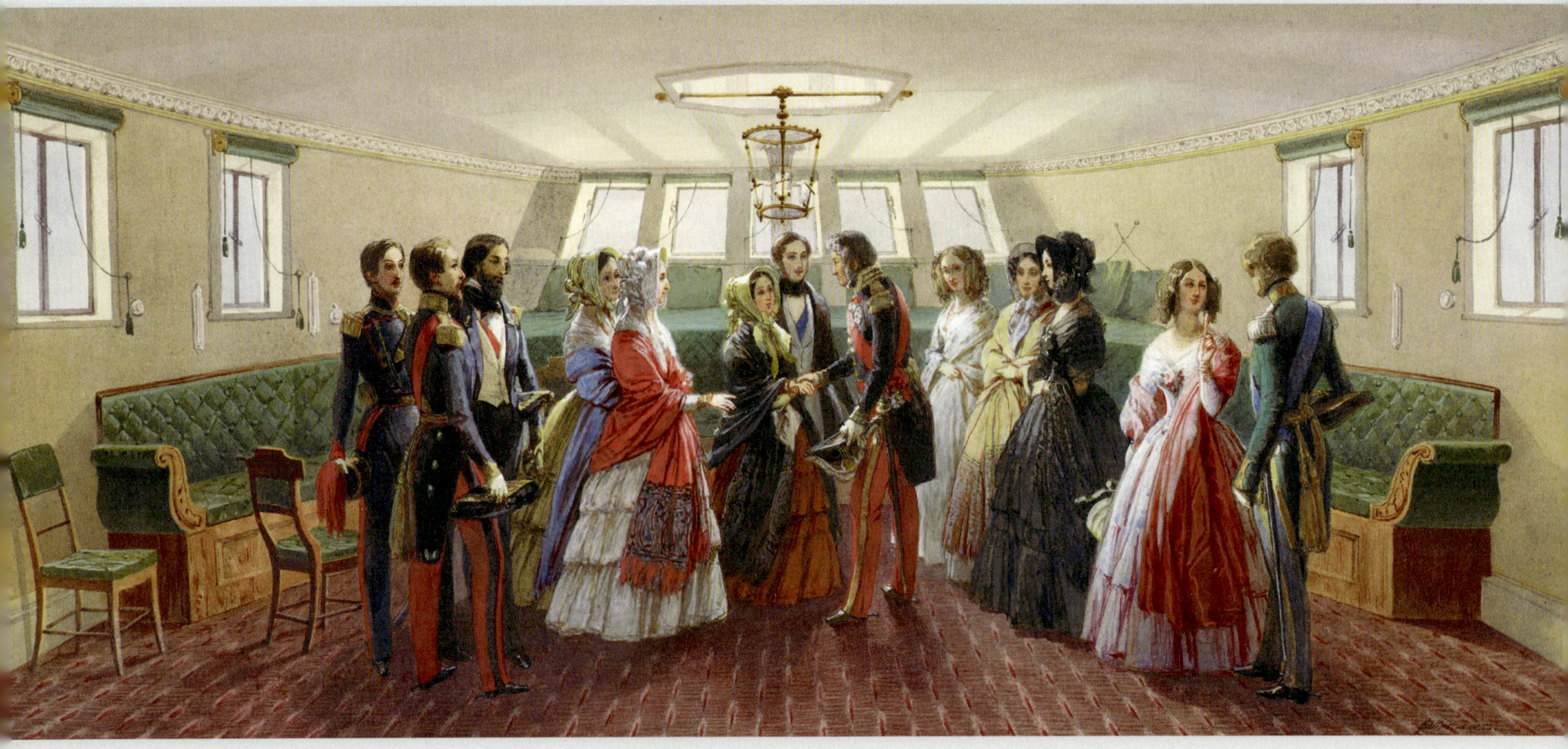

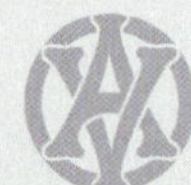

CHAPTER 3

France & Germany

'I would give millions to behold but for a day Brussels, Paris, Germany, Italy & Spain and envy all those who do!'[1]

– Queen Victoria

Queen Victoria had always yearned to explore the world beyond her own kingdom. Before her first excursion abroad in 1843, she could only encounter different places, traditions and customs second-hand, through the novels she read and the stories of travellers she knew, including Prince Albert. In her widowhood, she recorded that one of her 'greatest treasures' was an album sent to her by the Prince in 1837, compiled by Albert himself and containing watercolour views and mementoes – including a dried flower – of his recent tour of Italy and Switzerland.[2] When as a young princess she wrote to thank him for the gift, though, she could not help but admit her jealousy: 'I cannot say, how I envy you having seen Venice, which of all other places (Naples and Paris excepted) I would like to see.'[3]

While she did not visit either Italy or Switzerland until her widowhood, Victoria did travel abroad several times during her marriage, visiting France, Belgium and Germany. She felt profoundly grateful for her first experience of foreign travel. Writing in September 1843 to her uncle Leopold (whom she had recently visited in Belgium after travelling first to France), she confessed that she was finding 'Windsor and its daily occurrences very dull', but recognised that 'this is very ungrateful for what I have had, which is so much more than I ever dared to hope for'.[4] Although many of the trips Victoria and Albert made were ostensibly private ones to visit relatives at other European courts, these journeys were politically as well as personally significant. As was the case at home, newspaper proprietors sent reporters and artists to follow the royal family on their travels, providing extensive, illustrated first-hand accounts of their activities. Again, too, Victoria and Albert commissioned and collected watercolours documenting these journeys, which they mounted into their View Albums; some

Fig. 53

FRANZ XAVER WINTERHALTER

Louis-Philippe taking leave of Queen Victoria on board the royal yacht, c.1843–4

Pencil, watercolour and bodycolour with gum arabic, 19.4 × 44.0 cm

RCIN 920029

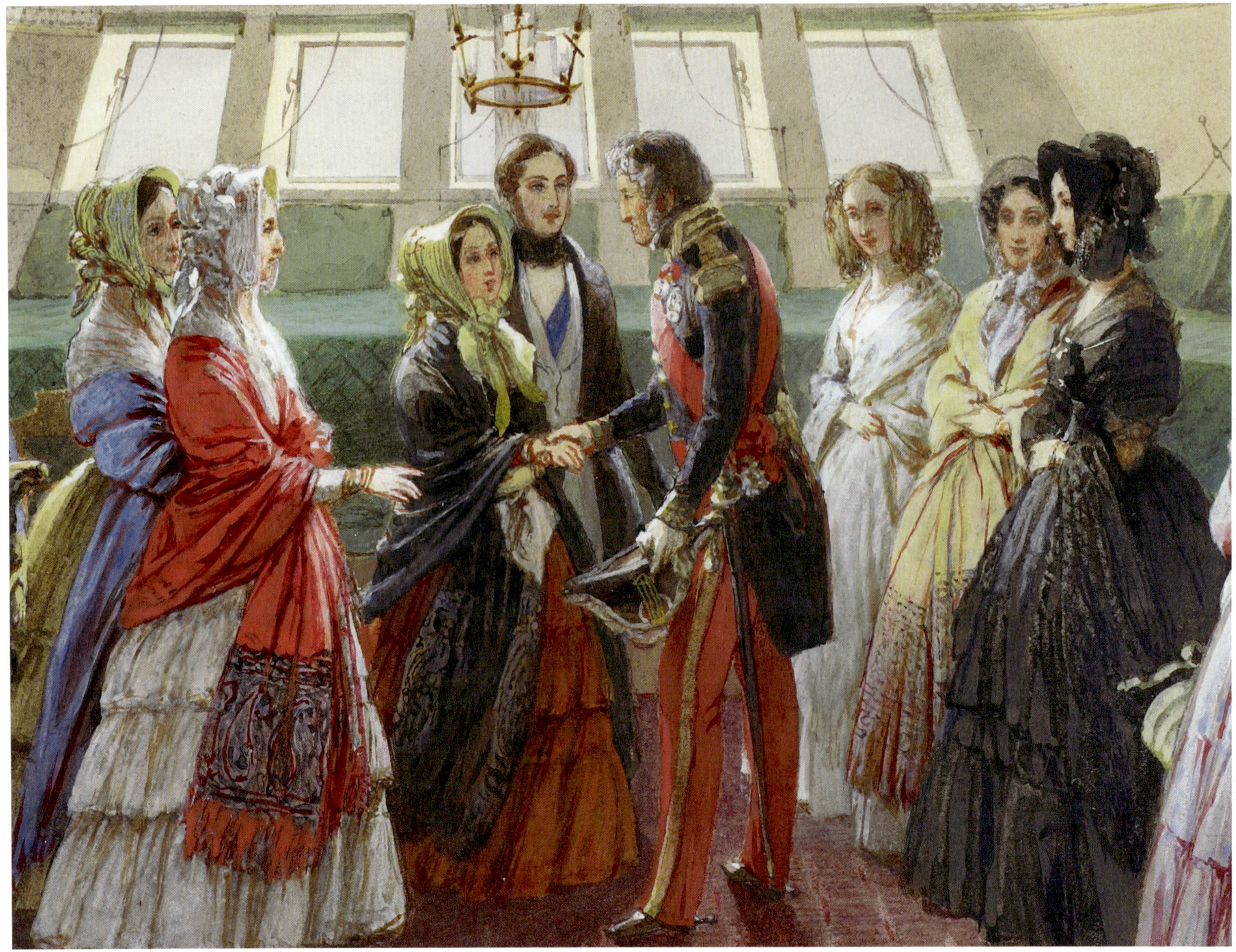

of their hosts also presented them with albums of watercolours as souvenirs. Thanks to this custom of gift-giving the royal couple were introduced to European artists whose work they came to appreciate. Victoria and Albert returned the favour on reciprocal visits, commissioning their own preferred artists to attend court functions and festivities in order to produce watercolours both for themselves and as mementoes for their guests.

'My beautiful Album d'Eu'[5]

In October 1844, it was widely reported that Louis-Philippe, King of the French (1773–1850), had presented an album of watercolours to Queen Victoria in commemoration of her and Albert's sojourn the previous year at the château d'Eu in Normandy. This visit, which took place 2–7 September, was a private one, made at the invitation of the King, but it was of especial significance. It was Victoria's first journey abroad, and also – as all of those involved were very aware – an historic moment for another reason; it was the first meeting of the sovereigns of France and Britain since the 'gorgeous festivities of the Field of the Cloth of Gold', the name given to the meeting of Henry VIII and François I in France in 1520.[6]

'It is one of the customs of the king of the French, to have the history of his times written by painters and sculptors.'

– Jules Janin

The form and content of Louis-Philippe's album appears to have been appropriately grand for the momentous occasion it celebrated. Press reports stressed its monumentality (using phrases such as 'of uncommon dimensions' and 'of unusually large size') and described its scarlet morocco leather binding decorated with the British royal arms and elaborate frontispiece. These accounts also noted that the 'first French artists' painted the thirty-two watercolours in the album, which illustrated events from the visit and some of the rooms in the château.[7] French journalists saw a nationalistic angle to the gift; *L'Illustration* stated 'England will undoubtedly find, by this precious collection, that France holds the sceptre for painting and drawing', and the *Gazette des Beaux-Arts* was pleased that Louis-Philippe was 'plac[ing] the works of our contemporaneous artists amongst the treasures of Windsor'.[8] The King chose his magnificent and simultaneously personal present extremely well – Victoria wrote in glowing terms in her journal of the 'really splendid album', awarding the watercolours her highest praise: 'they are beautifully executed & arranged & a most precious memento, as the greater part are so like what took place.'[9]

Fifteen artists produced watercolours for the Album d'Eu, some of whom collaborated on single scenes. It is unsurprising that the artist who painted the last and arguably the most personal of the watercolours in the album – of the leave-taking at the end of the visit (fig. 53), when Louis-Philippe and his relations boarded Victoria and Albert's yacht to say a final farewell to their guests – was Franz Xaver Winterhalter. By the autumn of 1843 Winterhalter was fast becoming Victoria and Albert's favourite portrait painter. Early in her reign Victoria had greatly admired portraits of her relations by him, such as that of her aunt and close friend Louise, Queen of the Belgians, with her eldest son, which Victoria considered 'quite lovely, so like her, and beautifully painted'.[10] It was Louise who recommended Winterhalter to Victoria and Albert, praising him as 'particularly lucky in catching a likeness' and a 'very excellent man full of zeal for his art, of good will, obligingness, and real modesty'.[11] These artistic and personal qualities would have particularly appealed to them – the ability to achieve a good likeness especially by the Queen. In the space of just his first year working for the British court

Winterhalter painted Victoria three times and Albert twice, as well as producing a portrait each of their two eldest children. Winterhalter had also worked extensively for the French court, painting the king, queen and a number of their children – one of whom was Louise of the Belgians. The artist therefore was already familiar with the family group he represented in his Album d'Eu watercolour.

It appears that Winterhalter did not personally witness the 'affectionate leave[-taking]', as it was termed by one of Victoria's maids of honour;[12] he spent the period from July to September in Britain, working on large oil portraits of Victoria and Albert, and his name is not referred to in the accounts of the visit either by the Queen or her ladies, nor in newspaper reports. Louis-Philippe perhaps described the scene to the artist himself. There is a clear emphasis on intimacy in the watercolour, conveyed in several different ways: its unusual horizontal format, which concentrates attention on the figures; the central focus on the joining of Victoria and Louis-Philippe's hands, further emphasised by the gesture of Queen Marie-Amélie (1782–1866); and (on the far right) Princess Clémentine (1817–1907, the youngest daughter of the French king) and her husband, engaged in conversation, suggesting the capturing of a brief personal encounter.

The album also brought the talents of Eugène-Louis Lami, another artist especially favoured by Louis-Philippe, to Victoria and Albert's attention. According to the contemporary writer and critic Jules Janin (1804–74), Lami was in attendance during the visit at the request of Louis-Philippe, 'for it is one of the customs of the king of the French, to have the history of his times written by painters and sculptors.'[13] As Janin went on to explain, in addition to the watercolours for the presentation album, Louis-Philippe had also commissioned a group of artists to make large-scale oil paintings to be displayed in what came to be known as the Galerie Victoria at Eu; Janin reported in 1843 that 'the artists are already at their task, and you may be sure they will not delay, so much are they pleased with the heroine, the beauty of the scene, the magnificence of the sea and sky.'[14] A specialist in depicting court festivities, Lami painted seven of the album watercolours, all of which are scenes busy with action and figures. The first of the watercolours in the album to feature close-up depictions of people was by Lami (fig. 54), and in it clasped hands (those of the two queens) are again the focal point at the centre of the composition. Thus the album began and ended with a visible manifestation of intimate friendship – or, as Louis-Philippe termed it, the *cordiale entente*.[15] Victoria herself wrote that

Fig. 54

EUGÈNE-LOUIS LAMI (1800–90)

Marie-Amélie, Queen of the French, greets Queen Victoria at Le Tréport, c.1843–4

Pencil, watercolour and bodycolour, 23.0 × 36.3 cm

RCIN 919996

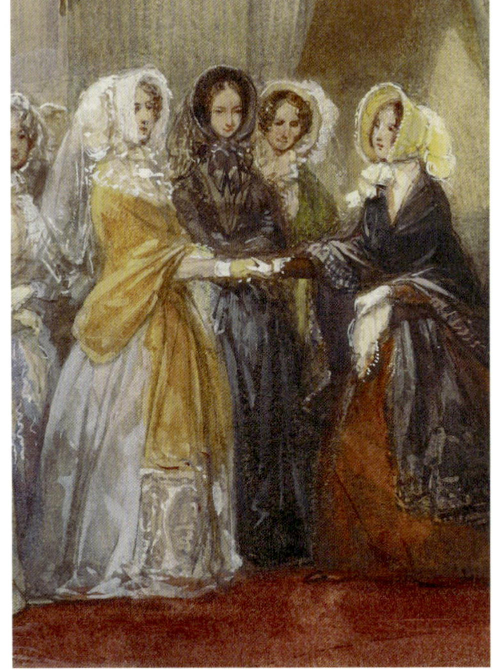

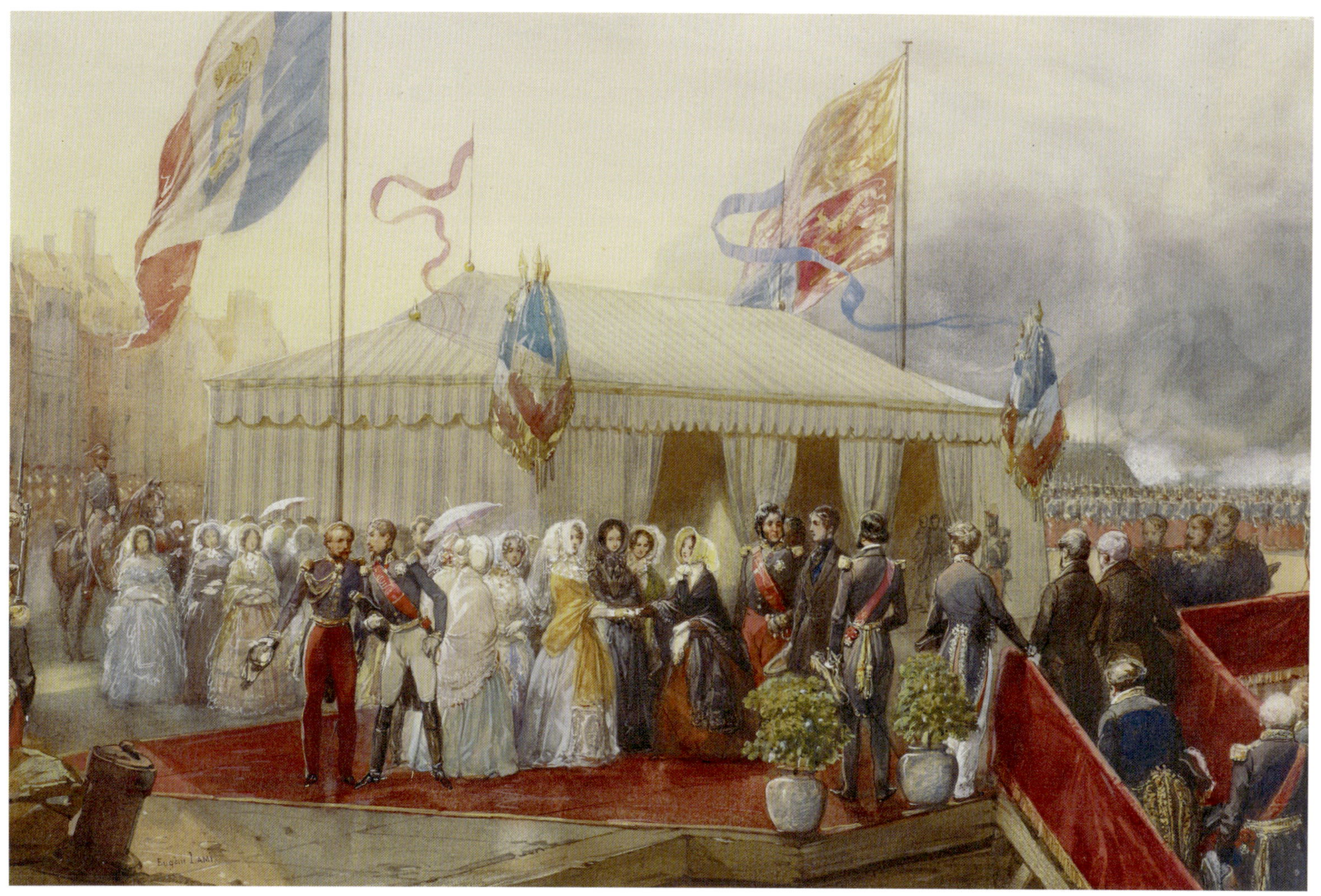

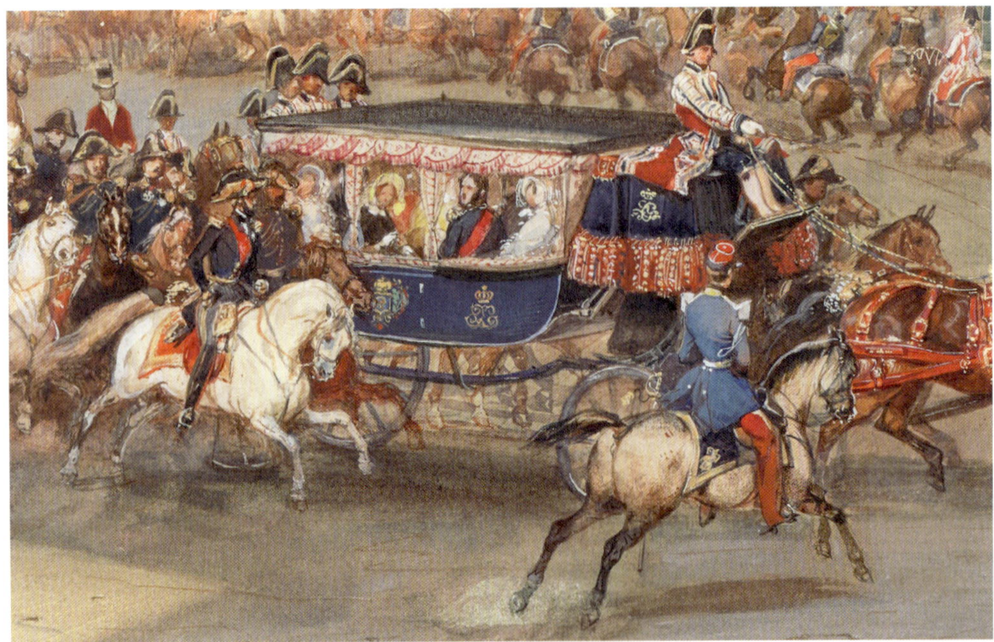

Fig. 55 (opposite)

EUGÈNE-LOUIS LAMI

The arrival of Queen Victoria at the château d'Eu, *c.*1843–4

Pencil, watercolour and bodycolour, 36.0 × 55.2 cm

RCIN 919998

Marie-Amélie gave her 'the kindest welcome', and newspapers emphasised the 'deep feeling' of this first meeting of the two queens.[16]

Both this watercolour and the next one by Lami in the album, depicting the arrival of the King and his guests at the château d'Eu (fig. 55), are richly coloured, conveying the pomp and pageantry of the occasion. The most distinctive element in this scene is the carriage in which the royal party is riding. This was a charabanc, an open-sided carriage with benches, drawn by eight horses, which Victoria described as 'a curious old carriage'; clearly intrigued by the vehicle, the next day she made a rapid sketch of one in her journal (fig. 56).[17] Georgiana Liddell, a maid of honour in attendance, thought that the whole procession of charabancs to Eu was 'quite mediaeval',[18] an effect Louis-Philippe may well have been intending. Certainly, the focus on this spectacle in Lami's watercolour bears comparison with the attention given to the long and stately procession of Henry VIII at the Field of Cloth of Gold depicted in a large oil painting made, probably, for the Tudor king himself (fig. 57).

Fig. 56 (below)

QUEEN VICTORIA

A French charabanc, 3 September 1843

Pen and ink with wash and watercolour, 2.6 × 4.0 cm

RA QVJ 3 September 1843

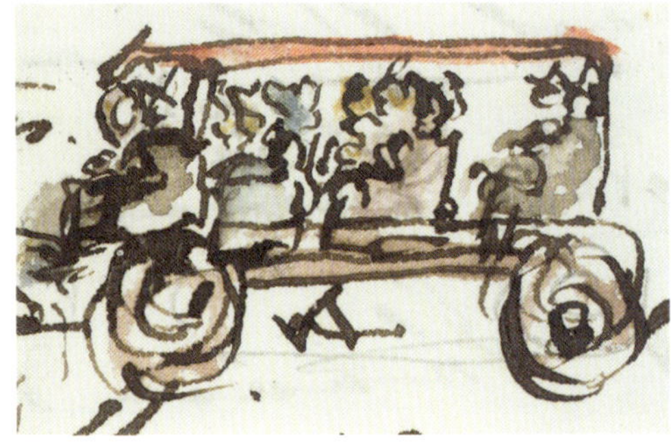

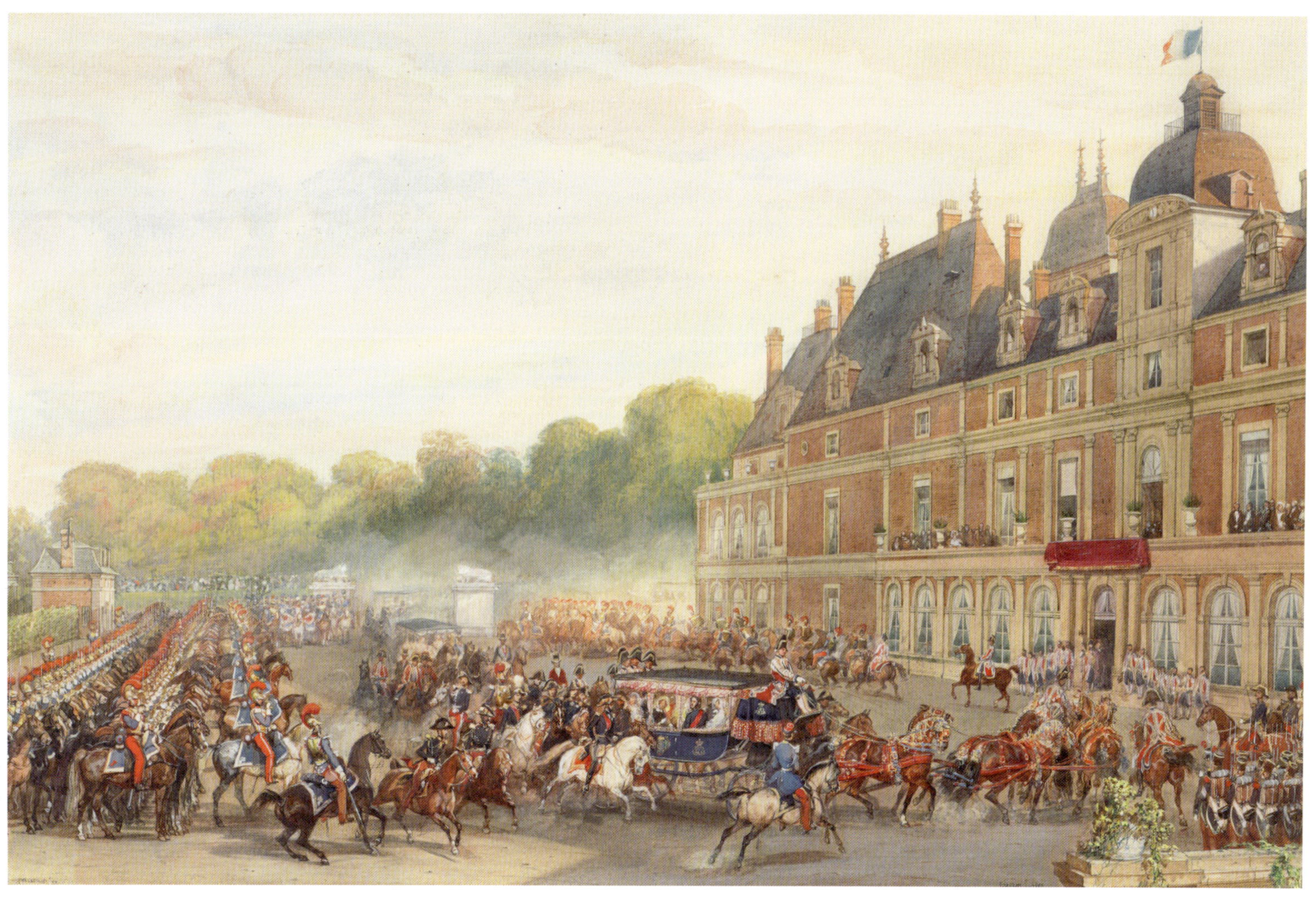

Fig. 57

BRITISH SCHOOL

The Field of the Cloth of Gold, *c.*1545

Oil on canvas, 168.9 × 347.3 cm

RCIN 405794

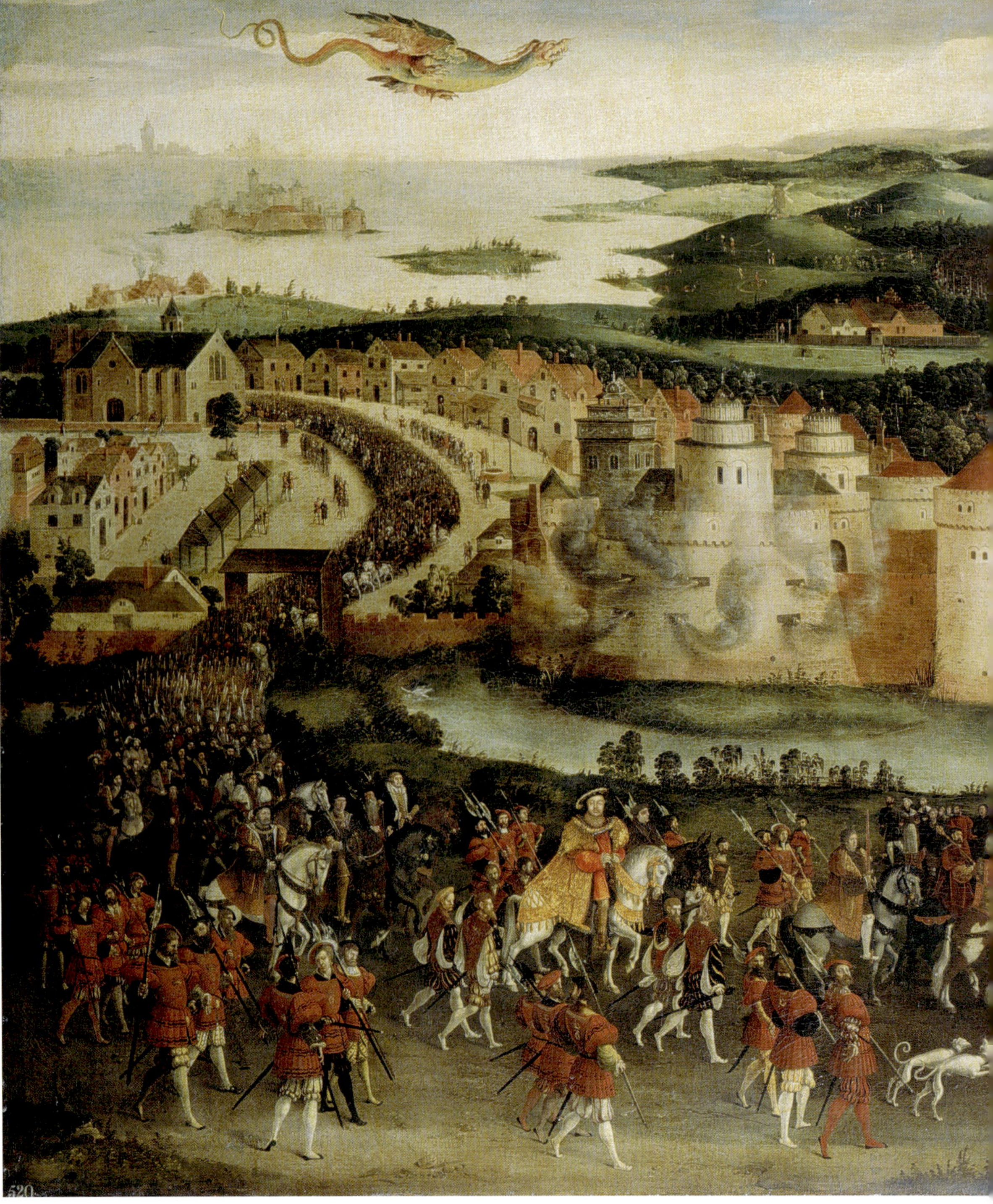

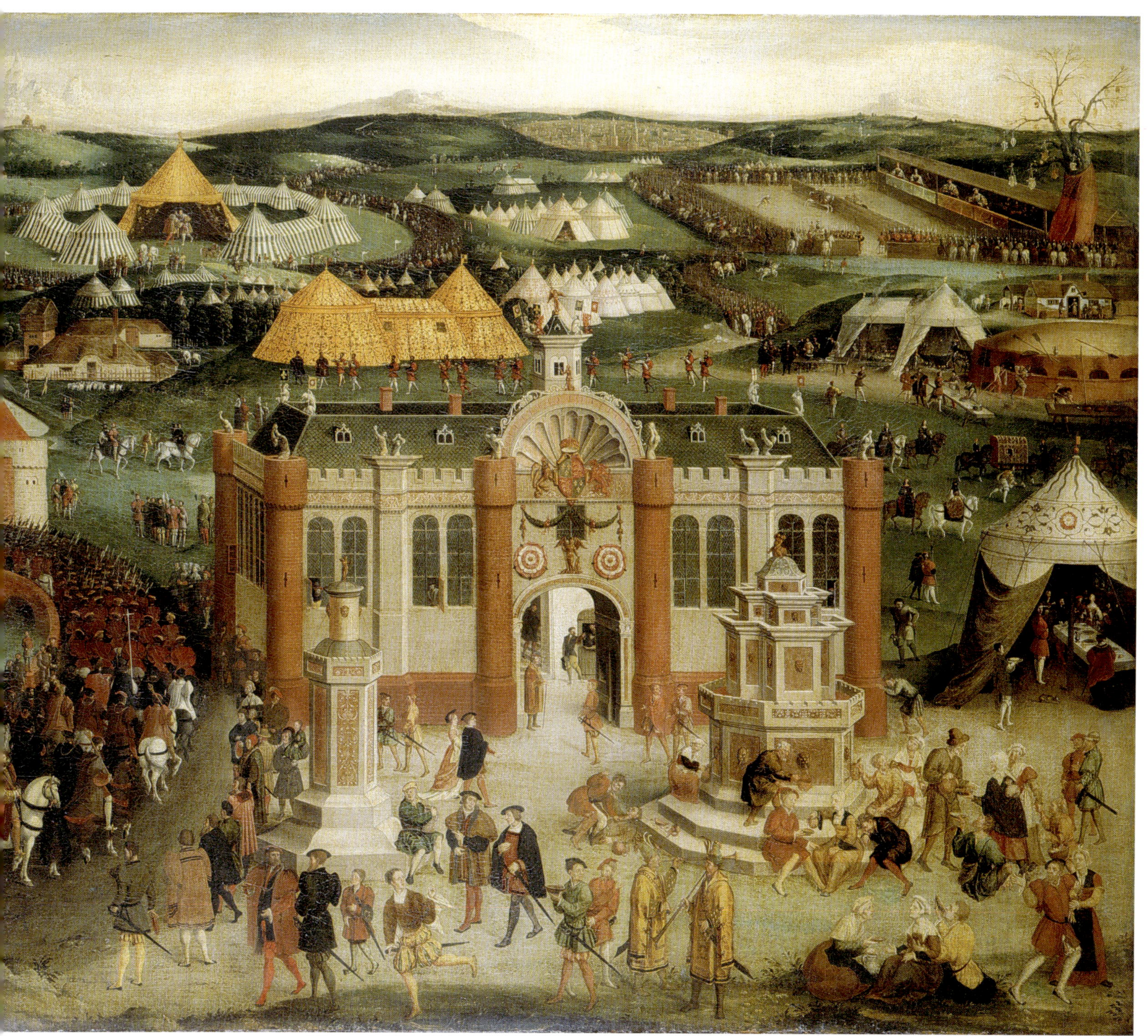

Louis-Philippe in Windsor – 'a truly affectionate reception'[19]

A charabanc also features prominently in a watercolour Queen Victoria commissioned to commemorate Louis-Philippe's reciprocal visit to England in October 1844. In the scene captured by Joseph Nash (fig. 58), the bright blue carriage is departing from Windsor Castle for a drive, with Victoria and the French king in the front seat, the Duchess of Kent in the second and Albert in the third. Louis-Philippe had sent the Queen a charabanc of her own as a present – and when they used it during Louis-Philippe's visit to Windsor, Victoria stated that it 'reminded us *so* much of the time at Eu'.[20] Though they are similar in content, Nash's watercolour is very different in appearance to that by Lami of the arrival at Eu. As one would expect of an English artist trained in the traditions of topographical and architectural draughtsmanship, the landscape forming the backdrop to Nash's scene (dominated by the Round Tower and part of the Upper Ward of Windsor Castle) is composed of loosely applied washes of pure colour and meticulously delineated architectural features. To make the central elements in the foreground of

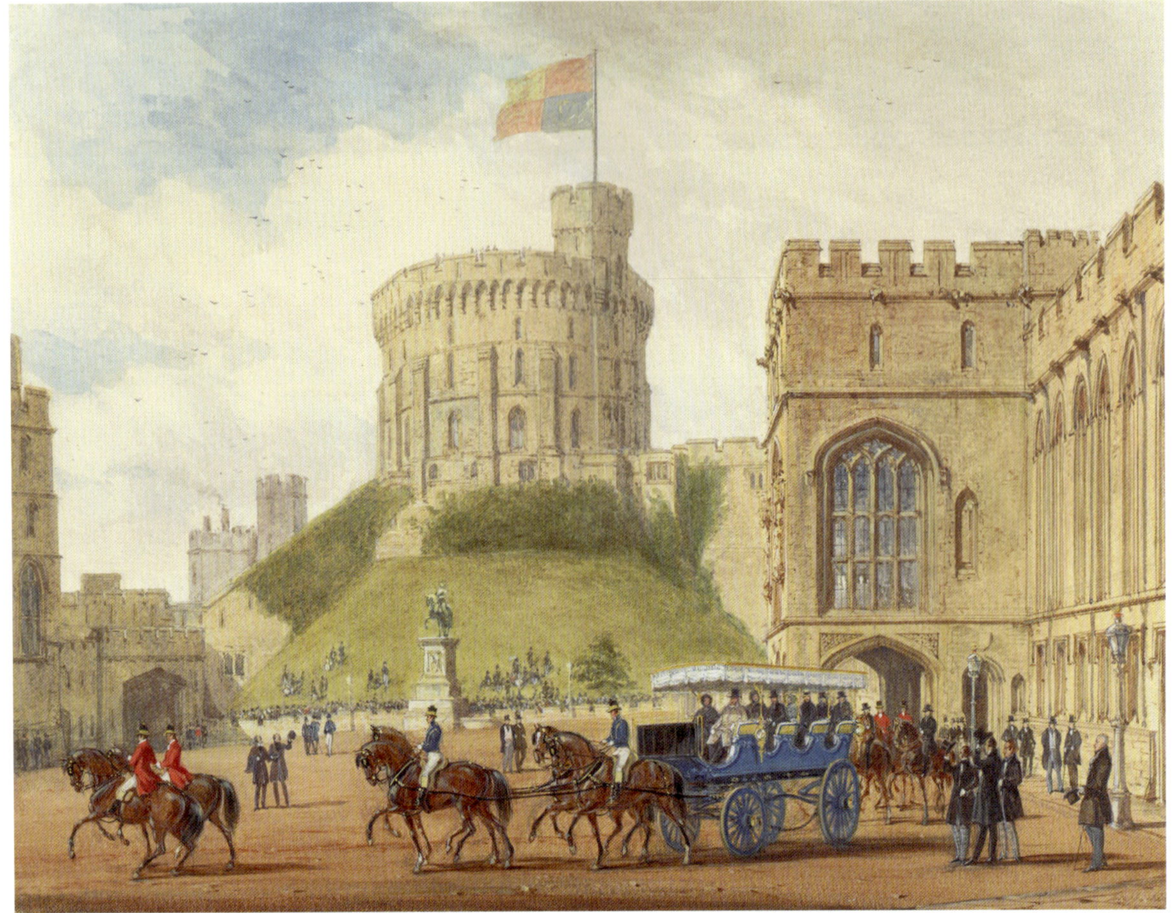

Fig. 58

JOSEPH NASH

Queen Victoria driving out with Louis-Philippe from the Quadrangle, Windsor Castle, 1844

Pencil, watercolour and bodycolour with gum arabic, 31.0 × 40.6 cm

RCIN 920031

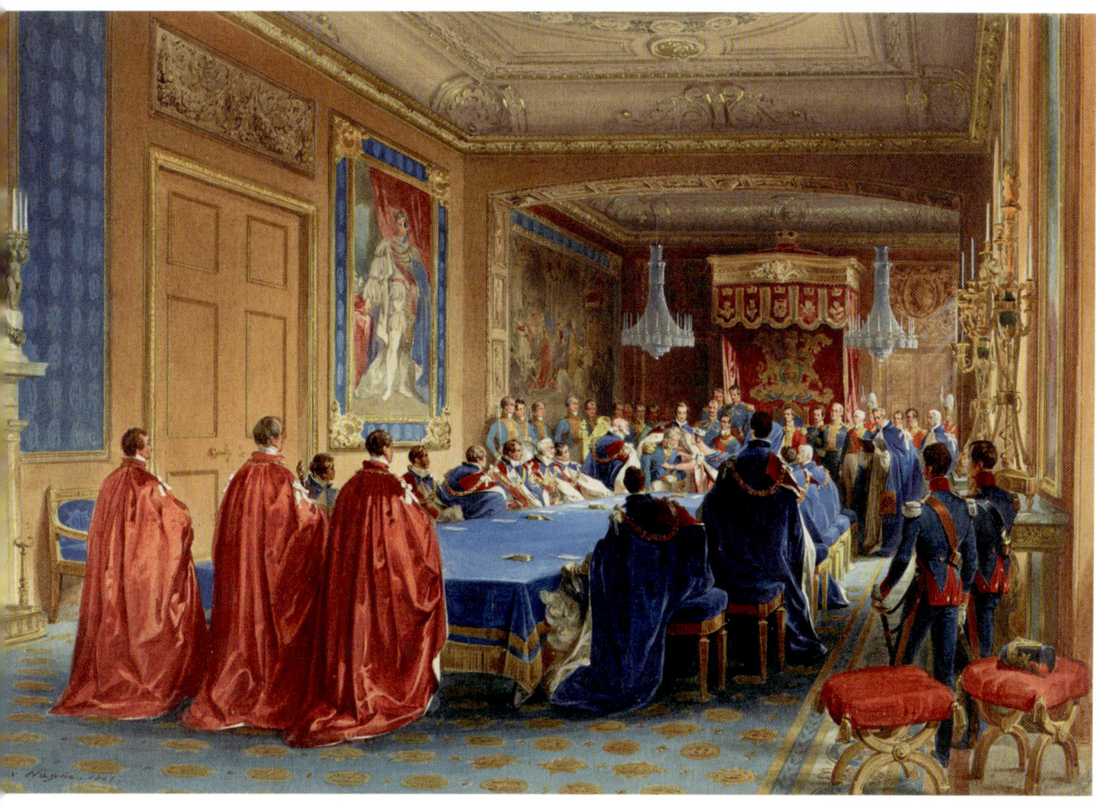

Fig. 59

LOUIS HAGHE

Queen Victoria investing Louis-Philippe with the Garter, 11 October 1844, 1845

Pencil, watercolour and bodycolour with gum arabic, 29.7 × 43.9 cm

RCIN 919793

the composition – the carriage, horses and surrounding figures – more prominent, Nash used opaque bodycolour, and applied spots of gum arabic on the flanks and tails of the horses to deepen their colour and convey the lustre of their coats. Lami's watercolour, however, encompasses a much wider and more sophisticated tonal range, evoking the setting sun with pinks and greens which are blended and reflected in the foliage below, and, in the middle distance, depicting a large cloud of dust in the wake of the carriages to emphasise the drama and excitement of Victoria and Albert's arrival at the château.

In addition to the watercolour painted for her own album, Victoria commissioned Nash to make a copy of it for presentation to Louis-Philippe. She probably also gave the French king a watercolour by Louis Haghe that must have pleased him greatly, as it depicted his investiture into the Order of the Garter (the oldest and most senior order of chivalry in Britain and the highest honour the monarch could award). In the version pasted by Victoria and Albert into their View Album (fig. 59), the shaft of sunlight entering the Garter Throne Room from a window on the right illuminates the figures of the British and French monarchs (Haghe also used this compositional device in an earlier watercolour he painted for the couple, of the christening ceremony of the Prince of Wales in January 1842). Victoria has just placed the ribbon of the order over the King's shoulder with the assistance of her uncle Adolphus, Duke of Cambridge (1774–1850), immediately in front of Louis-Philippe, while Albert looks on from behind. Just four years later, in 1848, political revolutions swept parts of Europe resulting in the King's abdication. Victoria and Albert –

horrified by this turn of events – afforded the French royal family safe haven in England. By the 1850s France's political landscape had fundamentally shifted and it continued to change dramatically. It became imperative that Queen Victoria and Prince Albert set aside their close personal relationship with the 'admirable and truly amiable' French royal family and make connections with the new regime in the national interest.[21]

The Second Empire

Prince Albert first met Napoleon III (1808–73), ruler of France from 1849 as the 'Prince-President' and from 1852 as Emperor, at a military camp in Boulogne, northern France, in September 1854. The backdrop to this visit was the recent outbreak of the Crimean War, occasioned by Russia's invasion of Turkey. To the surprise of many, Britain and France had become allies in the attempt to stop Russian expansionism and protect both Turkey and key trade routes.[22] Albert's visit to Boulogne was made at the Emperor's request, and was intended to both boost morale among the troops and provide a demonstration of the 'intimate union of the two countries', as Napoleon III described it in a letter to Victoria.[23] Albert, the Emperor and many commentators judged the visit to have been a great success.

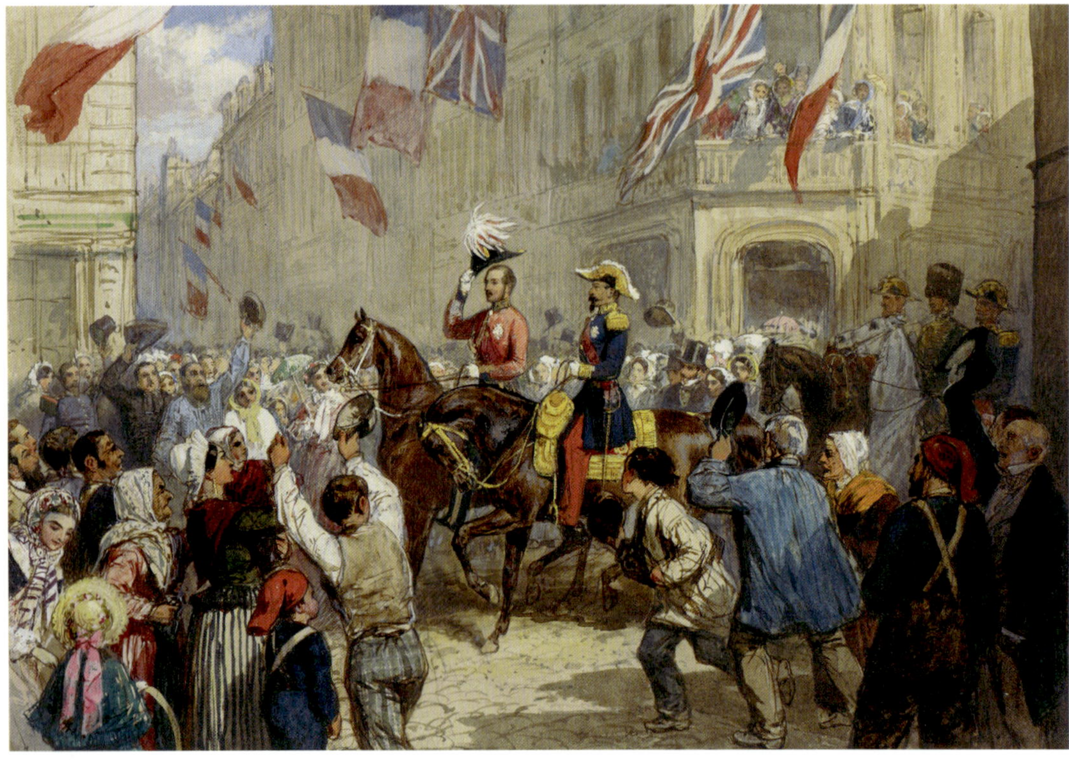

For Christmas 1854, Prince Albert presented his wife with three watercolours depicting events from his four-day sojourn in Boulogne. Two of these were smaller-scale works intended for the View Albums and the third was considerably larger, already framed for hanging. Victoria had confided to her journal while Albert was away that she had 'rather minded being left behind',[24] and perhaps the watercolours were, in part, by way of an apology. The first of the scenes shows Albert and Napoleon III riding through the streets of the town on their first afternoon there (fig. 60), intimating little of the serious purpose of Albert's visit and the surrounding framework of conflict. Vibrantly coloured and lively, the watercolour emphasises the rapturous welcome the Prince received in Boulogne. This was memorably described by Charles Dickens (1812–70), spending

Fig. 60

GEORGE HOUSMAN THOMAS (1824–68)

Napoleon III and Prince Albert in Boulogne, 1854

Pencil, pen and ink, watercolour and bodycolour with gum arabic, 24.8 × 35.0 cm

RCIN 920050

[Boulogne] looks like one immense flag, it is so decked out with streamers … the Prince in a blazing uniform … It was almost as fine a sight as one could see under a deep blue sky.'

– Charles Dickens

the summer in the city with his family: 'The town looks like one immense flag, it is so decked out with streamers; … as the royal yacht approached yesterday … the Prince in a blazing uniform … a stupendous silence, and then such an infernal blazing and banging as never was heard. It was almost as fine a sight as one could see under a deep blue sky.'[25]

The artist responsible for all three watercolours was George Housman Thomas, who worked extensively for the *Illustrated London News*. According to *The Times*, it was Thomas's illustrations of the 1849 siege of Rome in the *Illustrated London News* that first caught Victoria's attention, but the latter publication itself, well-placed to have inside information on the patron–artist relationship, stated instead that 'The Queen … had taken much pleasure, as we are proud to believe she usually does, in the Engravings presented in our Paper', and was 'particularly struck' with one after a sketch by Thomas of a review of the Baltic Fleet in March 1854.[26] This, it said, was the catalyst for the beginning of the artist's extensive royal patronage. Victoria herself, however, remembered that it was Albert who discovered Thomas – perhaps in Boulogne itself. Although the *Illustrated London News* only partially reproduced one of the three watercolours the artist painted at Prince Albert's request, their style and overall dynamism is a perfect example of the 'qualities of speed and vigour and accuracy' necessary for producing successful and engaging newspaper illustrations.[27]

Thomas was subsequently given a series of commissions from Victoria and Albert for both oil paintings and watercolours relating to both the Crimean War and new blossoming Anglo-French relations of the mid-1850s. The next watercolour he executed for the View Albums (fig. 61) commemorated the six-day state visit of Napoleon III and the Empress Eugénie (1826–1920) to England in April 1855. On the day of the French couple's arrival, Victoria wrote vividly of her heightened anticipation – shared by her family and many of her subjects – in her journal: 'All is in a state of bustle, excitement & expectation … All the Children on the tip top of expectation.'[28] Thomas painted a moment soon after the arrival of Napoleon III and Eugénie at the castle when the royal and imperial party ascended the Grand Staircase to the Throne Room, with the Emperor accompanying the Queen and Albert the Empress, and the eldest royal children Vicky and Bertie following behind. The treatment of the event in this watercolour, especially compared with that of Albert and Napoleon III in Boulogne, is more highly finished and overall very static – arguably more appropriate

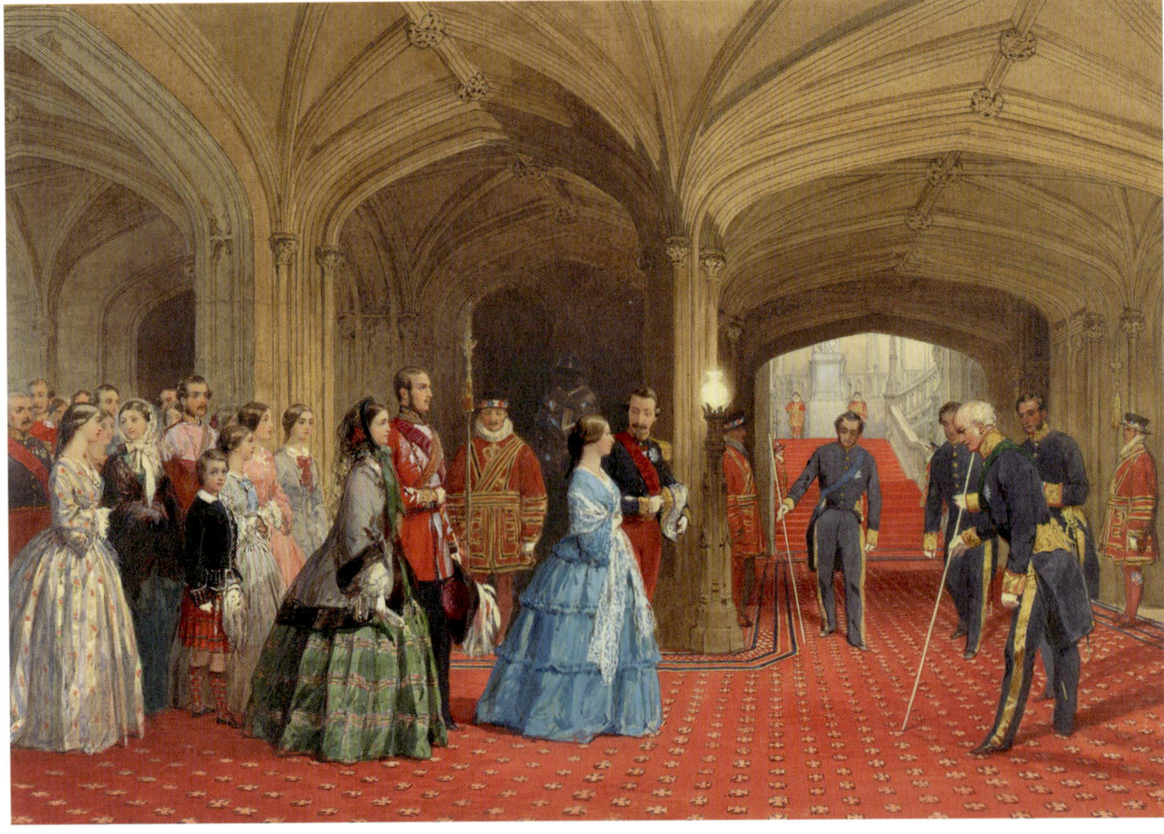

Fig. 61

GEORGE HOUSMAN THOMAS

The reception of the Emperor and Empress of the French at Windsor Castle, 1855

Pencil, watercolour and bodycolour with gum arabic, 32.4 × 47.5 cm

RCIN 919799

to a processional scene of this type. More naturalistic is the portrayal of thirteen-year-old Bertie, who – his attention having wandered – looks outwards with curiosity, appearing to meet the viewer's eyes. This watercolour was reproduced as the first illustration to *The Visit of Their Imperial Majesties the Emperor & Empress of the French, to Her Most Gracious Majesty The Queen, April 1855*, published by Paul and Dominic Colnaghi in December 1855. Both the subtitle of this publication and advertisements for it emphasised its royal credentials, stating that the illustrations derived 'from drawings executed at the command of Her Majesty'. Three artists were involved in the Colnaghi publication, with Thomas contributing the most watercolours – five in total.

Of these, Thomas's depiction of Victoria investing Napoleon III with the Order of the Garter (fig. 62) makes an interesting comparison with that of Louis-Philippe just over a decade previously (see fig. 59). The setting for both events was the Throne Room

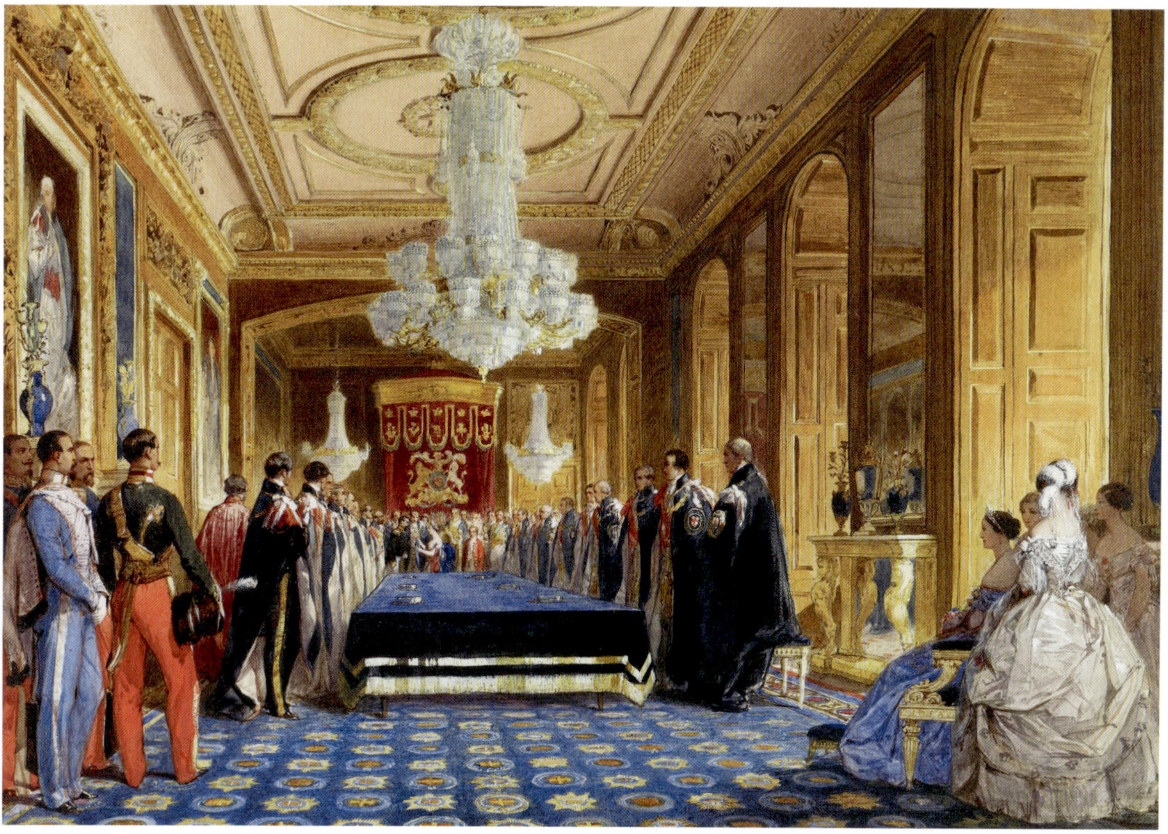

Fig. 62

GEORGE HOUSMAN THOMAS

Queen Victoria investing Napoleon III with the Garter, 1855

Pencil, watercolour and bodycolour with gum arabic, 32.7 × 47.3 cm

RCIN 920054

at Windsor, but Thomas's view of the room is head-on and taken from slightly further back than that by Haghe, allowing for the inclusion of two groups of figures in the foreground – the seated Empress, with Bertie standing by her side and Vicky and other ladies behind her chair, balanced by a group of French cavalry officers on the other side.[29] Thomas made much of the many textural contrasts presented by the clothing and accessories of a more diverse group of subjects than Haghe portrayed. The folds of the rich satin gown worn by the closest standing lady in the foreground are described with a network of dynamic watercolour lines and shapes, which intersect with splashes of white bodycolour to represent light falling on the material; bodycolour is also used to pick out her delicate lace shawl and feather headdress, as well as the shimmering tiara worn by Eugénie. This acts as a foil to the members of the order lining either side of the table who all wear homogeneous, sumptuous velvet robes. Those of Victoria are lighter and brighter than

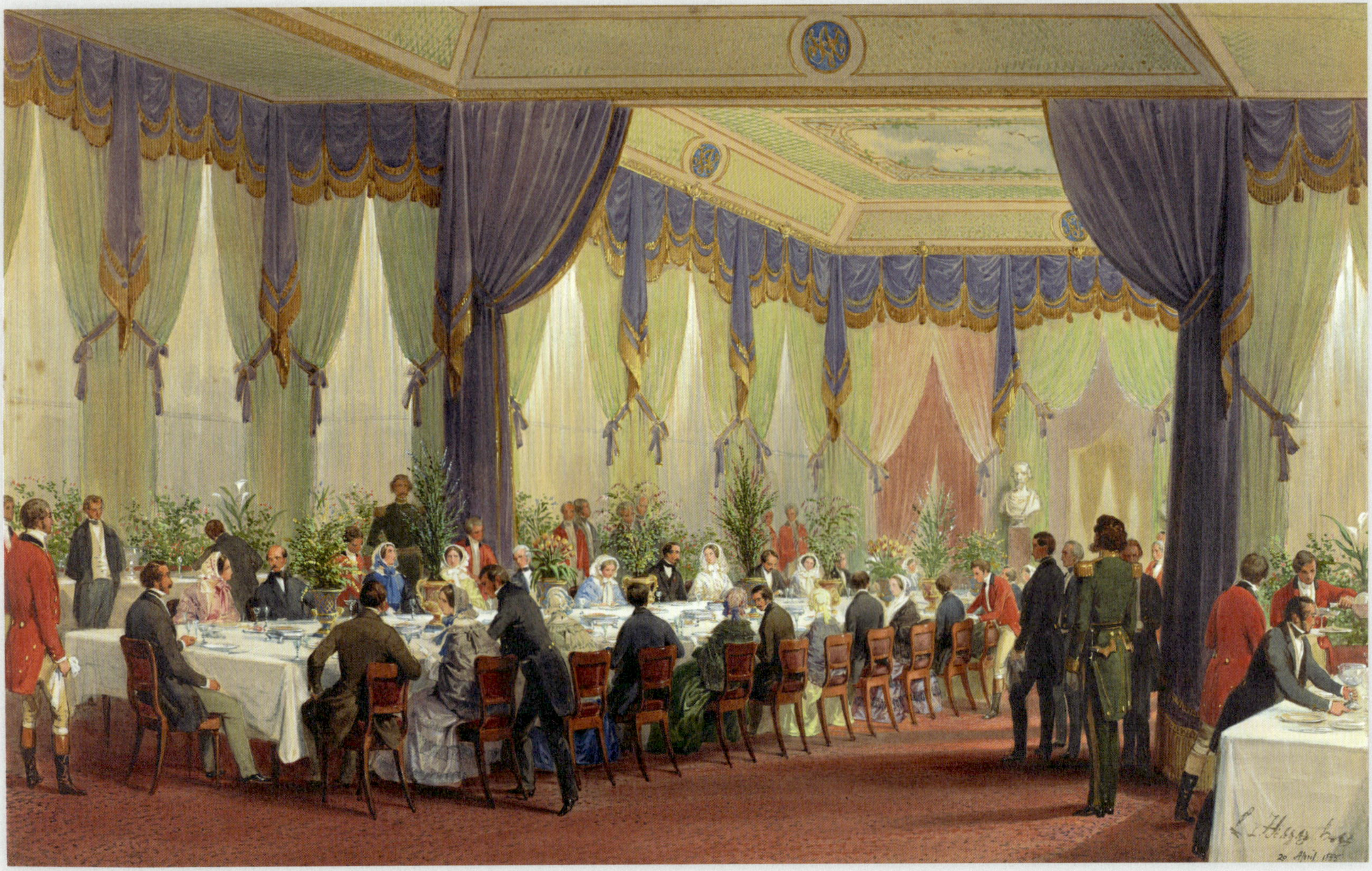

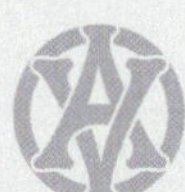

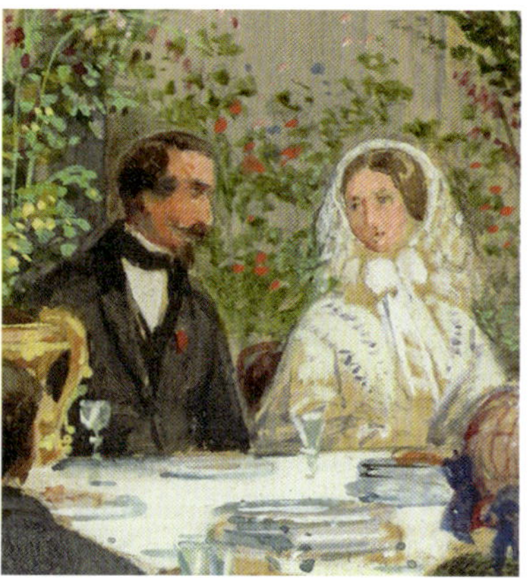

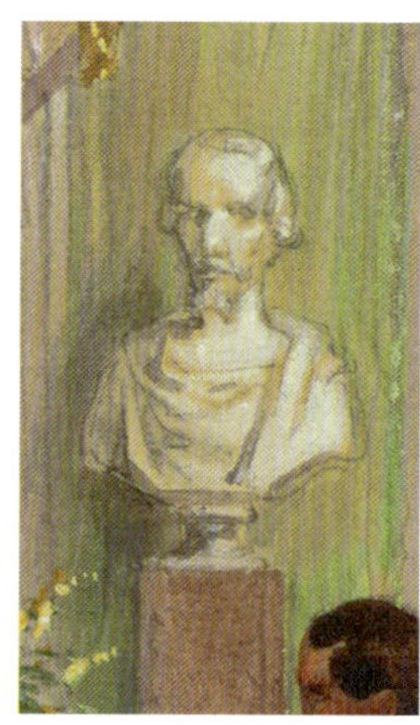

Fig. 63

LOUIS HAGHE

Queen Victoria and Prince Albert lunching with the Emperor and Empress of the French at the Crystal Palace, Sydenham, 1855

Pencil, watercolour and bodycolour, 29.7 × 48.4 cm

RCIN 920231

the rest, and Thomas's watercolour shares with Haghe's the inclusion of a shaft of light illuminating and thus drawing focus to the central group of characters. Whether Thomas had seen the earlier watercolour is unknown.

Haghe himself was employed by Victoria and Albert to record another significant event of the imperial visit. On the last full day the couples spent together, they visited the Crystal Palace, newly erected in Sydenham as a centre for leisure and entertainment. Victoria's journal entry is typically detailed and full of amused asides, such as when she heard the cry '"Vive le Hempereur", in cockney English!' from the enthusiastic crowds lining their route.[30] At the Crystal Palace, the sovereigns toured the galleries and then shared a luncheon, after which they sat before the public on a dais to hear the French national anthem played. Haghe produced two watercolours illustrating both public and private moments in the day. One, the dais scene, was included in the volume published by Colnaghi. The other watercolour, not reproduced there, shows the private lunch given by Victoria and Albert for the Emperor and Empress (fig. 63). The *Illustrated London News* explained that the luncheon room ordinarily functioned as the picture gallery and was transformed in the space of a week (Victoria thought it 'had been very prettily decorated for the purpose'), and thus Haghe's watercolour is an important record of an ephemeral decorative scheme.[31] The green and purple drapes were chosen as they were the colours of the Emperor, and the same colours featured heavily in the decoration of the rooms prepared for the French couple's private use at Windsor Castle and Buckingham Palace.[32] The entwined initials of Victoria and Albert, and those of their guests, which decorate the coving are also visible, and a portrait bust of Napoleon III can be seen placed at the head of the table as a compliment to the guest of honour.[33]

Victoria and Albert in Paris: 'the pleasantest & most interesting & triumphant ten days that I think I ever passed'[34]

In August 1855 the Queen and Prince made a reciprocal state visit to Paris. They took Vicky and Bertie, who had greatly charmed the Emperor and Empress in April, as well as a large suite of ministers and courtiers. Determined to dazzle his guests, Napoleon III convened a busy programme of private and public events that included two grand balls, a military review, a hunt and a tour of Versailles. The royal visit also coincided with the Exposition Universelle, the first of a series of world fairs held in Paris that emulated the Great Exhibition in London in 1851 (see pp. 109–17). Such a packed itinerary might have been overwhelming for some, but, as Albert told his mother-in-law the Duchess of Kent, 'Victoria bore the great fatigues remarkably well, and won the hearts of all by her endeavours to make herself agreeable to the people.'[35]

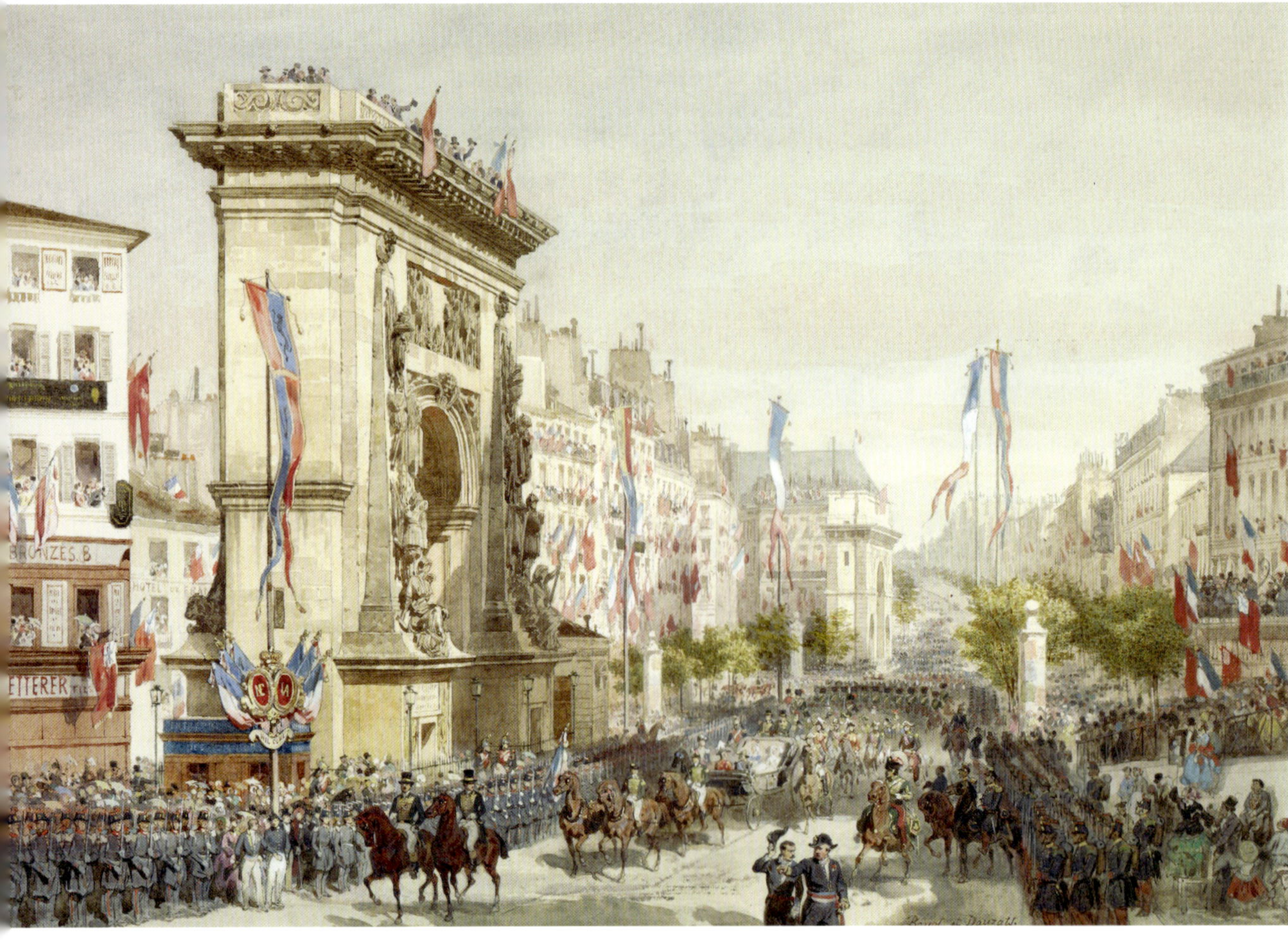

Fig. 64

ADOLPHE-JEAN-BAPTISTE BAYOT (1810–71) and ADRIEN DAUZATS (1804–68)

The entry of Queen Victoria into Paris, 1855

Pencil, watercolour and bodycolour, 32.6 × 47.7 cm

RCIN 920059

Not surprisingly, the royal couple were keen to ensure that there was a visual record – in colour – of this very significant event, and Victoria made enquiries of Winterhalter, who was based in Paris, as to artists who might be suitable for the task. Winterhalter clearly knew something of Victoria and Albert's existing watercolour collection and taste as he recommended (among others) the fashionable Eugène Guérard (1821–66) based on his similar style to Eugène-Louis Lami, whose watercolours the royal couple particularly esteemed.[36] Although, according to Winterhalter, Guérard was 'very good and not too expensive', neither he nor the other three artists Winterhalter suggested received direct commissions from Britain. In the end, the ten French artists who between them painted fifteen watercolours (all of which were mounted in the seventh View Album) were engaged for the Queen through the offices of the Empress Eugénie.[37]

The first of the watercolours, a collaboration between Adrien Dauzats and Adolphe-Jean-Baptiste Bayot (who specialised in architectural views and genre scenes, respectively), depicts the arrival of the royal party in Paris (fig. 64).

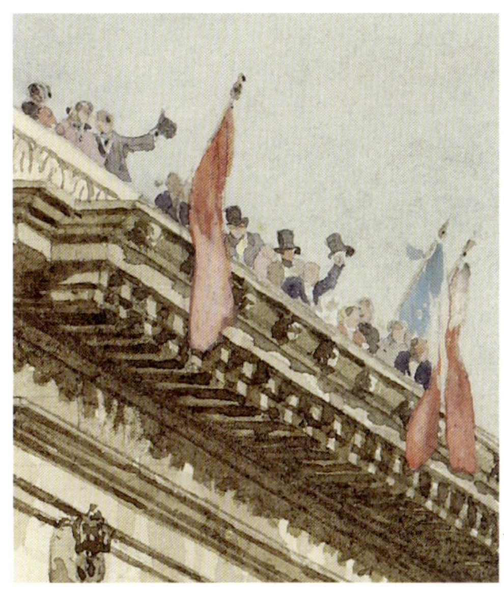

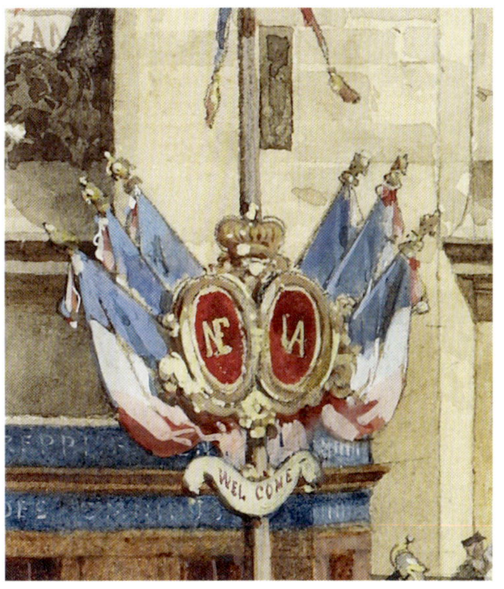

Victoria, Albert and their children landed at the port of Boulogne where the Emperor met them at just after 1pm on Saturday 18 August. Following a long journey by train, the state carriages drove through Paris to the château of Saint-Cloud, Napoleon I's favourite residence in the west of the city. The watercolour corresponds perfectly with Victoria's description of the scene: 'Paris is the most beautiful & the gayest town imaginable. The very high houses, with their endless stories [*sic*], were crowded from top to bottom & decorated in the most tasteful manner with banners, flags, arches, flowers, inscriptions & finally illuminations.'[38] The carriage is shown passing the Porte Saint-Denis, on the left in the watercolour, and between troops stationed either side of the processional route; the boulevard and the windows and balconies of the surrounding buildings – and indeed even the top of the triumphal arch – are thronged with spectators. Flags and banners flutter in the breeze, creating repeating accents of red, white and blue, and at the bottom left can be seen a temporary decoration comprising the initials of the imperial and royal couples surmounted by a crown and the word 'welcome' lettered on a scroll underneath. However, this atmosphere of gaiety and enthusiasm is misleading, as is the fact that the scene appears to be occurring during the day.

> *'The very high houses, with their endless stories* [sic]*, were crowded from top to bottom & decorated in the most tasteful manner with banners, flags, arches, flowers, inscriptions & finally illuminations.'*
>
> – Queen Victoria

In reality, the party's arrival was significantly delayed, and a number of contemporary sources attest to the disappointment of the crowds who, after long hours waiting, saw the spectacle of the procession only in the dim twilight.[39] The American socialite and writer Octavia Walton Le Vert (1810–77), in Paris for the Exposition Universelle, evocatively described how the expectant mood changed among the spectators:

> *It is a glorious day … All Paris is abroad, all smiling, all in good humour, and joyous expectation of seeing the English Queen … [later in the day] Wearied by the long delay, the multitude had lost much of their enthusiasm, and darkness was fast coming on. Thus the absolute reception seemed but tame, when judged by its expectation.*[40]

Four years after the visit, a further watercolour was incorporated into the View Album. This was painted by George Housman Thomas, who was in Paris during the state visit in 1855 on behalf of the *Illustrated London News*; the Queen particularly admired his work reproduced in the paper, writing to a relative shortly after her return to England that she thought 'the illustrations in the *Illustrated London News* of our visit to Paris [were] very good.'[41] Victoria and Albert commissioned Thomas to produce a large oil painting of the military review held by the Emperor for his guests on the Champ de Mars.[42] Exhibited at the Royal Academy in 1859, Victoria put it at the head of a list in her journal of the finest things on show.[43] The oil and the watercolour (fig. 65) are almost identical. Napoleon III and Prince Albert are on horseback (in the lower centre) before a series of marching infantry regiments, with cavalry in the distance, and Victoria, Vicky, Bertie and Eugénie watch proceedings from the balcony of the Ecole Militaire on the far right. This distant view of the 'truly magnificent' spectacle gives a clear sense of the vastness of the military ground and the brilliance of the uniforms and manoeuvres of the thousands of troops arrayed before the royal guests.[44]

Of the fifteen watercolours that Victoria herself commissioned, only four depicted public events, with the rest comprising exterior and interior views of the places the visitors stayed in and toured. This choice of subjects was probably dictated by a desire not to duplicate the contents of two albums of watercolours she was given as presents by, first, the Emperor and Empress, and second, Baron Georges-Eugène Haussman (1809–91), the high-ranking government official who was responsible for significant rebuilding in Paris. His present depicted scenes from a ball he hosted at the Hôtel de Ville in honour of Victoria and Albert's visit.[45] The album of ten watercolours given as a Christmas present in 1855 by Napoleon III and Eugénie was the idea of the latter, and it was exceptionally well-received by Victoria, who wrote to thank them for the 'ravishing drawings'.[46] These illustrated some of the public events of the state visit, including the arrival and departure of the British guests, the military review and the ball at Versailles hosted by the Empress on the penultimate night of Victoria and Albert's stay. As with the Album d'Eu, the presentation of this gift was reported by the British press, who described the watercolours as having been painted by 'the most renowned French masters'.[47]

A depiction of the gala performance attended by the royal guests at the Paris Opéra

Fig. 65

GEORGE HOUSMAN THOMAS

The military review on the Champ de Mars, 24 August 1855, 1859

Pencil, pen and ink, watercolour and bodycolour, 28.5 × 45.8 cm

RCIN 920091

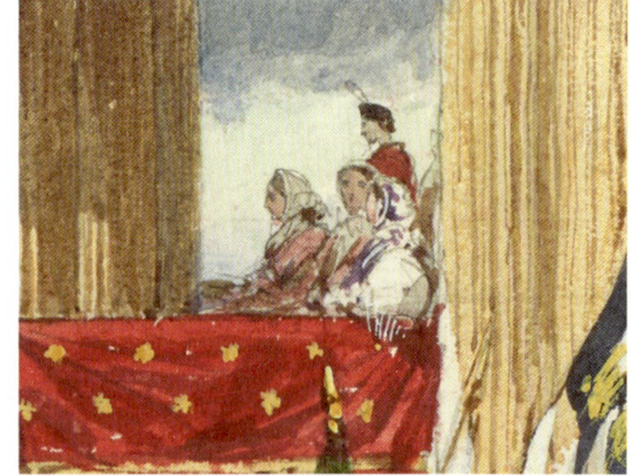

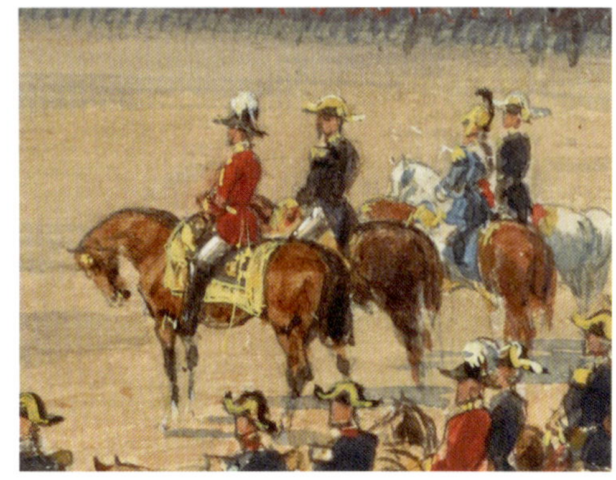

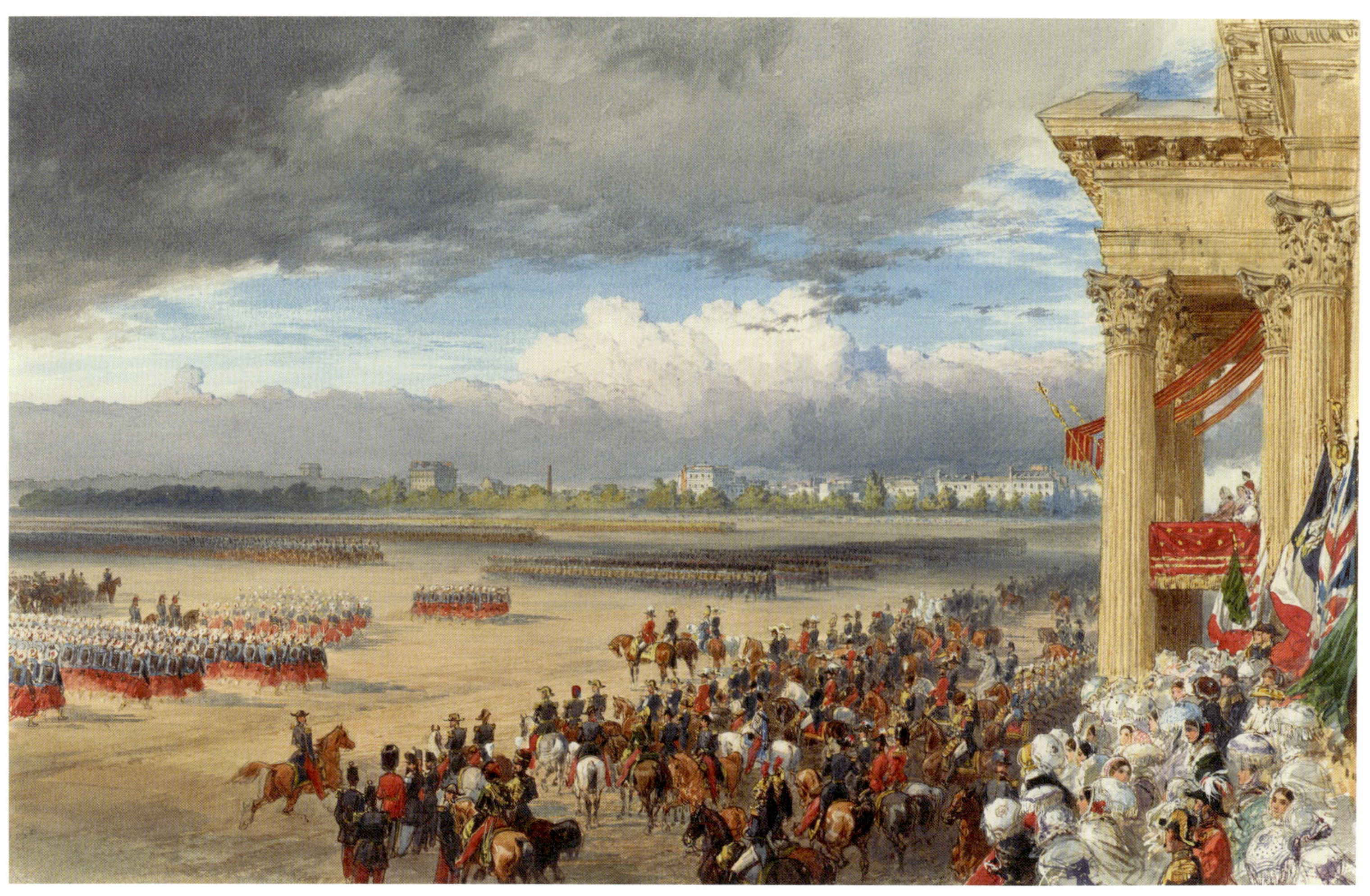

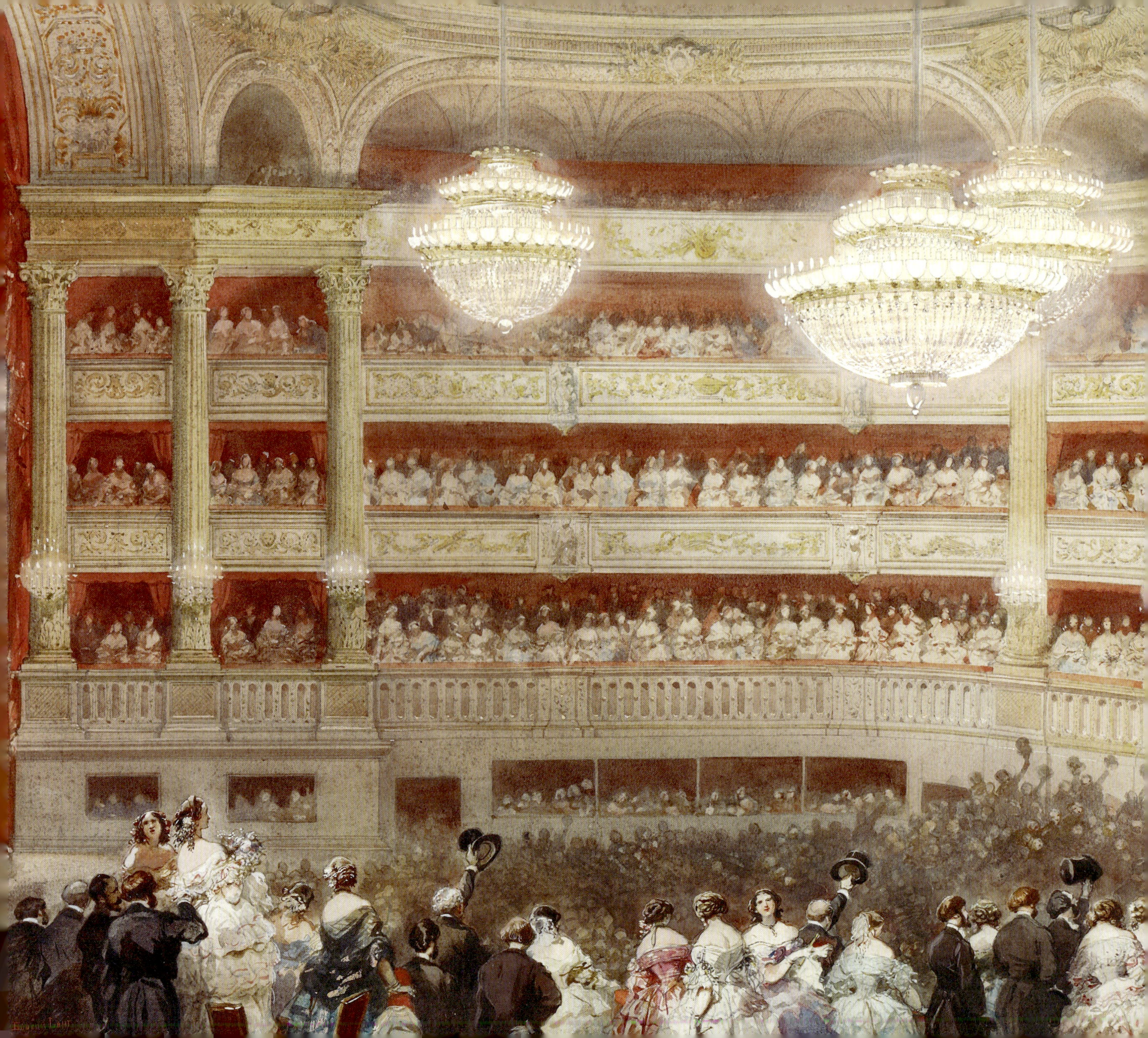

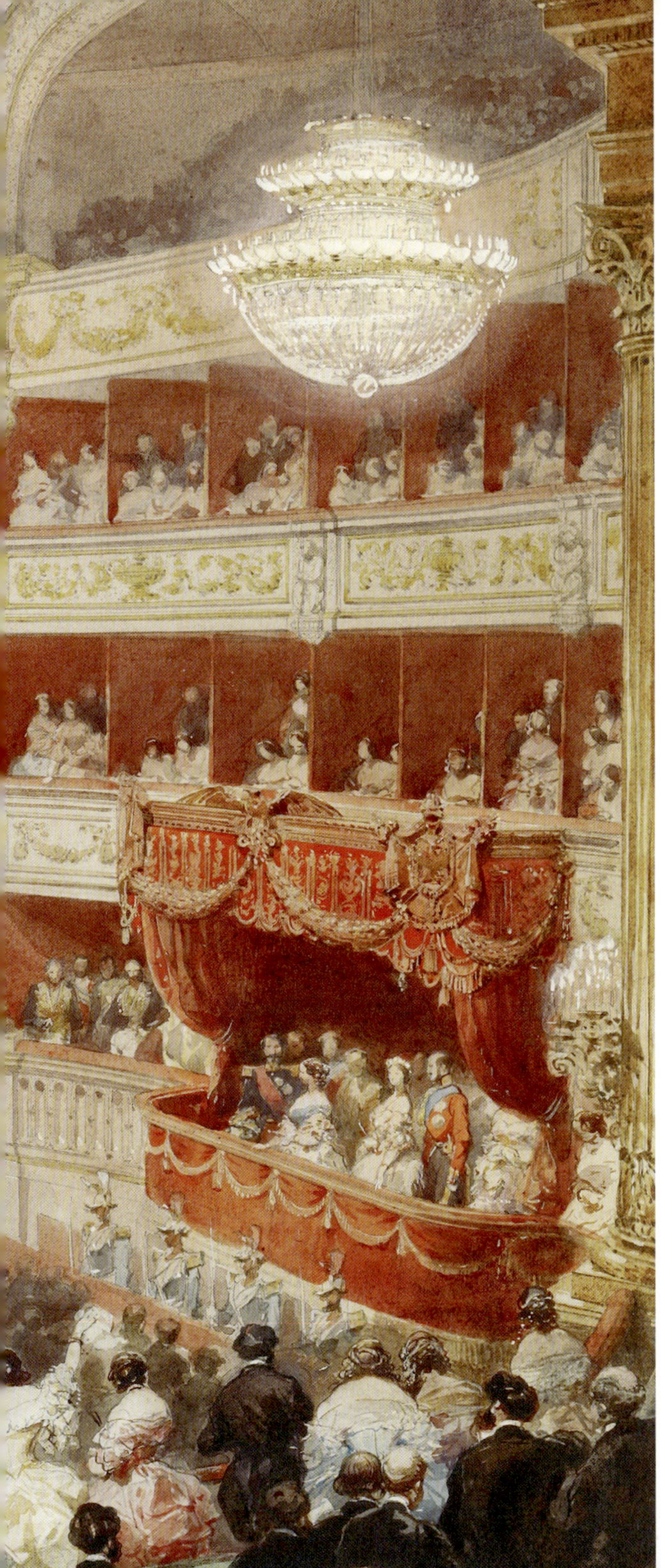

(fig. 66), a collaboration between Eugène-Louis Lami (who drew the figures) and Jules-Pierre-Michel Diéterle (responsible for the architecture) is a distillation of the purpose of the souvenirs commissioned by the imperial couple. The carefully chosen scene, showing the arrival of the party in the royal box on the far right, illustrates a moment of enthusiastic obeisance to the British queen as all those in attendance turn away from the stage and towards the more significant spectacle at hand. Victoria later reported to her uncle Leopold that their reception there was '<u>most magnificent</u>'.[48] Additionally, Lami's painterly representation of the luxurious fabrics worn by the affluent female patrons in attendance, coupled with the richly decorated opera house skilfully portrayed by Diéterle, clearly conveys the splendour and opulence of the Second Empire.

Fig. 66

EUGÈNE-LOUIS LAMI and
JULES-PIERRE-MICHEL DIÉTERLE (1811–89)

The gala performance at the Paris Opéra, 1855

Pencil, watercolour and bodycolour, 35.6 × 57.0 cm

RCIN 920071

The first visit to Germany – 'The Queen is enchanted'[49]

In the summer of 1845 Victoria and Albert realised a long-held dream when they travelled together to Coburg, the Prince's birthplace. Albert exchanged a number of letters with his elder brother Ernest, Duke of Saxe-Coburg and Gotha, in the months leading up to the visit, expressing the royal couple's excitement and their desire to 'have an opportunity of seeing the neighbourhood and the family'.[50] The trip was clearly of great personal and emotional significance to Victoria. On the day they arrived in Coburg, she wrote in her journal: 'I cannot say how much affected I felt in entering this dear old Place & with difficulty I resisted crying.'[51] A series of watercolours of their trip, which also incorporated stopovers in the Kingdom of Prussia and the Electorate of Hesse, made up the majority of the third View Album. Almost half of these works were by Charlotte Canning, Victoria's lady-in-waiting – all landscape views, among them a romantic sunset depiction of Cologne (fig. 67). The Queen noted rather disingenuously on 15 August 'Ly Canning has been sketching delightfully', but the previous day Charlotte had herself recorded that she was 'ordered to draw all day long'.[52] Victoria and Albert were very satisfied with her work, though, and enjoyed looking 'at the beautiful sketches Lady Canning made, during our Tour, which are all so like the places'.[53]

The most commonly represented subject from the first German trip in the View Album was Rosenau castle, the birthplace of Prince Albert, and its environs. *The Times* correspondent following the tour described it as 'the beau-ideal of a summer residence', and indeed Albert and his brother had spent many happy periods during their childhood there, and particularly playing in the Swiss Cottage on the estate.[54] After their first night at the castle, Victoria wrote with strong emphasis in her journal of 'How happy, & how joyful we felt on awaking to feel ourselves here, at the dear Rosenau, my dearest Albert's Birth Place & favourite place! I told him I was so delighted, so over happy, so over thankful to be able to come here at last, which we so wished.'[55]

Douglas Morison's depiction of the Gothic Revival Rosenau (fig. 68) was the only exterior representation of it in the View Album. Although the residence itself is small in scale, Morison's low viewpoint serves to exaggerate the size of the building; an effect further

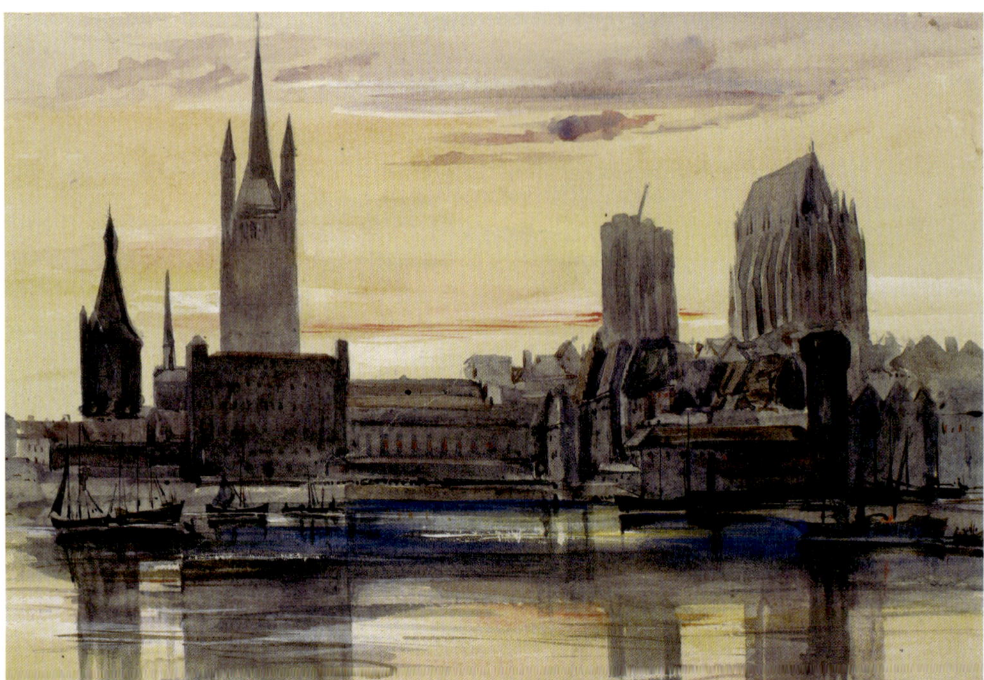

Fig. 67

CHARLOTTE CANNING

***Cologne from the Hôtel de Belle Vue at Deutz*, 1845**

Pencil, watercolour and bodycolour, 15.8 × 24.0 cm

RCIN 920523

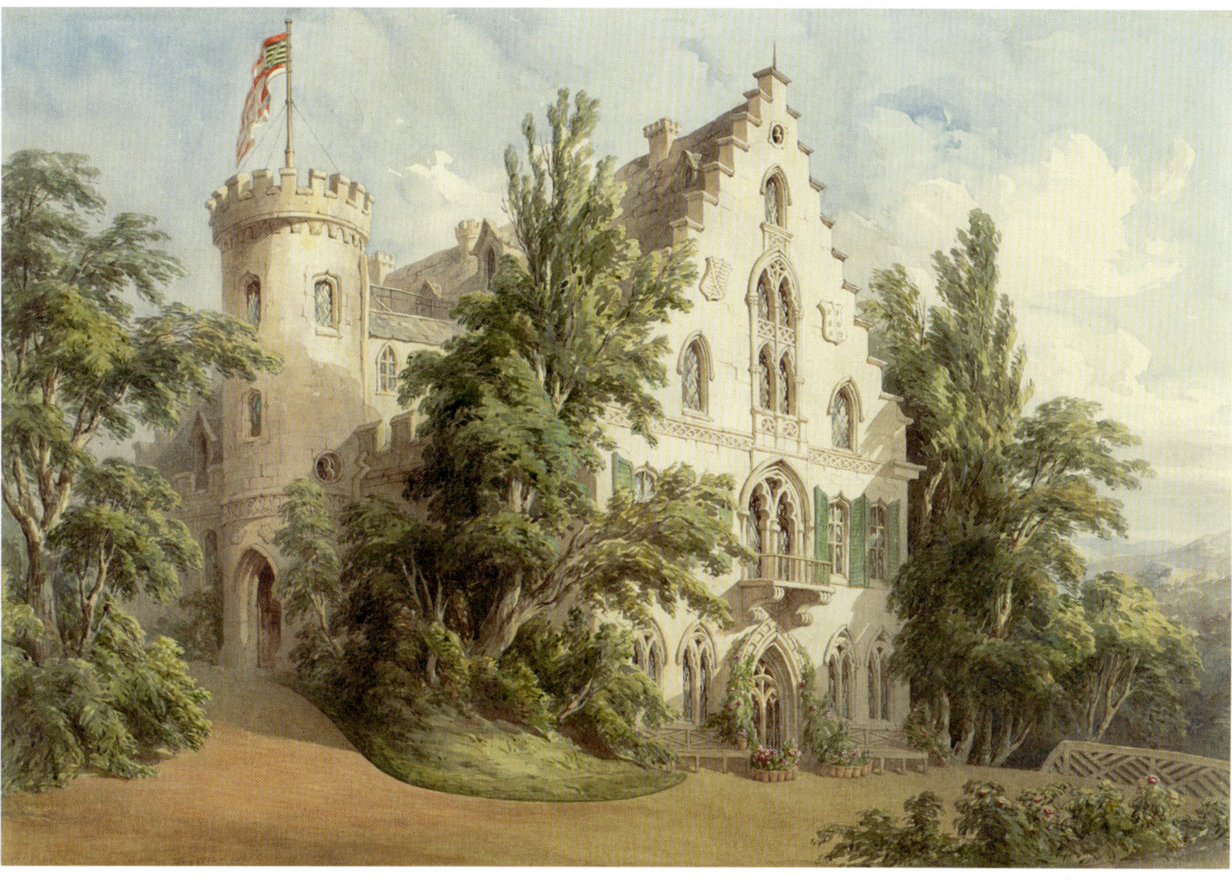

Fig. 68

DOUGLAS MORISON (1814–47)

Schloss Rosenau, 1845

Pencil, watercolour and bodycolour, 29.2 × 43.7 cm

RCIN 920430

accentuated by the distant mountains to the right over which it appears to loom. The artist, who specialised in architectural subjects, was paid for this watercolour in 1846, meaning it was likely commissioned as a souvenir following Victoria and Albert's first joint visit to the Rosenau.[56] Notably, Morison had already drawn other residences in Coburg and Gotha at the behest of Prince Albert, who sent him there in 1841 and 1842 to paint views of his homeland.[57] This was probably in connection with Albert's father Duke Ernest I's idea for a publication of views and descriptions of its palaces, castles and hunting seats – perhaps a canny attempt to capitalise on the increased interest in the duchy generated in Britain by Victoria and Albert's marriage. The volume comprised twenty-one lithographs made by Morison after his own drawings, including this one, and was published in 1846, two years after Ernest I's death, under the patronage of Victoria and Albert.[58]

The marriage of the Princess Royal

On 25 January 1858, Vicky, Princess Royal, Victoria and Albert's eldest child, married Frederick William, Prince of Prussia (1831–88), forging new close familial links with Germany. Victoria and Albert commissioned an official record of the event in the form of a large oil painting by the Scottish artist John Phillip (1817–67), which was then reproduced as a print in 1865 and thus widely available to the public. An image that remained private was the watercolour of the ceremony (fig. 69) that Prince Albert gave his wife as a present and which was then mounted in the seventh View Album. This was painted by Egron Lundgren, the Swedish artist who had already captured an important family occasion (the christening of Victoria and Albert's youngest child Princess Beatrice the previous year) and who, in 1859, would spend time at Balmoral (see p. 36). Although the features of some of the figures present at the ceremony are indistinct, a sense of intimacy and solemnity pervades Lundgren's evocation of the scene. Vicky and her new husband, to whom Queen Victoria sent a photograph of the watercolour in March 1858, were delighted with the depiction, telling her that it 'gave them the greatest pleasure'.[59]

Both Victoria and Albert greatly mourned the departure of their 'darling child' to Berlin, and the desire to see her again prompted their second visit to Germany together the summer after the wedding.[60] The reunited family members spent just over two weeks together at Potsdam, and again watercolours document some of their tourist experiences. On 16 August the party travelled by rail to Berlin for some sightseeing. According to Victoria's journal entry, they had a busy day, touring both the royal palace, where they also had lunch, and the palace of the Crown Prince. On their carriage drive into the city the Queen noted travelling through the Brandenburg Gate and along the boulevard of Unter den Linden ('under the lime trees') which she admired: '[it is] the Bond S[t] of Berlin, a broad street, with trees … very fine & gay, with pretty shops'.[61] She also particularly praised 'Rauch's fine equestrian statue of Frederick the Great'.[62] The composition of a charming watercolour by the genre painter Max Michael, who later became a professor at the Berlin Art Academy, was probably suggested by Victoria and Albert themselves via the agency of Vicky's mother-in-law, Augusta, Crown Princess of Prussia (1811–90).[63] Michael's view (fig. 70) is taken from a spot on Unter den Linden

Fig. 69 (opposite)

EGRON SELLIF LUNDGREN

The wedding of the Princess Royal and Prince Frederick William of Prussia, 1858

Pencil, watercolour and bodycolour, 28.0 × 38.8 cm

RCIN 919928

Fig. 70 (below)

MAX MICHAEL (1823–91)

*Unter den Linden with the statue of Frederick the Great, Berlin, c.*1858

Pencil and watercolour, 21.6 × 30.5 cm

RCIN 920689

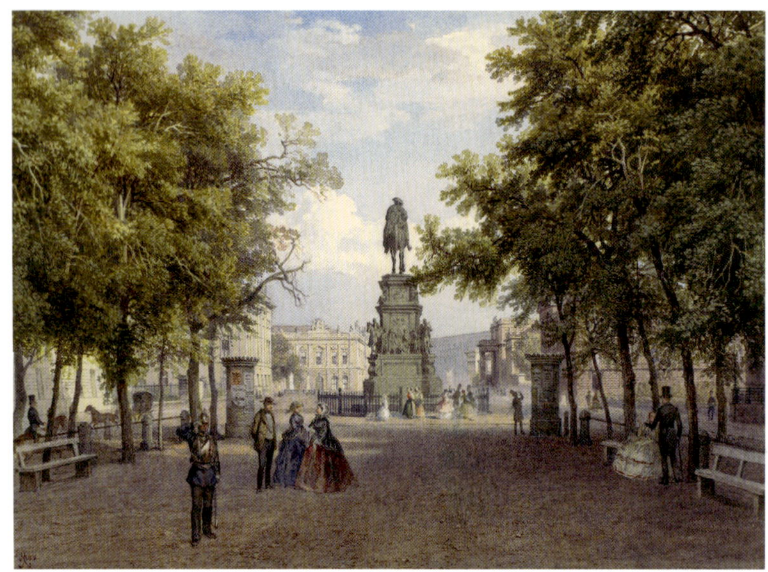

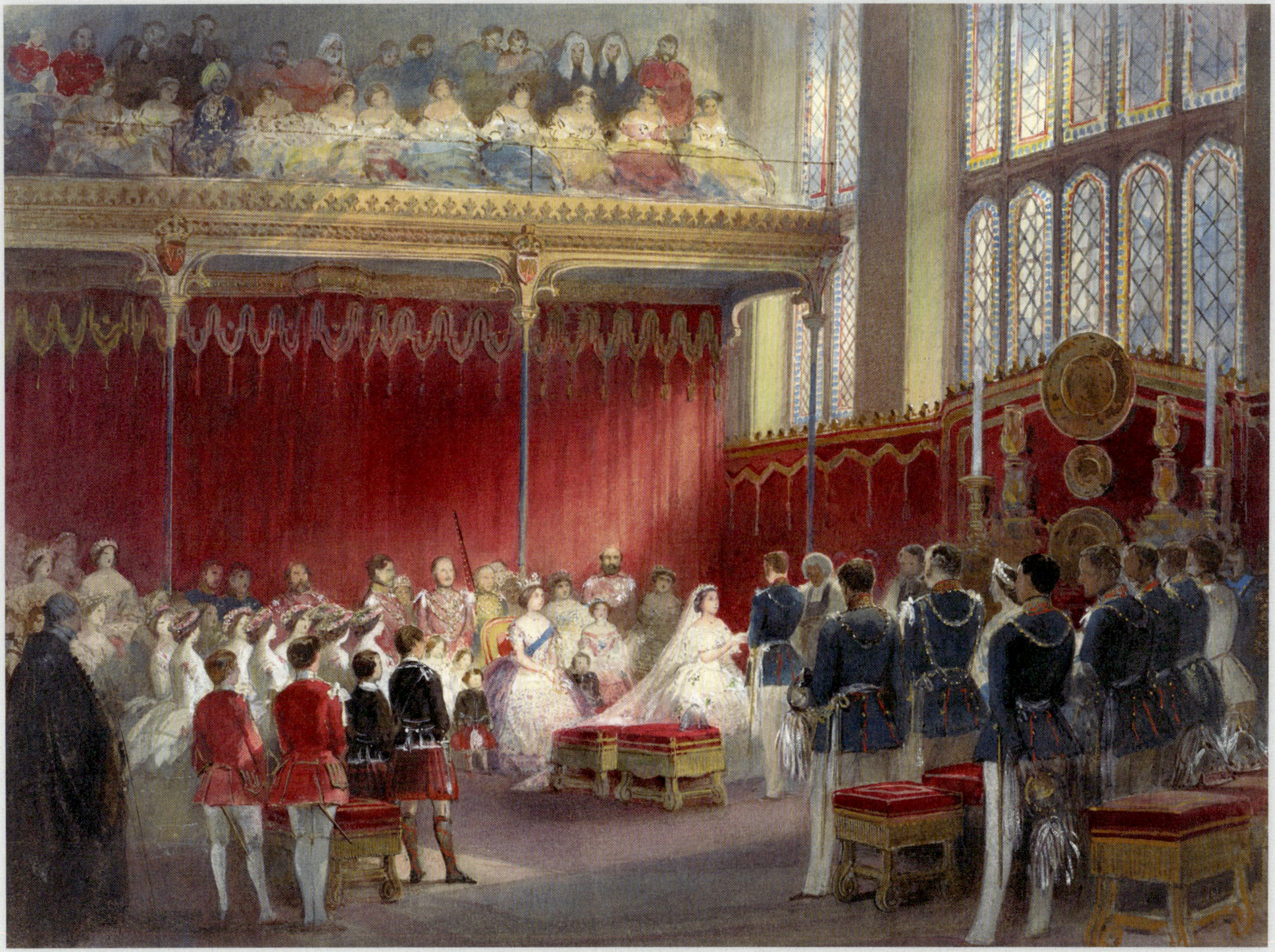

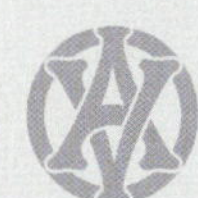

'[We breakfasted] in a charming spot, just outside the Casino, close above the water, with a beautiful view.'

– Queen Victoria

a few metres behind Rauch's statue and looks east, with the Zeughaus (the city arsenal) and the Crown Prince's palace on the left and right respectively in the distance. Fashionably dressed figures promenade on the boulevard, which is shaded by the lime trees that lend it their name; these trees also serve to frame the composition neatly.

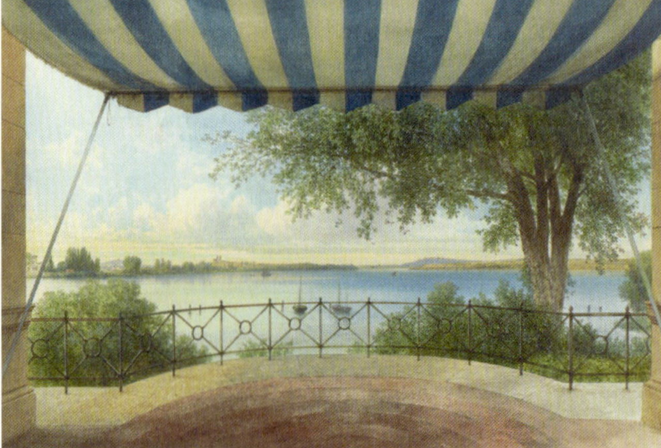

Fig. 71

CARL GEORG ANTON GRAEB (1816–84)

The view from the terrace of the Casino, Glienicke, c.1858–9

Pencil, watercolour and bodycolour, 22.2 × 31.7 cm

RCIN 920705

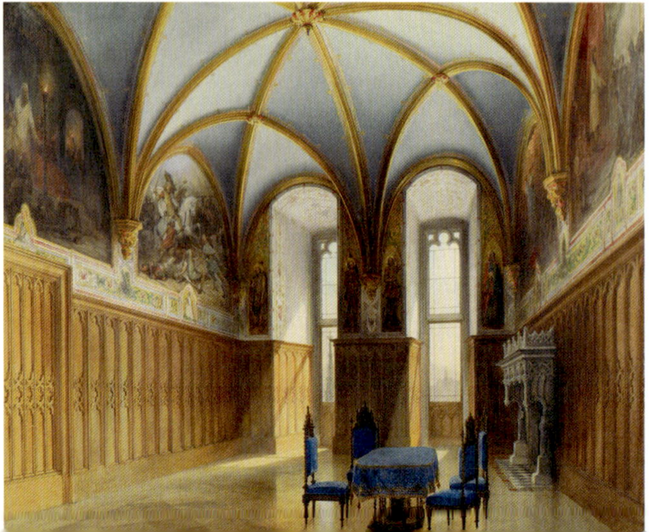

Fig. 72

CARL GEORG ANTON GRAEB

The Small Knights' Hall, Schloss Stolzenfels, 1847

Pencil, watercolour and bodycolour, 31.5 × 37.5 cm

RCIN 920422

A different German view, also mounted in the eighth View Album, illustrates a more atypical approach to composition. During their stay at Potsdam Victoria and Albert twice visited the palace of their new son-in-law's aunt and uncle, Prince Charles (1801–83) and Princess Marie (1808–77) of Prussia. On their second visit the British couple breakfasted with their hosts 'in a charming spot, just outside the Casino, close above the water, with a beautiful view'.[64] Victoria clearly expressed her appreciation of the view at the time, as letters between her and Prince Charles attest to the latter having promised to send her a record of it – and Victoria was very grateful to receive, in December 1859, a watercolour (fig. 71) by Carl Graeb. Taken from a spot on the terrace of the Casino, looking out towards the Belvedere on Pfingstberg Hill, it is unusual in its framing of the view with the striped awning prominent above. Victoria and Albert already owned examples of Graeb's work, the earliest of which were presented to them by the King of Prussia in 1847 as part of an album. This album contained watercolour views by different German artists of Schloss Brühl and Schloss Stolzenfels, two of the King's palaces at which he hosted the royal couple in 1845, among them Graeb's atmospheric view of a hall (fig. 72) in the latter residence.

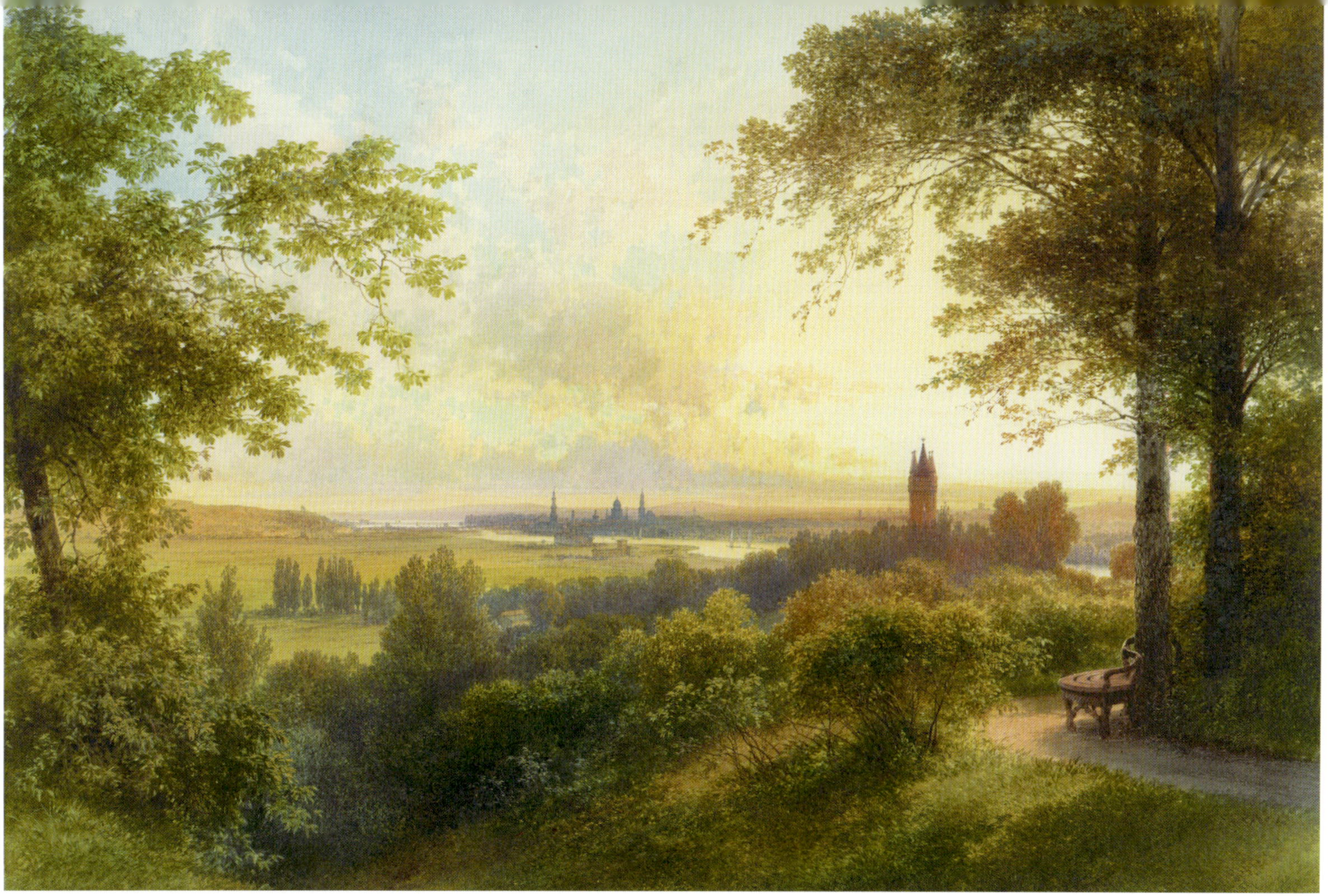

Although Prince Charles of Prussia apologised to Victoria for the delay in sending her the view from his palace and partially attributed it to the laziness of the artist, Graeb did paint a landscape quickly at the command of Prince Albert.[65] This (fig. 73) was given by Albert to Victoria as a Christmas present in 1858. The overt romanticism of this watercolour surely appealed strongly to Victoria, who had commented one evening towards the end of their stay in the city that 'Potsdam lit up by the setting sun looked splendid.'[66] With a background in stage design, Graeb was skilled at organising a composition and used strong, complementary colours to create an almost theatrical view of the distant skyline.[67]

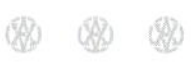

Fig. 73

CARL GEORG ANTON GRAEB

A distant view of Potsdam at sunset, 1858

Pencil, watercolour and bodycolour, 31.6 × 43.6 cm

RCIN 920706

Fig. 74

EUGÈNE-LOUIS LAMI

The Salon de Famille, château d'Eu, 1843

Pencil, watercolour and bodycolour, 27.6 × 42.9 cm

RCIN 920007

> ‘*the Princess showed us the Album [of watercolours] presented to the Pce on their Silver Wedding ... It contains some beautiful paintings.*’
>
> – Queen Victoria

It is clear that Victoria and Albert's large network of familial connections provided a fertile source for their knowledge and patronage of European artists. Artists were recommended by relatives or fellow princes directly, as was the case with Winterhalter, or indirectly through gifts of works of art, as with Graeb. The opportunities afforded by travel itself were a stimulus, too. The royal couple were attentive to schemes of decoration and works of art in the palaces and castles they visited, and while abroad, as at home, they enjoyed visiting exhibitions – Albert, for example, spent an entire morning at the Exposition Universelle in 1855, following the visit he had made with Victoria and Napoleon III three days previously. Finally, looking at albums of prints and watercolours in company was a common after-dinner activity and one that Victoria and Albert engaged in often with their fellow rulers and relations, thereby enjoying the opportunity to see works by a variety of European artists. At Koblenz in 1860, for example, Victoria noted that after dinner ‘the Princess [Josephine, of Hohenzollern] showed us the Album presented to the Pce on their Silver Wedding ... It contains some beautiful paintings.’[68] Eugène-Louis Lami perfectly captured the sociability of looking at albums in his watercolour depicting an evening at the château d'Eu in 1843, in which Victoria (facing the viewer) is deep in conversation across the table, while gesturing to the open album in front of her (fig. 74).

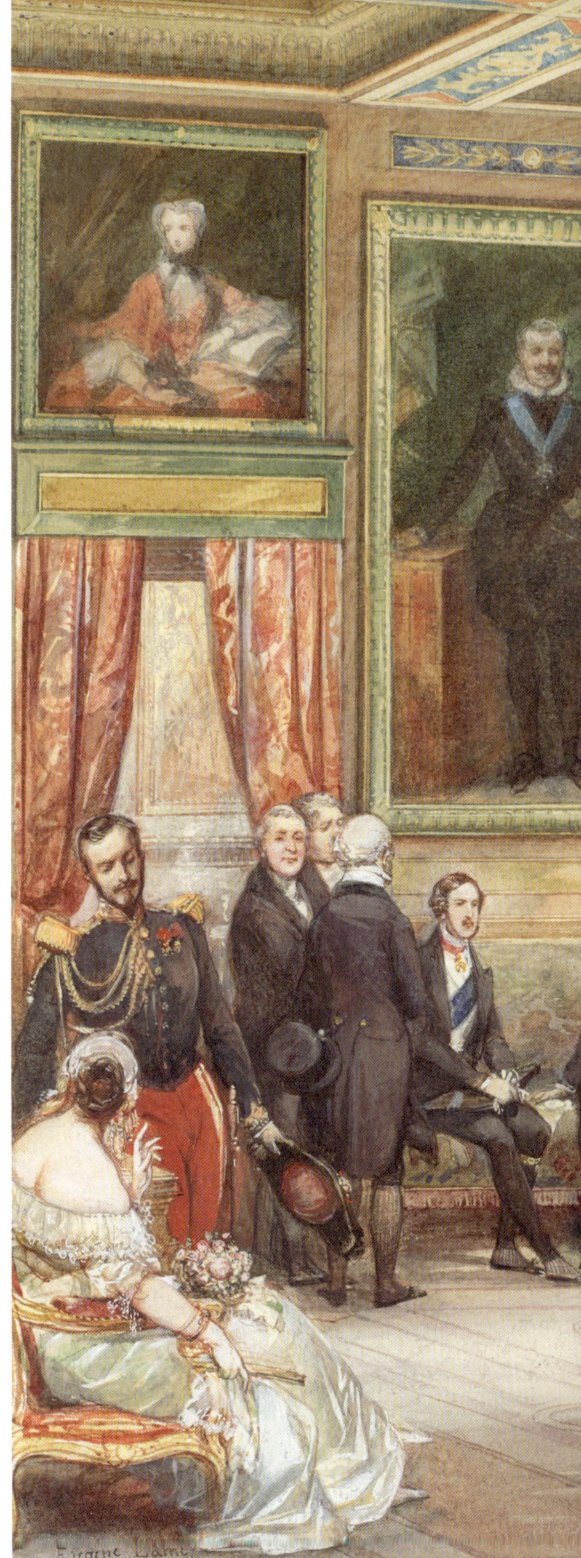

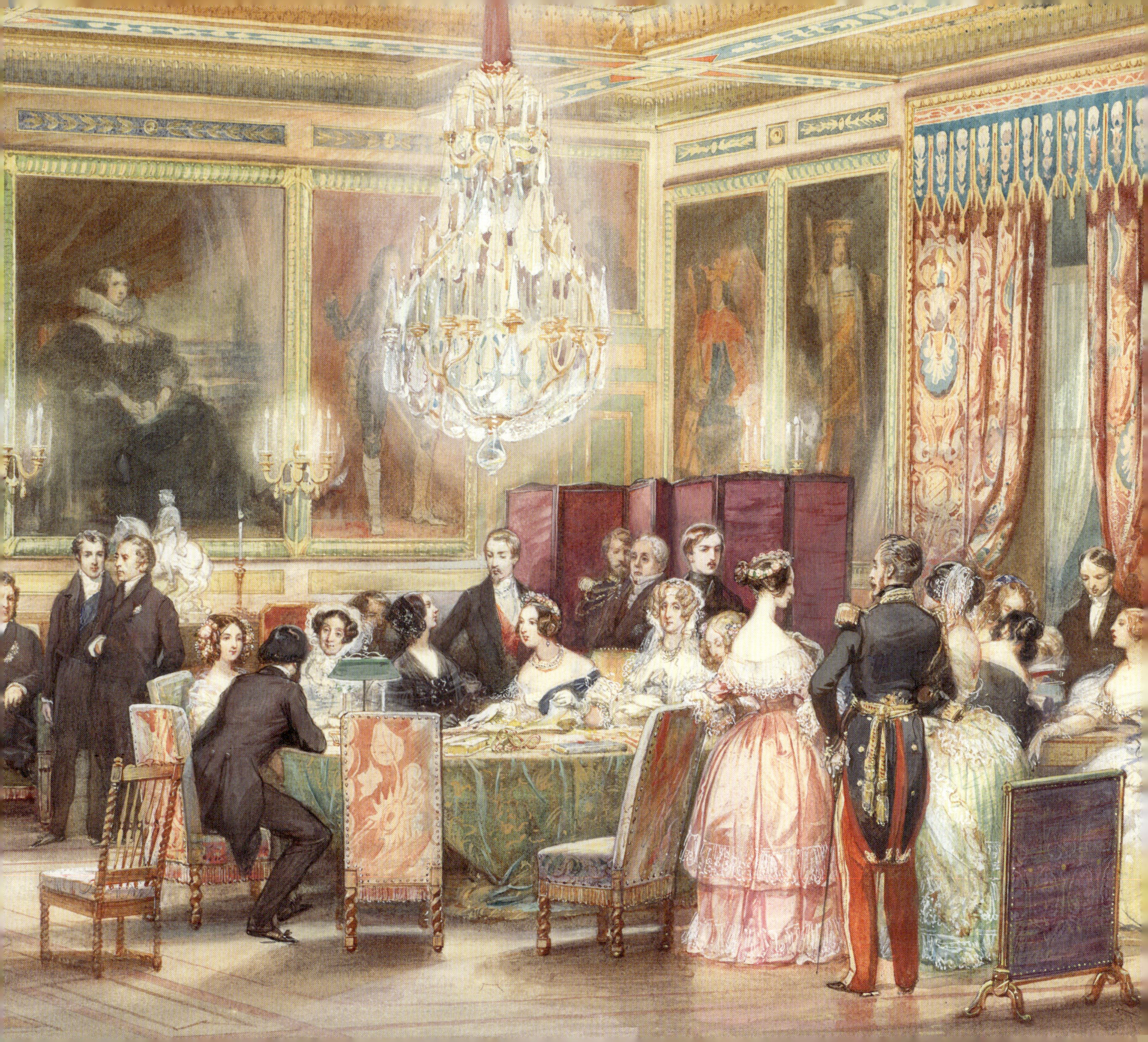

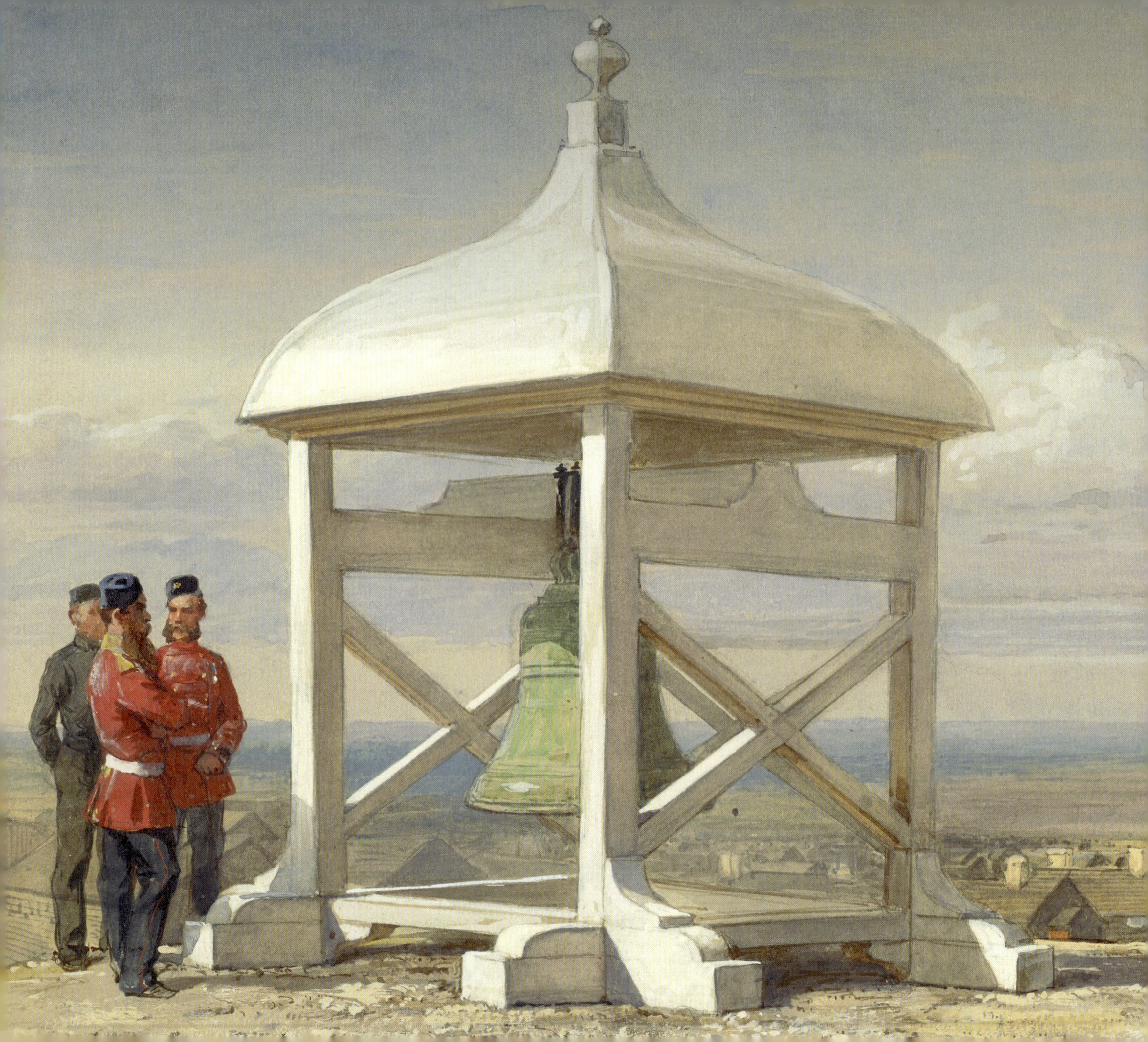

CHAPTER 4

PUBLIC SPECTACLE IN PEACE & WAR

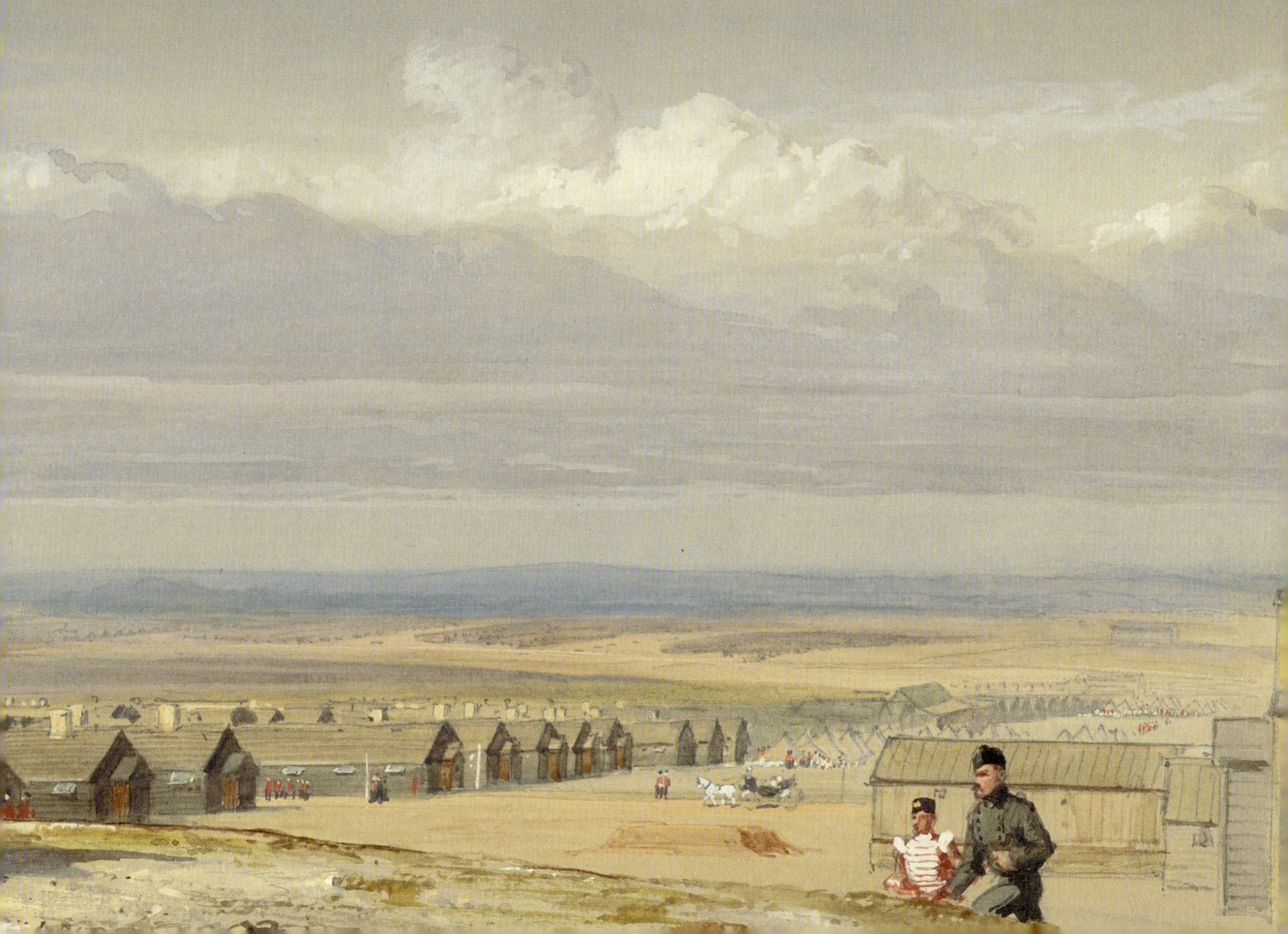

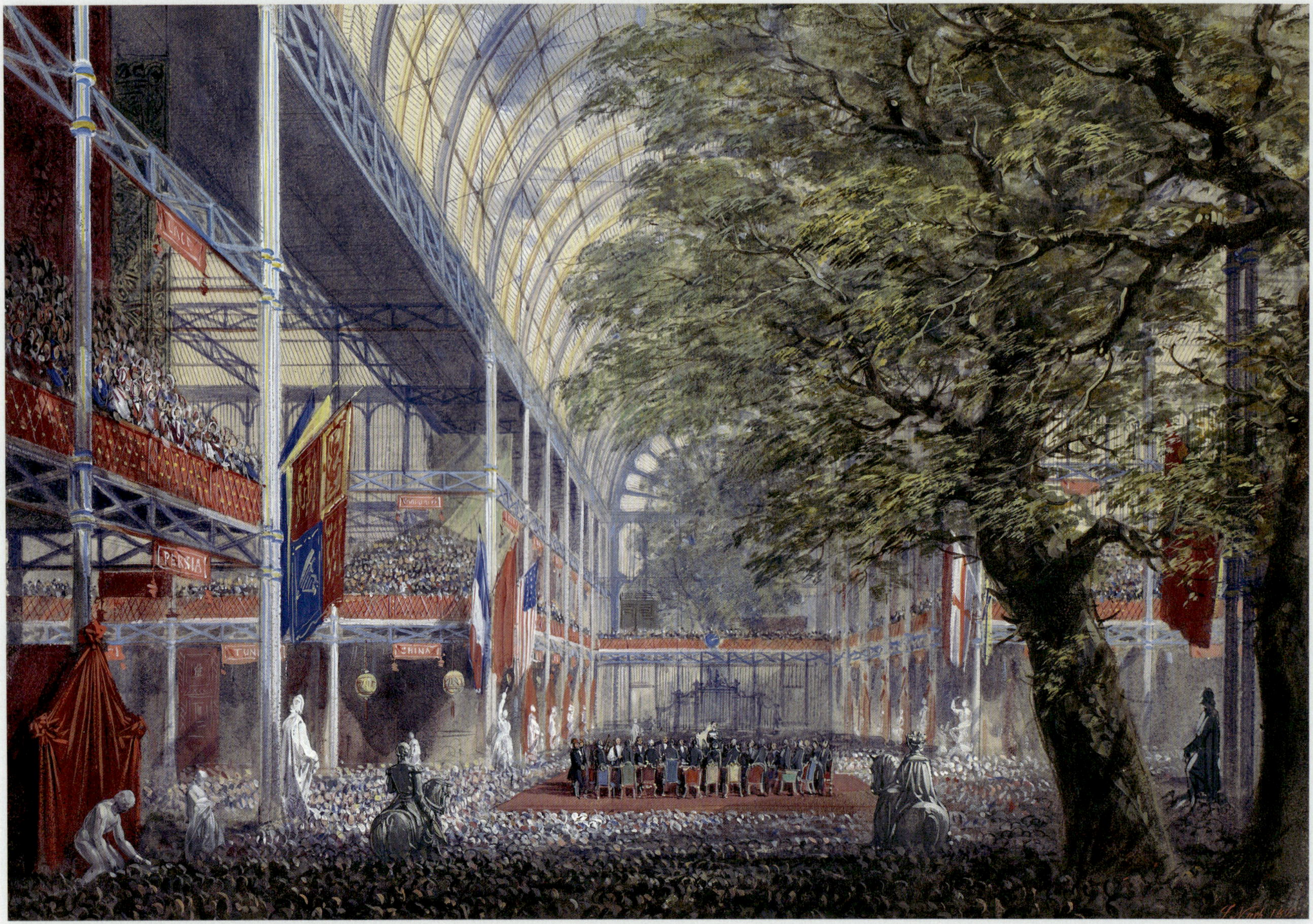

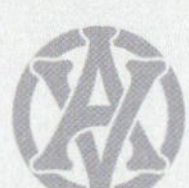

CHAPTER 4

Public spectacle in peace & war

> ‘A large crowd was assembled outside the railings & … great cheering being heard, as well as the distant sounds of music, we stepped out on to the balcony [at Buckingham Palace] & were loudly cheered.’[1]
>
> – Queen Victoria

Fig. 75

JOSEPH NASH

Prince Albert's closing address at the Great Exhibition, 15 October 1851, 1852

Pencil, watercolour and bodycolour, 32.2 × 48.2 cm

RCIN 919975

In 1876 the *Art-Journal*, writing about royal commissions given to the war artist William Simpson (1823–99), briefly described for its readers the Queen's watercolour albums, which 'preserv[ed] mementoes of all the interesting ceremonials and events in which she has herself personally appeared and publicly borne a part'.[2] Though the View Albums began rather introspectively, filled with topographical views of the royal residences and places Victoria and Albert visited, they soon expanded in scope to include scenes of court events and those of much wider public magnitude. In many of these, despite the *Art-Journal*'s statement, there is no royal presence, though of the subjects of this type chosen by Victoria and Albert for inclusion in the albums there was always a degree of personal resonance.

The Great Exhibition – 'this wonderful creation of my beloved Albert's'[3]

The first day of May 1851 saw an event take place in London of huge significance nationally, internationally and personally for the royal family. This was the opening of the Great Exhibition of the Works of Industry of All Nations, a world fair of industry and manufacturing unprecedented in its scale and scope (it encompassed over 100,000 exhibits) and visited by more than six million people. It was the catalyst for a whole sequence of exhibitions held in Europe and the United States of America during the second half of the nineteenth century. The leading figures in the event's organisation were Prince Albert and the civil servant Henry Cole (1808–82). The Prince was the President of the Society for the Encouragement of Arts, Manufactures and Commerce, from which the germ of the idea originated, and then the President of the Royal Commission under whose auspices the project was developed and carried out.[4] Albert wrote to his brother Ernest in July 1849 that he was 'working out a plan for a large industrial exhibition in London, for the whole civilised world, with all its competitors', and his proposals were advanced enough to be known of outside Britain by the following summer, when the painter Winterhalter confided to the Queen's dresser Marianne Skerrett that '[In Paris] we admire very much the Prince's beautiful and grand idea of a general exhibition for the next year, as well as all the efforts for its success; it is an admirable effort!'[5]

The exhibition was held in a vast and technologically innovative purpose-built structure that came to be known as the Crystal Palace – 'a real work of art', as Albert himself noted.[6] Approximately half of the floor space of the building was given over to the display and promotion of goods and manufacturing from Britain and its empire, and the remainder showcased the industry of world nations including Russia, India, France and Switzerland. The categories of display encompassed raw materials (such as coal and cotton), machinery and the fine arts, meaning that the visitor could trace the history of many objects through the process of their creation to the finished product.

Both Victoria and Albert were keen to capture what was only ever intended to be a temporary spectacle in a permanent visual record. They commissioned a number of artists to paint views in both watercolour and oils of the Crystal Palace and the grandeurs of the opening ('the greatest day in our history', wrote Victoria to uncle Leopold) and closing ceremonies (fig. 75) at which Prince Albert presided.[7] Victoria engaged James Roberts to paint a series of nine watercolours for the View Albums. The majority of these were views, from different angles, of the transepts and down the nave of the building, with a couple recording specific displays. Victoria and Albert together also instigated a more public project, commissioning two favourite artists – Joseph Nash and Louis Haghe – to produce forty-nine large watercolours for the purposes of reproduction in chromolithography (then still a relatively new and developing technology in colour printing, and thus in keeping with the ethos of the exhibition). These chromolithographs were published by Messrs Dickinson of Bond Street in two volumes with accompanying letterpress descriptions in 1854. In total the original watercolours cost £600, a large sum of which Victoria and Albert paid £300 each directly to Dickinson.[8]

Joseph Nash was responsible for the majority of the watercolours and, according to the Queen, he had made fifty views by 15 October 1851 (though at least four of his paintings of the Great Exhibition were not part of the Dickinson project). Unlike those painted by Roberts for the View Albums, the works commissioned for the publication were designed to be comprehensive, depicting the

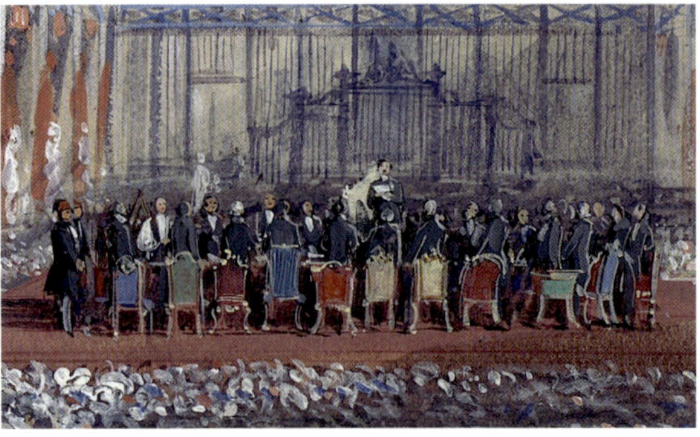

Fig. 75 (detail)

displays of the participating countries and those organised according to class of material or product. Nash painted one exterior view (fig. 76) as part of this series. This differed from others commissioned by the royal couple, which were intended to record the magnificence of the Crystal Palace, in focusing on depicting the raw materials that could not be housed inside the building, such as coal, cement and concrete, and large objects such as obelisks. The smoking factory chimney in the background of this exterior view further underscores the industrial purpose of many of the materials illustrated in the foreground.

In Nash's interior views the architecture is – perhaps surprisingly, given the artist's background and specialism – treated somewhat summarily. This may be because he painted the large group of watercolours in a short amount of time, and because the most important details needed for the reproductive prints were the objects on display. Indeed, it appears that for some of the watercolours Nash used a transfer method to copy the primary elements of the architecture from one sheet to another, presumably to speed up the painting process.[9] Furthermore, in the scene of the stained glass gallery (fig. 77), the paper has been left bare in places to represent the clear glass, another time-saving technique.

Of the watercolours Nash painted for the publication, seven depicted different views of the Indian display. This was the biggest of the colonial section, and in a prime position within the Crystal Palace. Victoria mentioned looking at its displays on six separate occasions in her journal. One of its most impressive exhibits was the howdah that she loaned (fig. 78), which had been presented to her by the Nawab Nazim of Bengal. It was displayed on a stuffed elephant borrowed from a museum in Suffolk.[10]

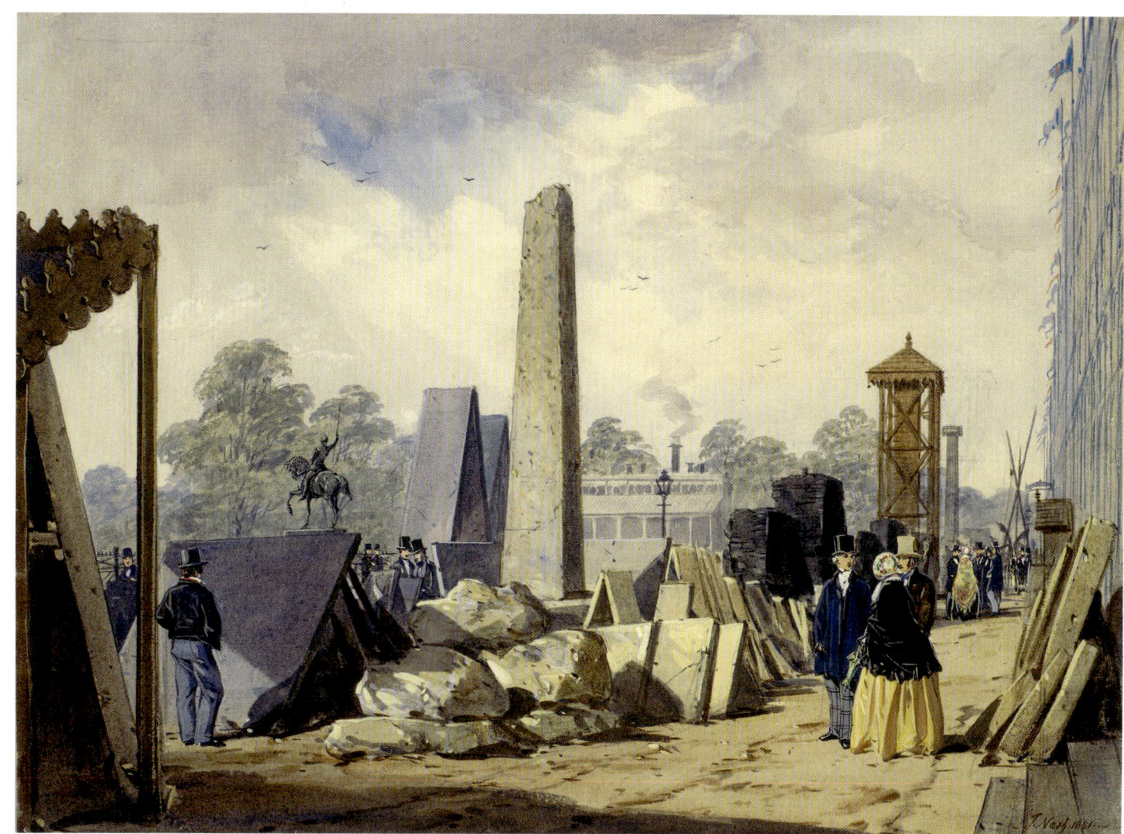

Fig. 76

JOSEPH NASH

The Great Exhibition: the exterior, 1851

Pencil, watercolour and bodycolour, 33.0 × 46.0 cm

RCIN 919931

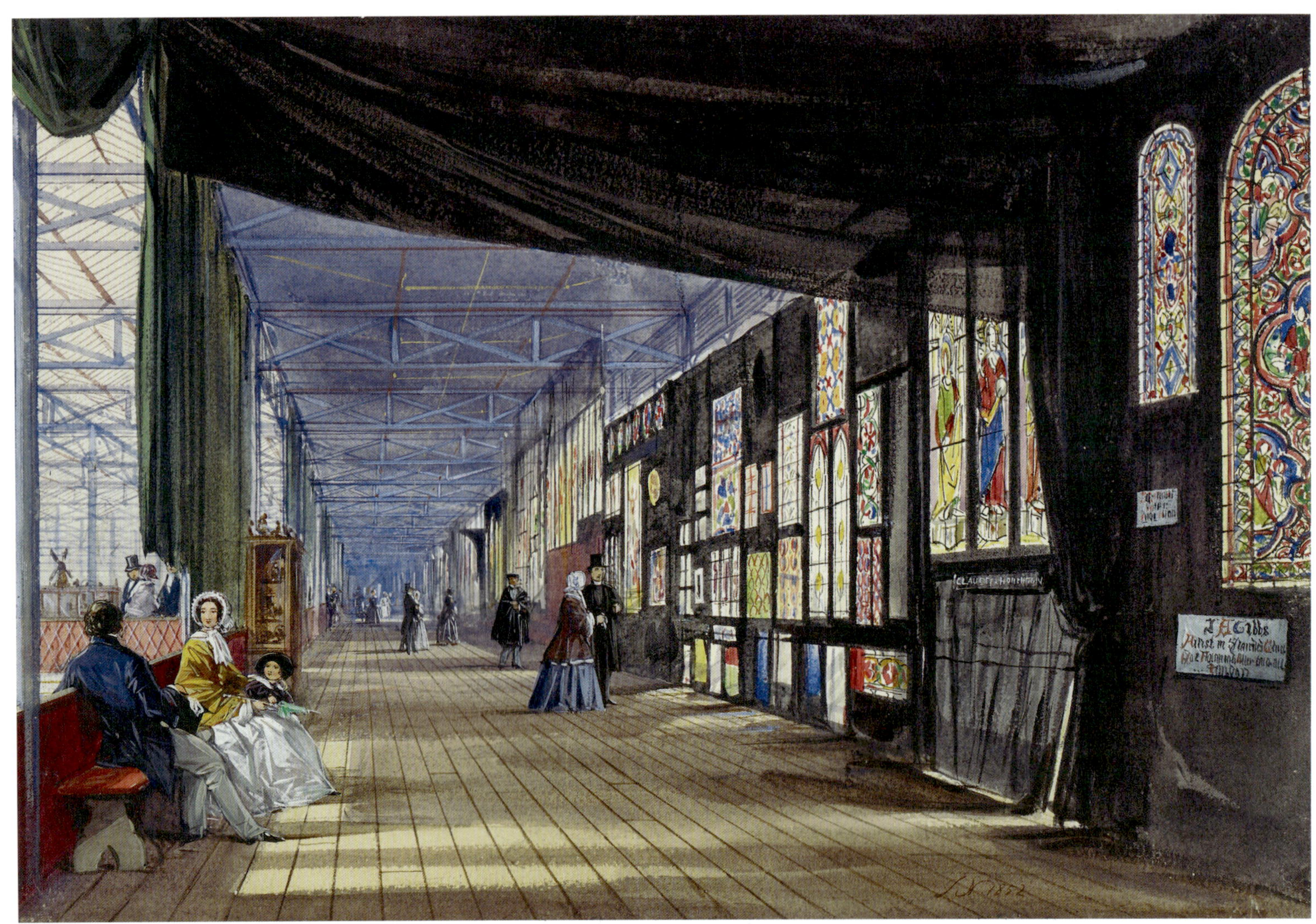

Fig. 77

JOSEPH NASH

The Great Exhibition: the stained glass gallery, 1852

Pencil, watercolour and bodycolour,
33.0 × 48.3 cm

RCIN 919941

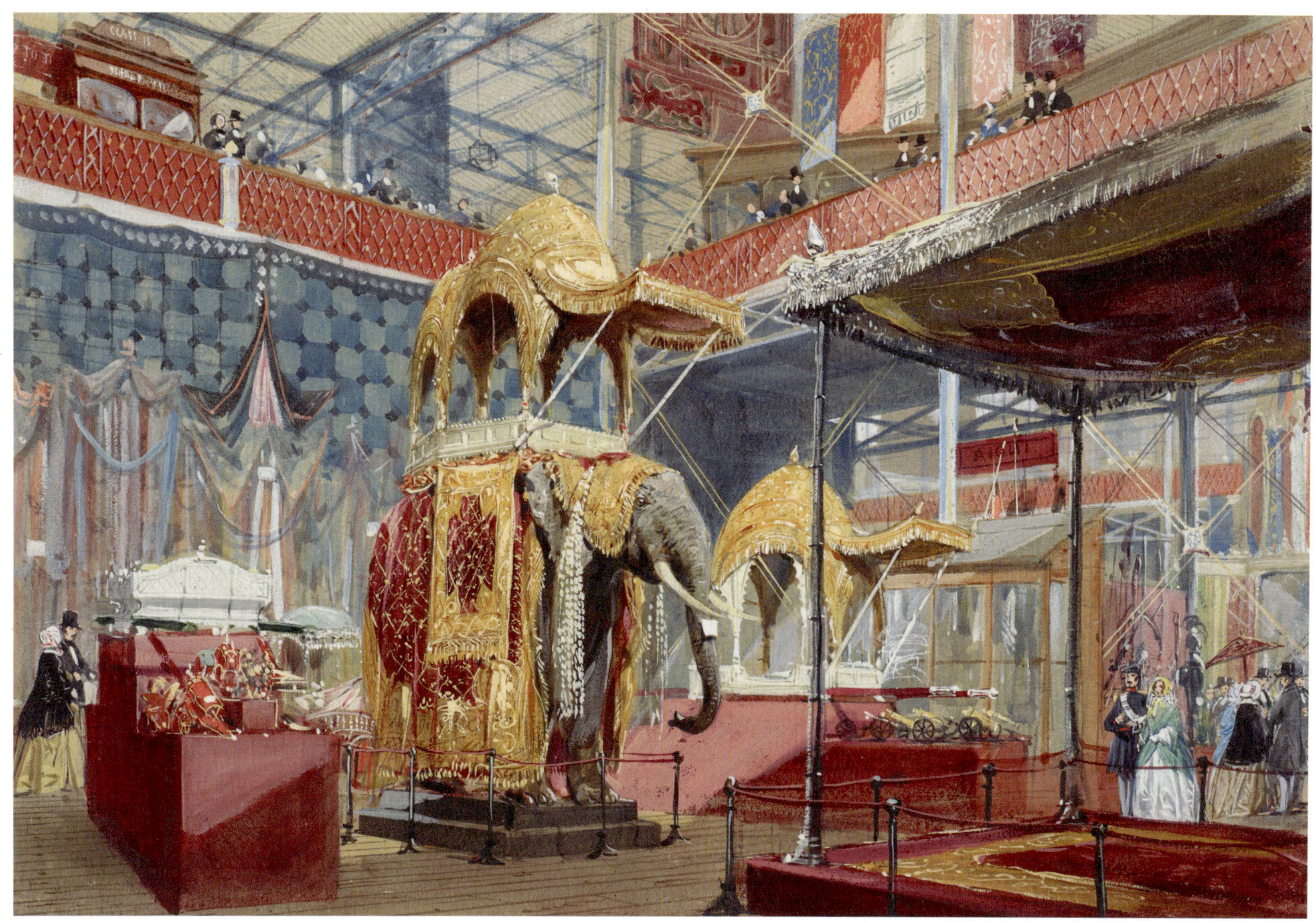

Fig. 78

JOSEPH NASH

*The Great Exhibition: India no. 4, c.*1851

Pencil, watercolour and bodycolour,
33.0 × 48.2 cm

RCIN 919942

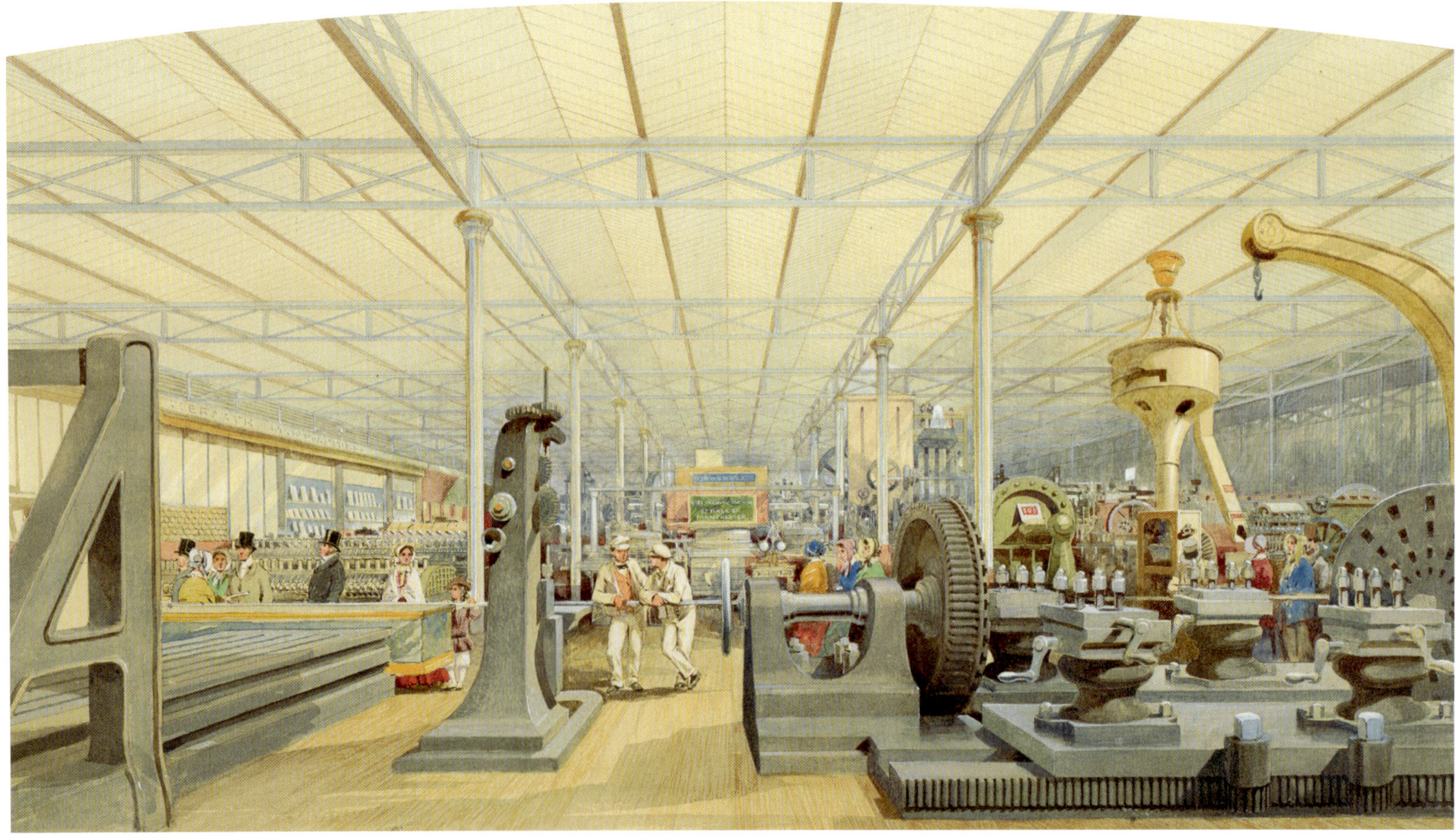

Fig. 79

LOUIS HAGHE

The Great Exhibition: moving machinery, *c.*1851–2

Pencil, pen and ink, watercolour and bodycolour with gum arabic, 29.5 × 54.5 cm

RCIN 919979

Haghe's six watercolours are much more highly finished than those by Nash. That depicting the hall of moving machinery (fig. 79) is particularly noteworthy for its almost modernist look. It is the only one of the Dickinson Great Exhibition watercolours to have an arched top, the exaggeratedly elongated format conveying the expansiveness of the space which was necessary to hold such large machines. Indeed the figures in Haghe's scene – visitors marvelling at the iron and steel tools of mass production and what are presumably two machine operators in the centre – are dwarfed by them. Haghe's limited use of colour, restricted primarily to various shades of grey and yellow, further implies the dominance of the machinery.

It is significant that all of the watercolours painted by Nash and Haghe are populated with figures (fig. 80). Staggered ticket pricing was applied during the period of the exhibition to ensure that it was accessible to

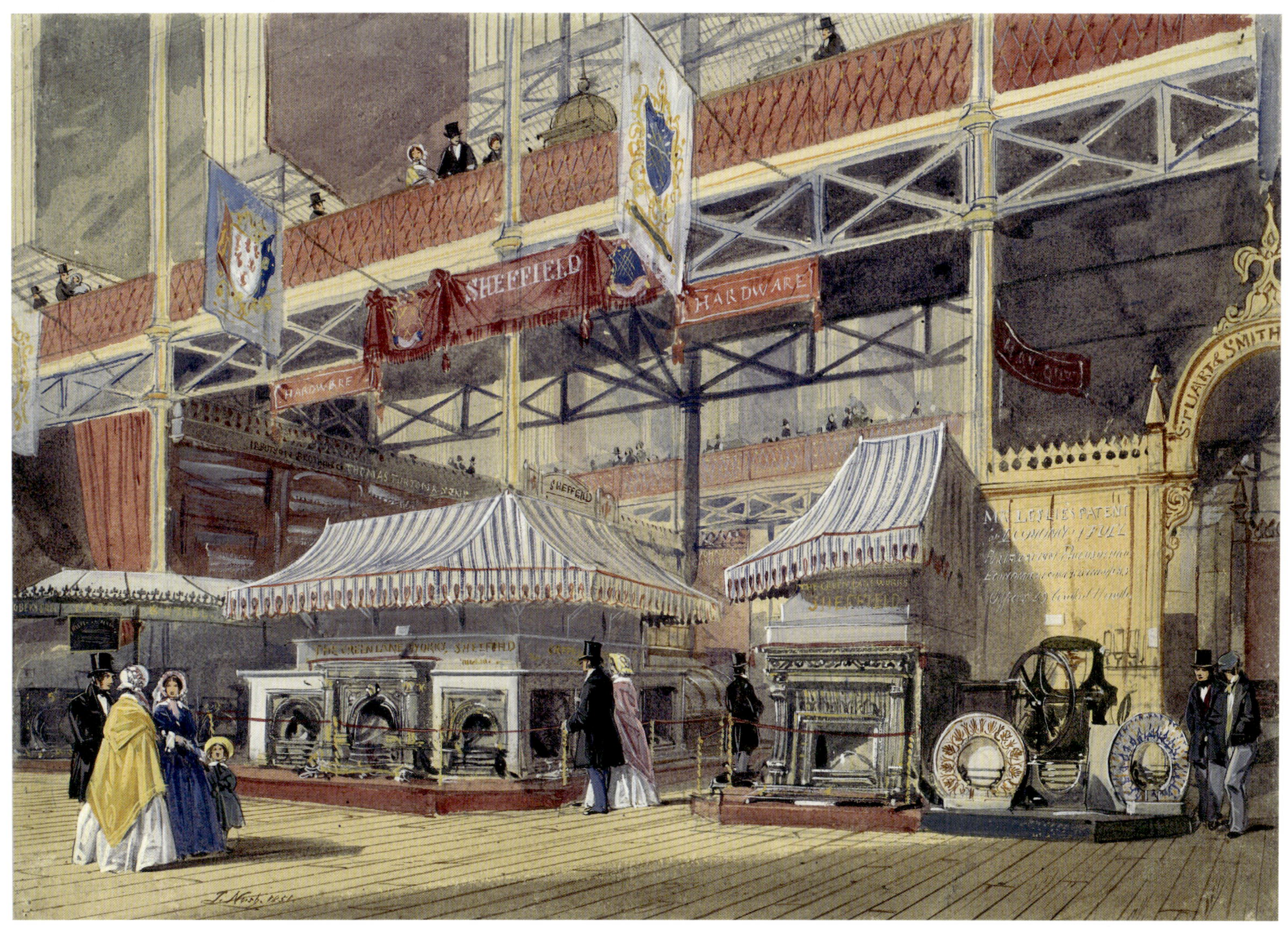

Fig. 80

JOSEPH NASH

The Great Exhibition: Sheffield hardware, 1851

Pencil, watercolour and bodycolour, 33.3 × 48.8 cm

RCIN 919936

a large proportion of the populace. Some of the figural groups in the watercolours demonstrate the sociable aspect of visiting the exhibition, but many – of a variety of ages and classes – are depicted engrossed in the exhibits, holding guidebooks and discussing the objects in front of them. The watercolours therefore do not just function as visual records of the temporary exhibition mounted in Hyde Park, but also emphasise the positive realisation of the Great Exhibition's aims to be didactic and universally beneficial.

In July 1851 Victoria and Albert were guests of honour at a ball held at the London Guildhall to celebrate the success of the endeavour. According to the *Illustrated London News*, the Queen's attendance enabled her 'to receive, in a scene of festivity, the Commissioners and other persons of our own and foreign nations by whose labours the Exhibition has been made so splendid and so successful, to add the last graceful touch to the great moral work of the year 1851'.[11] It is likely that a watercolour scene of the ball (fig. 81) – mounted in the fifth View Album – was presented to the royal couple as a souvenir of the event. The selection of William Wyld, an English-born artist based primarily in France, to paint this may have been consciously in keeping with the ethos of the exhibition, which celebrated and sought to facilitate relationships between nations.

Wyld's composition is skilfully organised. The Queen and Prince are on a dais under a canopy at the far end of the room, with elegantly dressed guests posed in small groups or pairs providing variety in the foreground. The figures are dwarfed by the vast Great Hall, and Wyld's depiction emphasises both the grandeur of the ancient space and the extravagance of the decorations created for the event. These included a large Gothic screen around the walls, floral garlands suspended from the ceiling and an arch above the throne inscribed with the message 'God save the Queen and Prince Albert' and surmounted with the Prince of Wales's feathers, 'seemingly of soft plumage, gracefully feathering over and swaying with a soft bend, yet made out of spun glass, and soaring to no less a height than nine feet!'[12] Wyld was well-suited to painting a subject replete with variety and detail – his watercolours are often heavily worked, with elaborate detail and rich colouring – and certainly there is, overall, a dense decorative effect to the scene. Whilst there is no record of her response to receiving Wyld's work, Victoria wrote in her journal that she thought the Guildhall 'beautifully decorated', and she and Albert ordered a letter of 'thanks for the splendid entertainment' to be sent to the Lord Mayor.[13]

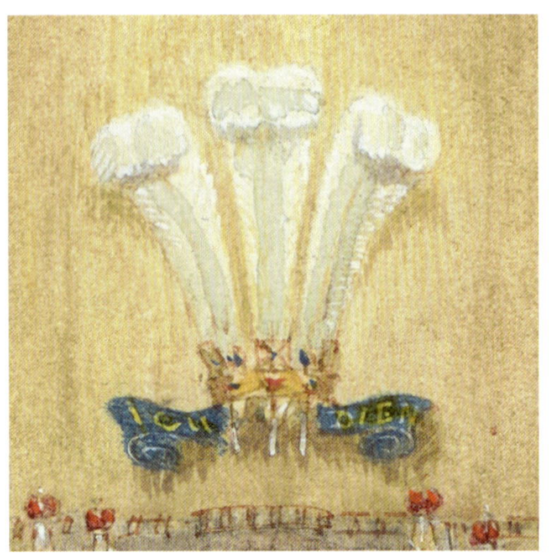

Fig. 81

WILLIAM WYLD

The ball at the Guildhall, 1851

Watercolour and bodycolour, 29.4 × 43.0 cm

RCIN 920218

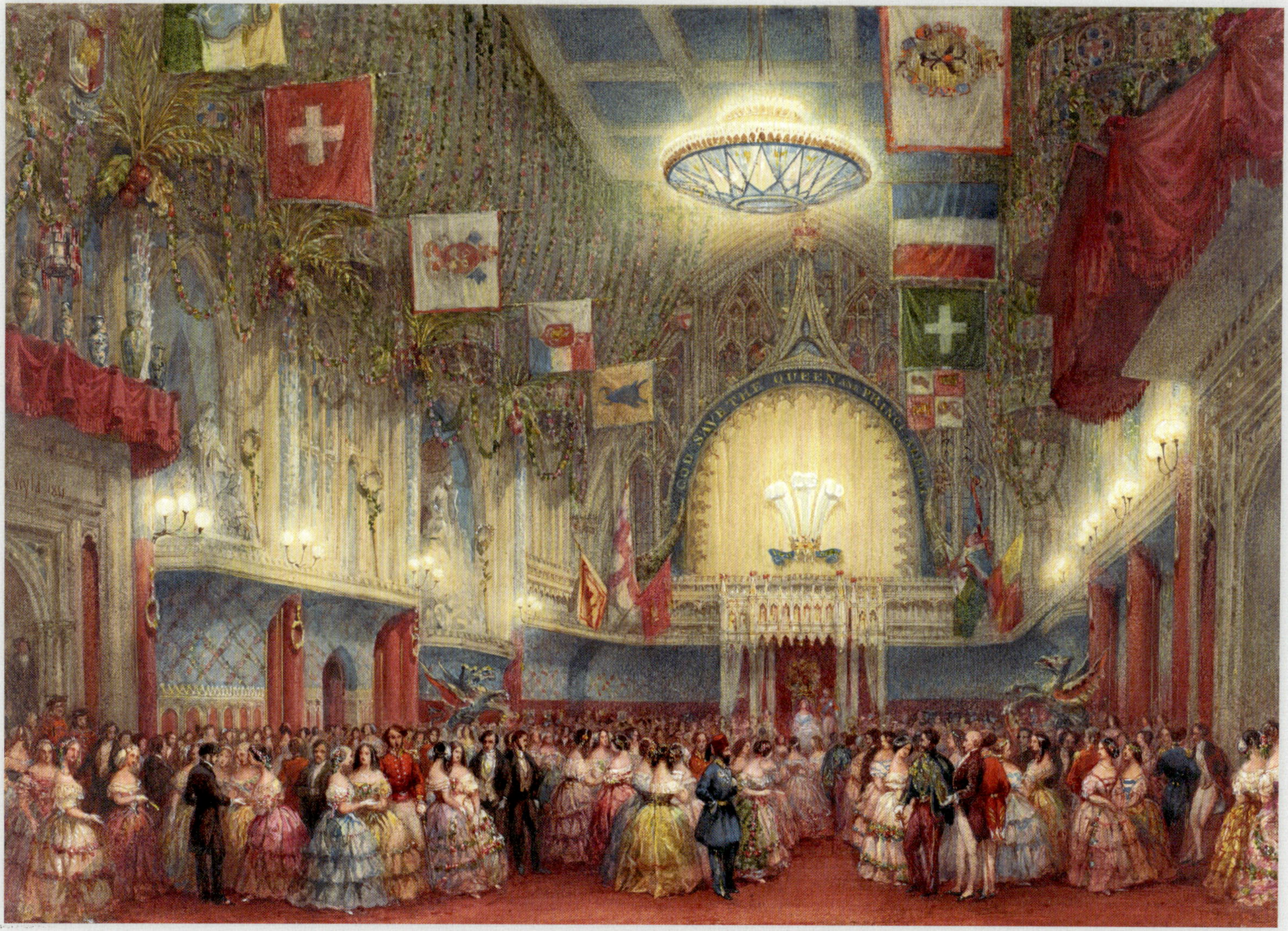

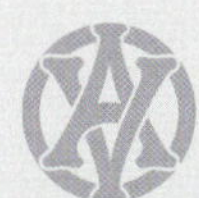

Court spectacle and entertainment

'Ere one ray of the splendour of that brilliant spectacle of the state ball has faded from memory, I will consecrate to the future its impressions on me.'[14] So began Octavia Walton Le Vert's detailed and enthusiastic account of a state ball she attended at Buckingham Palace in July 1853. The event was 'dazzling', according to the author, who keenly observed the splendour of the setting and the activities of the royal hosts – she noted, for example, that Albert and Victoria, 'in passing one another … constantly interchanged words, and pleasant, happy glances'. Such were the many and varied entertainments on offer – dancing, a supper, the opportunity to tour the state rooms of the palace – the evening passed quickly, and Octavia was amazed to be leaving at 'nearly 5 o'clock!'

Only a few of the many balls held or attended by Victoria and Albert during their marriage were represented in watercolours commissioned for the View Albums. Eugène-Louis Lami, described by his biographer as

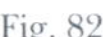

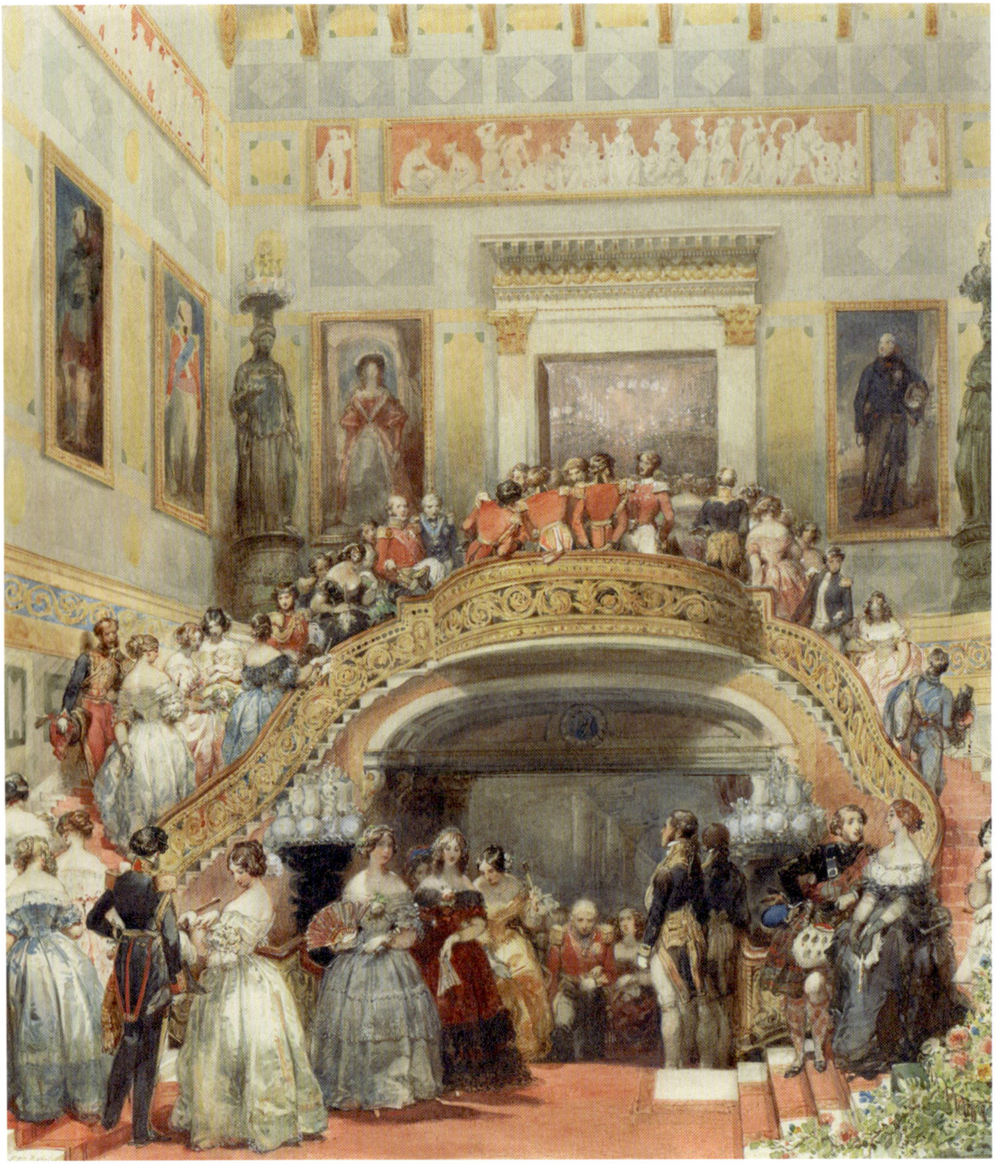

Fig. 82

EUGÈNE-LOUIS LAMI

The Grand Staircase at Buckingham Palace, 1848

Pencil, watercolour and bodycolour, 38.0 × 33.4 cm

RCIN 919902

being the most 'brilliant interpreter' of the fêtes of the July Monarchy of Louis-Philippe, was a natural choice to produce two such scenes.[15] The first of these depicts a throng of guests ascending the Grand Staircase towards the state apartments (fig. 82) on their arrival at a ball at Buckingham Palace. Staircases were a common theme in Lami's depictions of elegant society events such as this – incorporating them creates a sense of movement and dynamism among the large group of characters necessarily included in such scenes, and enables the viewer to read the depictions of different attitudes and costumes more easily than if all the figures were on the same level. The following summer, on a visit to the Duchess of Sutherland at Stafford House, Queen Victoria noted seeing 'the clever French artist ... working on a drawing of the staircase' there.[16] This was presumably the watercolour Lami sent for exhibition at the Royal Academy in 1850, where it was titled 'Her Majesty's visit to Stafford House', though the *Athenaeum*'s reviewer castigated the institution for hanging it – 'one of the choicest subjects and drawings' in its exhibition space – too low to be properly seen and enjoyed.[17] In the case of the Buckingham Palace staircase scene it seems likely that Lami's patrons determined the setting so as to take the opportunity of recording not just the specific event but also the recent renovation of the space. The desire to include the full decoration of the staircase ('most beautifully done up' according to the Queen on seeing the work in progress) may well account for the portrait format of this watercolour.[18] The gleaming, richly coloured dresses of the ladies and uniforms of the men in attendance harmonise beautifully with the colourful fictive marble panels on the walls surrounding the staircase. In the far right foreground a flower display is just visible; ascending the same staircase a few years later, Octavia Le Vert observed that 'on each side of the marble steps, masses of flowers were placed, so arranged they formed immense beds of gorgeous hue.'[19]

The 'clever French artist' had a number of points of contact with Victoria and Albert in the years around 1850. Lami followed the exiled French royal family to England in 1848 and remained close to them; two watercolour family group portraits by him entered Victoria and Albert's collection in 1850, one given to Victoria as a birthday present from Louis-Philippe and Marie-Amélie and the other commissioned by her.[20] In June of that year Lami seemingly witnessed the christening of Victoria and Albert's third son, Prince Arthur, as a watercolour by him of the event was mounted into the fifth View Album.[21] In 1851 the artist was an expert member of the committee charged with choosing the designs for the medals to be awarded at the Great Exhibition, and thus would have encountered Prince Albert in that context; Lami also painted a large-scale 'beautiful' watercolour for the Queen of the exhibition's opening ceremony.[22]

During the early summer of 1851 Lami was also busy playing a leading role arranging a costume ball Victoria and Albert hosted at Buckingham Palace on 13 June. This was the third and final event in a series of such balls the couple held, at which guests were required to come in a themed costume. The first, held in 1842, had celebrated the era of Edward III, and the second, in 1845, the Georgian court of a hundred years before; the final event looked back to the Restoration court of Charles II. The hosts intended these costume balls to encourage native textile manufacturing industries, and they took historical accuracy relatively seriously. In 1842, they employed James Robinson Planché (1796–1880), an expert in historical dress, to design their costumes (although Albert did wear a sword made for George IV's coronation as part of his outfit).[23] In 1851 the Queen recorded being 'much occupied' with Lami over the costumes on two separate occasions. Their hard work and attention to detail paid off; Victoria described their outfits, which had been 'most exactly carried out from Lami's drawings', as 'really beautiful & so correct' and Albert later informed a correspondent that the event 'went off … very brilliantly and transported us quite into [Charles II's] times'.[24] Victoria's magnificent dress survives in the Royal Collection today (fig. 83). Lami's close involvement with the design and staging of the ball made him an obvious choice to record it for the View Album (fig. 84). A variety of colourful period costumes dominate the watercolour, which shows an episode from the beginning of the evening when groups of dancers approached the dais on the far right and paid homage to Victoria and Albert.[25] Lami also carefully depicted the seventeenth-century hairstyles worn by many of the ladies in attendance; the Queen particularly admired their 'very becoming curls'.[26]

Though they did not always share exactly the same taste in the arts, both Victoria and Albert were great lovers of music, dancing, theatre and the opera. They were keen playgoers, making their first visit to the theatre in London as a married couple just two weeks after their wedding. Both appear to have been accomplished dancers; Victoria thought Albert 'a splendid dancer', an opinion a royal dancing master later endorsed, and her own gracefulness and enjoyment of dancing were frequently attested to in accounts of court entertainment – teaching the Queen a Scottish reel, for example, her maid of honour recorded that Victoria 'danced and skipped gloriously'.[27] Both husband and wife were also talented singers and pianists, which heightened their deep appreciation of music. Concerts, dances and theatrical performances therefore frequently featured in court entertainment. Some of the greatest musicians and actors of the day performed for the court, and the royal family themselves sang, played and acted to varying degrees in the same context.

The year 1848 saw the institution of a tradition of command performances of plays – the so-called Windsor Theatricals – at the British court in an effort to encourage the native theatrical industry.[28] Following the first performance of *The Merchant of Venice* by the company of Charles Kean (1811–68), a leading actor and theatre manager especially regarded for his revival of plays by Shakespeare, Victoria bestowed all the credit on her husband: 'It was a most successful performance … all this is dear Albert's idea.'[29] The theatricals took place most years during Victoria and Albert's marriage, the majority being held in the Rubens Room at Windsor Castle, where temporary staging and a dais for the royal party were erected specially. Despite

Fig. 83

Designed by EUGÈNE-LOUIS LAMI

Queen Victoria's costume for the Stuart Ball, 1851

Silk, lace, gold braid, silver fringing, seed pearls

RCIN 74860

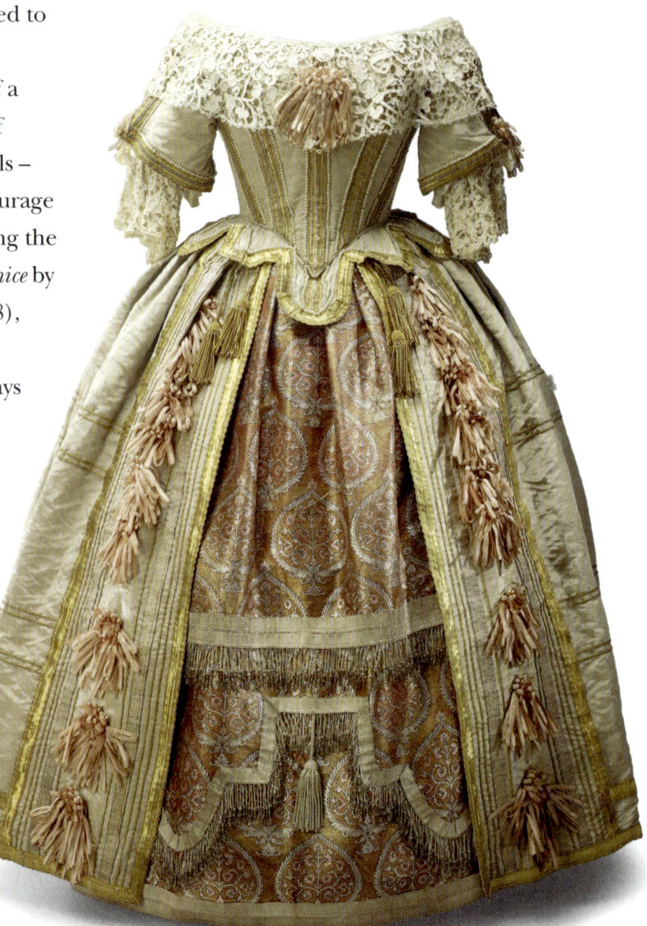

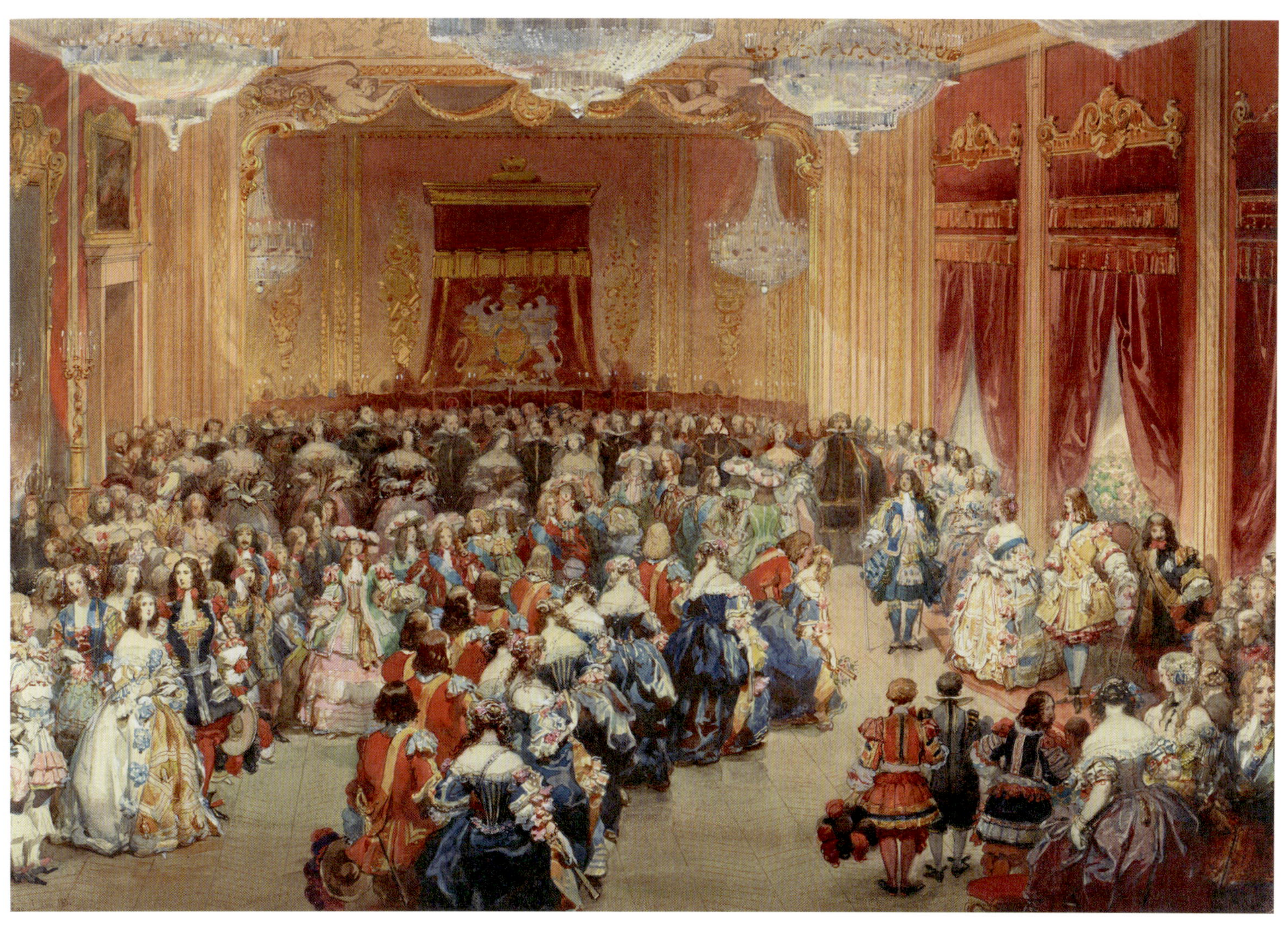

Fig. 84

EUGÈNE-LOUIS LAMI

The Stuart Ball at Buckingham Palace, 1851

Pencil, watercolour and bodycolour, 30.6 × 45.2 cm

RCIN 919904

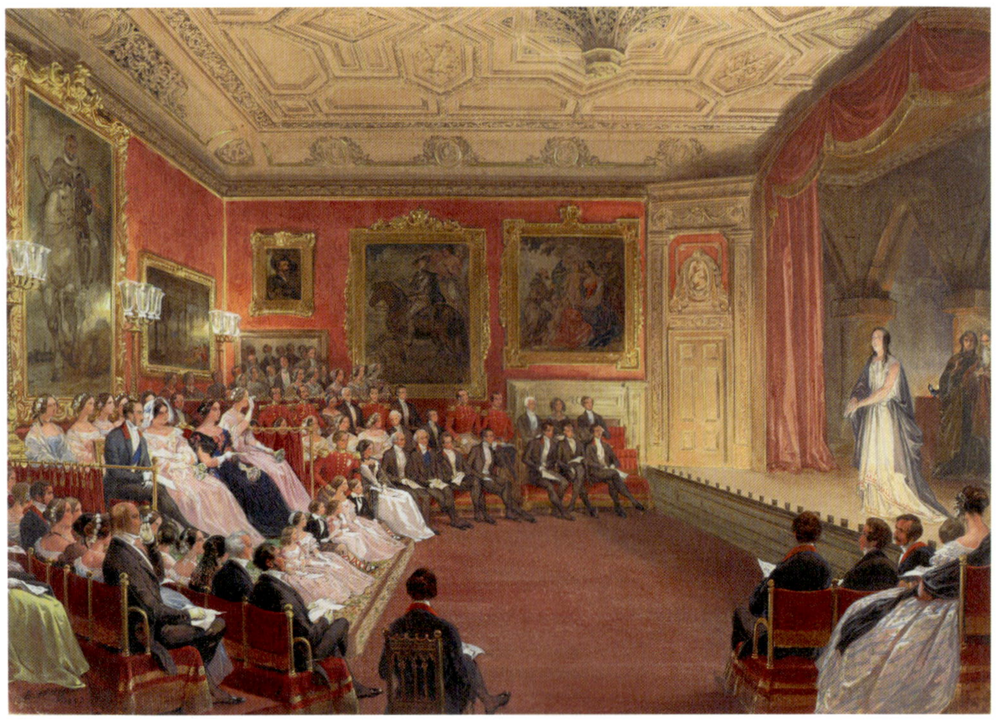

Fig. 85

LOUIS HAGHE

The performance of Macbeth *in the Rubens Room, Windsor Castle*, 1853

Pencil, watercolour and bodycolour with gum arabic, 33.4 × 48.2 cm

RCIN 919794

the royal couple's enjoyment and support of the theatre, only one watercolour mounted in the View Albums relates to such a production staged for the court – Louis Haghe's depiction of a performance of *Macbeth* in 1853 (fig. 85), which shows both the action on stage and the audience looking on. Victoria and Albert sit on the dais to the left with the Duchess of Kent, their niece Princess Adelheid ('Ada') of Hohenlohe-Langenburg (1835–1900) and their six eldest children. The composition gives a real sense of Haghe's field of vision from the position he was allocated for sketching (only the lap and one hand of the woman on the very far left are visible, for example). There is also a noticeable 'snapshot' quality to the watercolour in details such as Princess Ada, sitting beside her aunt Victoria, having seemingly just raised her theatre glasses to her eyes.

It was Haghe's patrons who specified that the audience as well as the action on stage should be included in the watercolour. This decision creates an interesting tension, for it is not just the actors being observed but also the royal family themselves, as is made clear by the direction in which the heads of the two men in the far right foreground are turning. Victoria's maid of honour Eleanor Stanley intimated this in a letter to her mother after a Windsor performance the following year, describing the six royal children seated on the royal dais 'all together look[ing] very nice'.[30] Haghe was also commissioned by the Queen to paint a further three watercolours of this new production of *Macbeth*, which was staged at Kean's Princess's Theatre in London in the spring of 1853. Victoria and Albert went to see it twice during its run. A letter from the artist to Marianne Skerrett reveals that he received specific instructions about one of the scenes Victoria wanted illustrated – moreover, there was to be an important distinction between this watercolour and the first he had painted, in that no part of the theatre should be included in the later work. Two of these watercolours were framed and hung at Osborne, and the third mounted in the Theatrical Album, which Albert gave to his wife in 1852 to house watercolours of scenes from plays they saw together.[31]

The royal children also put on plays for the court on several occasions, generally to celebrate special anniversaries such as the birthdays of their parents. These were often recorded in watercolour, as is the case with a large, ambitious painting titled *Rot Käppchen* (fig. 86). It depicts the seven oldest children, along with other cast members, in character for a tableau they composed at the end of a performance of the fairytale Red Riding Hood. The occasion was their parents' fifteenth wedding anniversary in 1855, and Albert commissioned a depiction of the tableau scene to give to Queen Victoria as a present for her birthday later that year from Edward Corbould, then 'Instructor in Drawing and Painting in Watercolour to the Royal Children'. It is seen in James Roberts's watercolour of Victoria's birthday table of that year, and was framed and hung at Osborne.

Fig. 86

EDWARD CORBOULD (1815–1905)

Rot Käppchen or Red Riding Hood, 1855

Watercolour and bodycolour,
36.8 × 53.5 cm

RCIN 450631

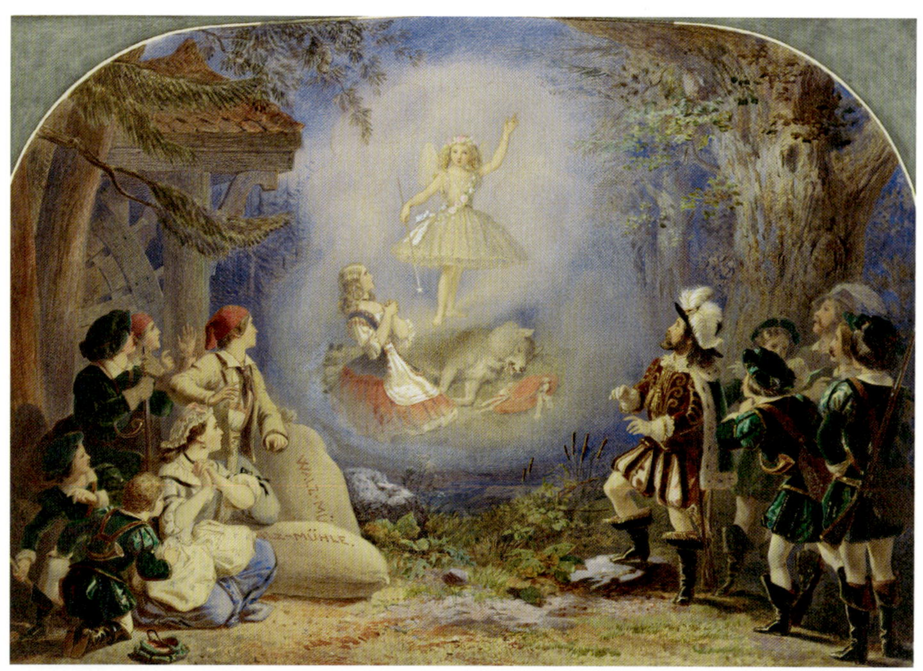

The Crimean War – Victoria's 'beloved troops'[32]

Between 1854 and 1856 such joyful occasions were in stark contrast to the ongoing conflict in the Crimea. Along with the rest of the country, Victoria and Albert followed the Crimean War closely from its inception; the Queen declared to her uncle Leopold: 'My whole soul and heart are in the Crimea.'[33] This was the first major conflict of her reign, and the key players involved were Britain, France, Turkey and Sardinia, who came together as allies to fight against Russia. Naturally the Queen had a privileged position in terms of receiving intelligence about the course of the war – its successes and setbacks, from the British point of view – meeting frequently with her Secretary of State for War, communicating directly with army commanders in the field and reading written reports from them, and receiving in person accounts from officers returned from the front.[34] Victoria and Albert's abiding concern was for the welfare of the soldiers, whom Victoria referred to repeatedly in her journal as our 'brave men', and the royal couple engaged practically and constructively with the war effort, encouraging their household to follow suit.[35] They sent supplies including food, soap, blankets and reading material out to the Crimea and to military hospitals at home, pressed government ministers to provide adequate facilities and care to wounded soldiers on their return from the front, and spearheaded a series of unprecedented visits to British military hospitals. Victoria recorded her vivid impressions of these events, as well as some occasions on which veterans were invited to Buckingham Palace, in her journal, noting the personal details – the names, ages and wounds – of many of the soldiers thus encountered.[36] This genuine concern and empathy is reflected in the inclusion of almost forty watercolours in the sixth and seventh View Albums relating to the war and its aftermath.

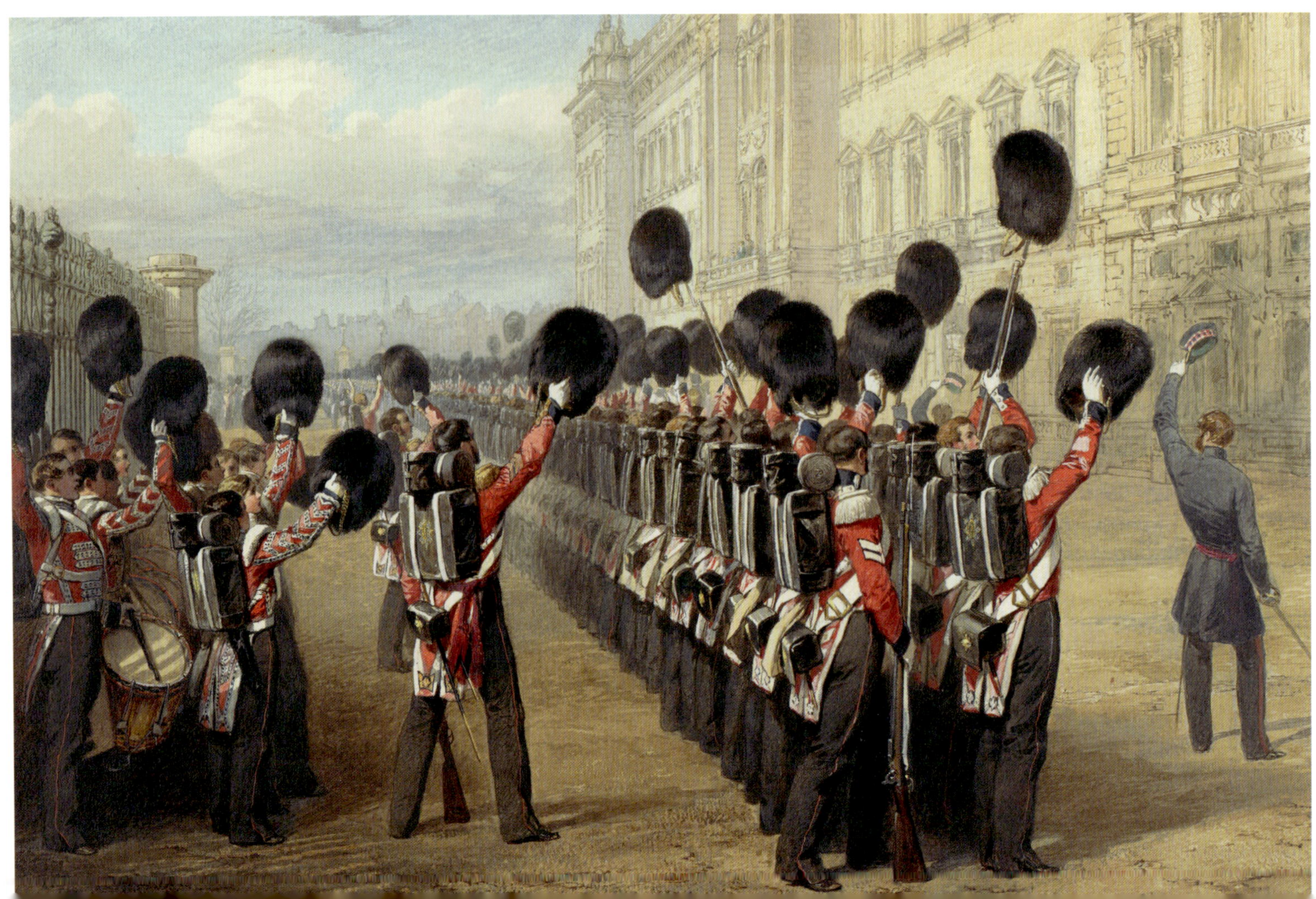

Fig. 87 (opposite)

GEORGE HOUSMAN THOMAS

The farewell to the Scots Fusilier Guards at Buckingham Palace, 1854

Pencil, pen and ink, watercolour and bodycolour with gum arabic, 32.5 × 47.5 cm

RCIN 916781

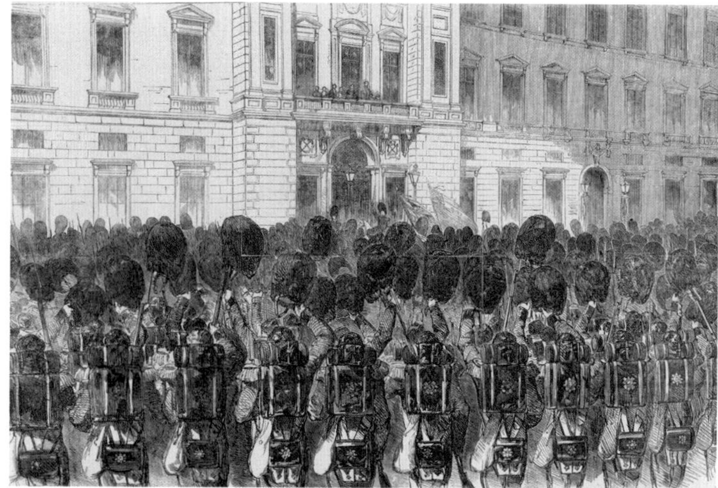

Fig. 88 (right)

Probably after GEORGE HOUSMAN THOMAS

Farewell of the first battalion of Scots Fusilier Guards at Buckingham Palace

Illustrated London News, 11 March 1854, p. 216

George Housman Thomas became one of Victoria and Albert's favourite military painters; after his death the Queen judged that the 'most talented artist Mr Thomas … was not to be equalled in his military, & indeed all other sketches.'[37] He was well represented in the View Albums of the mid-1850s, and indeed the first watercolour of a Crimean subject mounted in the sixth album was painted by him. This depicts a battalion of soldiers, en route to Portsmouth (from where they were to embark for the Black Sea), parading through the forecourt of Buckingham Palace early on a February morning in 1854 (fig. 87). This occurred at Victoria's request, and she wrote to her uncle Leopold later the same day that it was 'a touching and beautiful sight'.[38] The exact moment represented in Thomas's watercolour was described by Lieutenant Hugh Annesley, who took part in the parade: 'The Regiment halted in line … a thousand voices gave three hearty hurrahs for their Majesties, waving their bearskin caps in the air and by every gesture manifesting the most intense enthusiasm and loyalty.'[39] The Queen, who was watching with Albert and some of the older royal children from the balcony, 'appeared much affected, and bowed and smiled most graciously on her gallant third Regiment of Guards'.[40] It is notable that the soldiers are the focus of the watercolour, with the royal family group on the balcony almost imperceptible in the distance. The men in the immediate foreground are depicted obliquely, so that some of their faces and expressions can be seen. Thomas very much individualised these portraits, and particularly emotionally affecting are the two figures at the far left who look to be especially young men – a real note of pathos in what is ostensibly a moment of optimism and joyful demonstration of loyalty. Thomas may have been present at this event on behalf of the *Illustrated London News*, which published an illustration of it from a different viewpoint (fig. 88) – here the royal family figure more prominently and only the backs of the soldiers are seen.

Two years later Prince Albert commissioned Thomas to paint a series of watercolours of the British Army's first permanent military training camp, then being built at Aldershot in Hampshire at the Prince's initiative. Albert and Victoria were closely involved in the camp's development, making frequent visits.[41] Thomas's watercolours are views of different areas or features of the camp, such as an arresting depiction of a bell, hung inside a wooden frame or bellcote (fig. 89). This bell was one of two taken from the Church of the Twelve Apostles in Sebastopol following the allied victory there; one was sent to Aldershot and the other to Windsor Castle, where it now hangs in the Round Tower. In Thomas's watercolour the bell dominates the scene, towering over the group of three soldiers on the far left. The placement of the bell in the left foreground means that an elevated view over the south camp at Aldershot occupies the remainder of the scene, showcasing both the vast scope and orderly nature of the garrison. Eleanor Stanley described Aldershot as 'so different from anything I had seen, or had any idea of; nothing but huts and huts and cavalry barracks on all sides, and soldiers marching from every direction.'[42]

Other watercolours by Thomas are scenes of daily life at the camp, which accord with Victoria and Albert's particular concern for the mental as well as physical welfare of the British troops. The subjects of a number of them may have been inspired by a three-day visit Victoria, Albert and their three eldest children made to Aldershot in company with the Prince and Princess of Prussia in July 1856, as they correspond with a long, detailed entry in the Queen's journal. One scene shows soldiers with their wives and children engaged in domestic activities such as darning and playing games together, while another particularly characterful watercolour illustrates a group of 'Crimean heroes', as a later album caption designated them, in the canteen (fig. 90). The royal group visited one of the Aldershot canteens on 17 July, which Victoria found 'quiet and orderly'; Thomas's evocation of the scene is rather livelier, implying that the group of infantrymen seated at the table are having a spirited discussion.[43] Framed almost like a photograph, the close focus on the facial expressions and gestures of the men means that the bottoms of the legs of those at the front are cut off. There is also an unfinished quality to this watercolour that would have contributed to a sense of variety in treatment among the ten successive Aldershot views by Thomas in the seventh View Album. The Queen presumably would have appreciated

Fig. 89

GEORGE HOUSMAN THOMAS

The bell brought from Sebastopol, at Aldershot, 1856

Pencil, watercolour and bodycolour, 24.6 × 34.8 cm

RCIN 916804

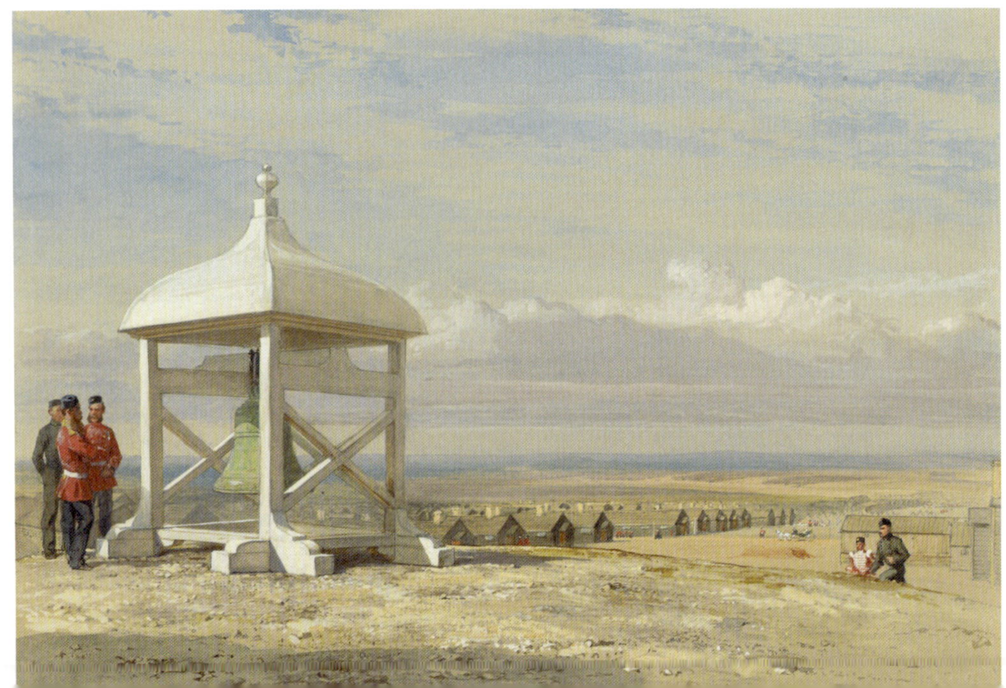

looking over this series in her album and relieving her memories of the visit, as she confided to her journal on the evening of 17 July that she had 'greatly enjoyed having been in the midst of all, amongst & close to the troops'.[44]

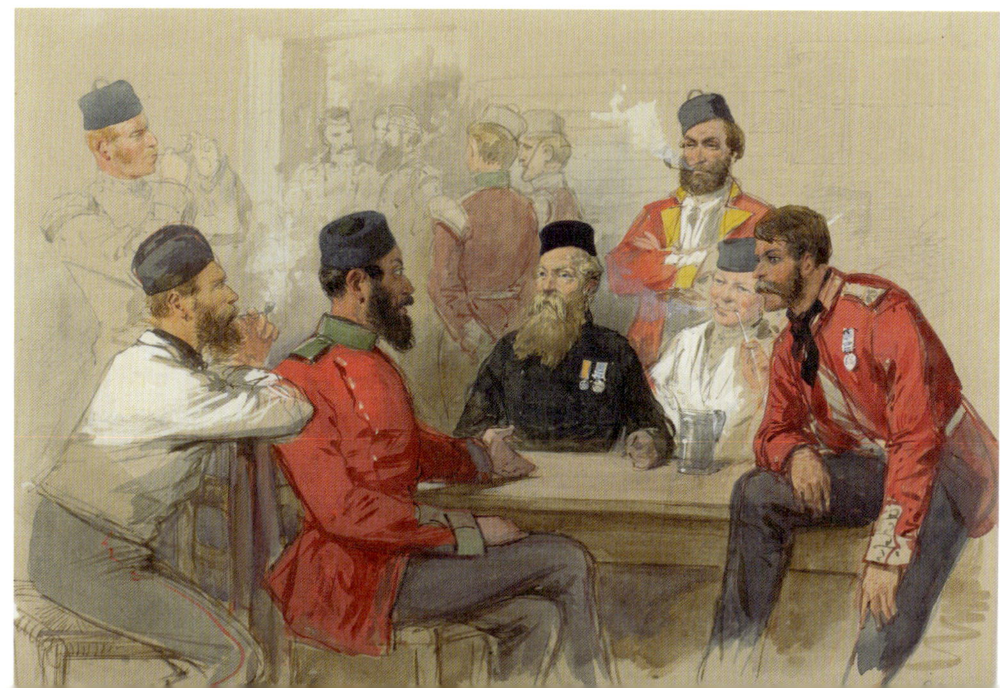

Fig. 90

GEORGE HOUSMAN THOMAS

Crimean heroes at the canteen, Aldershot, 1856

Pencil, watercolour and bodycolour, 24.7 × 35.2 cm

RCIN 916803

'Peace is signed!' Victoria informed her uncle Leopold joyfully on 1 April 1856.[45] The Treaty of Paris, which marked the end of the Crimean War, had been ratified two days previously. Just over a month later Victoria, Albert and their four eldest children presided over the unveiling of models for two monuments to the war at the Crystal Palace in Sydenham. The Scutari Monument and the Peace Trophy were created by the Italian sculptor Baron Carlo Marochetti (1805–67), who later sculpted Victoria and Albert's tomb effigies. A watercolour painted by John Tenniel (fig. 91) depicting the moment of the unveiling of the first of the two monuments was mounted in the View Album. Tenniel was primarily a cartoonist and illustrator but

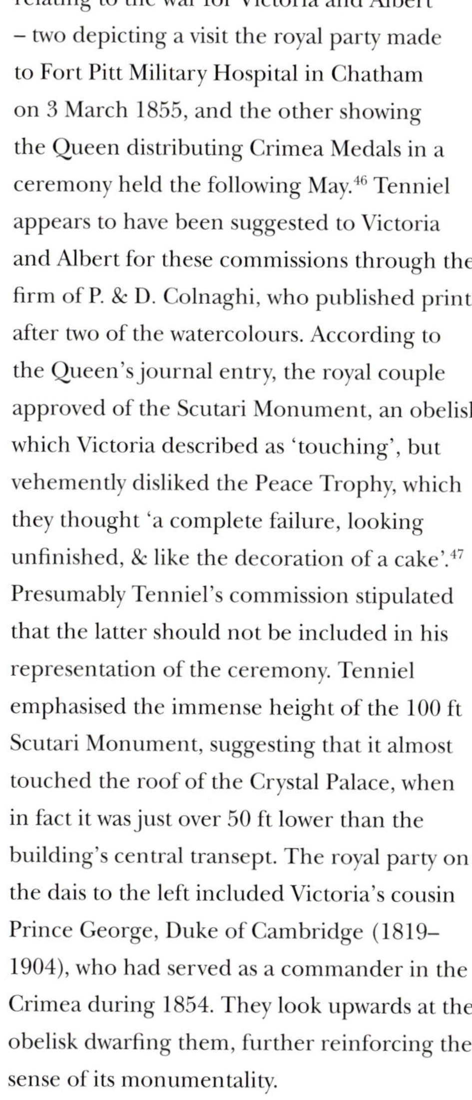

had already painted three other watercolours relating to the war for Victoria and Albert – two depicting a visit the royal party made to Fort Pitt Military Hospital in Chatham on 3 March 1855, and the other showing the Queen distributing Crimea Medals in a ceremony held the following May.[46] Tenniel appears to have been suggested to Victoria and Albert for these commissions through the firm of P. & D. Colnaghi, who published prints after two of the watercolours. According to the Queen's journal entry, the royal couple approved of the Scutari Monument, an obelisk which Victoria described as 'touching', but vehemently disliked the Peace Trophy, which they thought 'a complete failure, looking unfinished, & like the decoration of a cake'.[47] Presumably Tenniel's commission stipulated that the latter should not be included in his representation of the ceremony. Tenniel emphasised the immense height of the 100 ft Scutari Monument, suggesting that it almost touched the roof of the Crystal Palace, when in fact it was just over 50 ft lower than the building's central transept. The royal party on the dais to the left included Victoria's cousin Prince George, Duke of Cambridge (1819–1904), who had served as a commander in the Crimea during 1854. They look upwards at the obelisk dwarfing them, further reinforcing the sense of its monumentality.

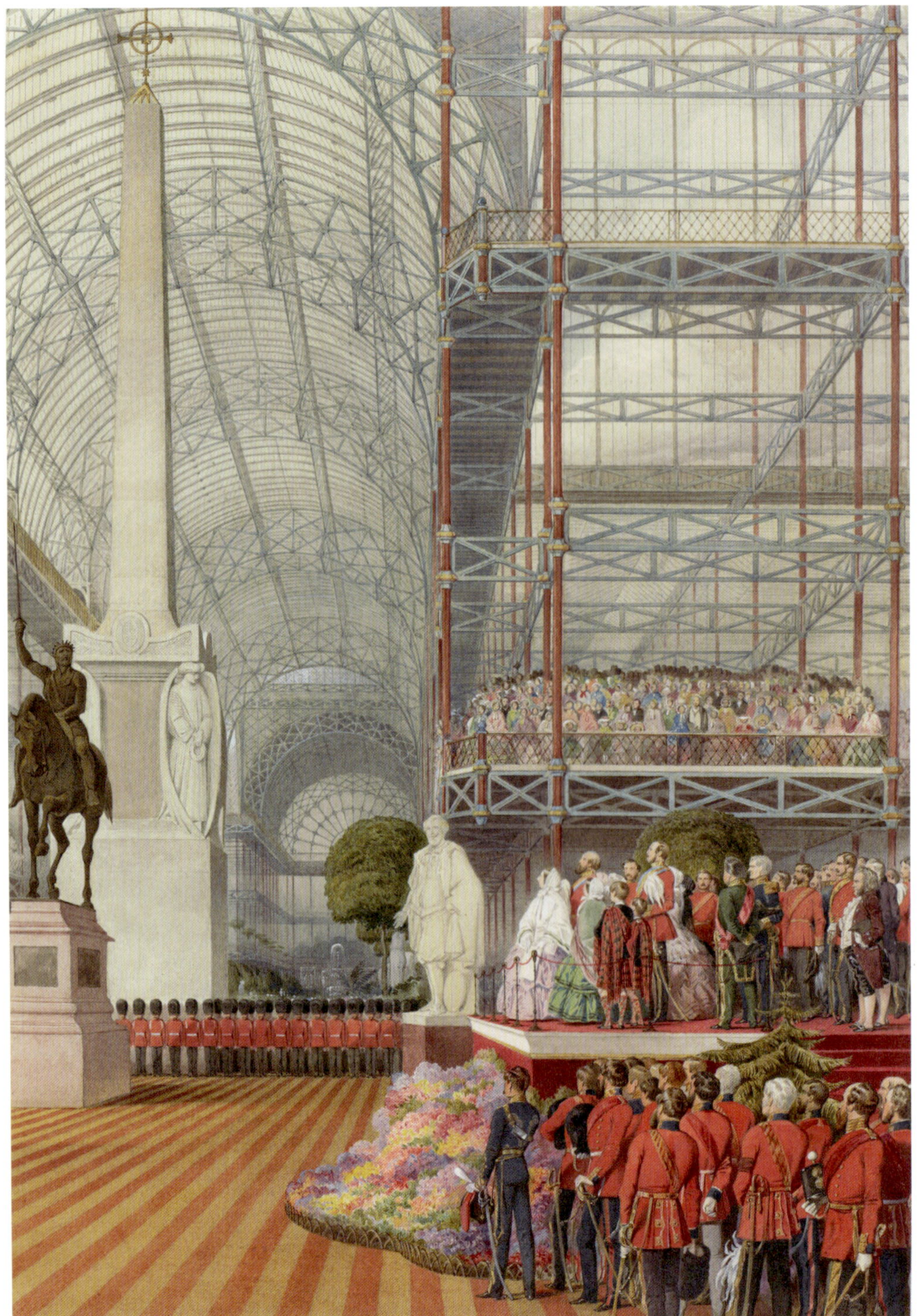

Fig. 91

SIR JOHN TENNIEL (1820–1914)

The inauguration of the Scutari Monument and the Peace Trophy at the Crystal Palace, Sydenham, 1856

Pencil, watercolour and bodycolour, 47.7 × 33.6 cm

RCIN 916788

Ceremony and pageantry

The magnitude in the national consciousness in the first half of the nineteenth century of Arthur Wellesley, 1st Duke of Wellington (1769–1852) – whose renowned victory at the Battle of Waterloo in 1815 ended the Napoleonic Wars – cannot be overestimated. Wellington also had a close personal relationship with the royal family. In the 1840s Victoria noted some of the Duke's birthdays in her journal, sending him a 'souvenir' on his eightieth in 1849, and when the following year Victoria and Albert's third son was born on Wellington's birthday, the infant prince was named Arthur after him and the Duke invited to be one of his godparents. On hearing of Wellington's death in 1852, the Queen wrote 'he was to us a true, kind friend and a most valuable adviser'.[48] A memorandum dictated by Albert at the same time further reflects his importance, instructing, 'Victoria wishes the Army to mourn for the Duke as long as for a member of the royal family'.[49]

The Queen and Prince were closely involved in the arrangements for the state funeral the Duke was afforded on 18 November. This became a huge public event, with over a million spectators thronging the streets of London to watch the procession of the funeral cortège to the internment ceremony at St Paul's Cathedral. Louis Haghe witnessed both the lying-in-state and funeral of Wellington, perhaps under a joint commission from Victoria and Albert and the publishers and printsellers Ackermann & Co. The latter exhibited watercolours by him in December 1852 prior to publishing them as large chromolithographs the following spring; these were described by the *Art-Journal* as 'the best illustrations of the solemn and imposing ceremony that have as yet been published'.[50] Haghe also painted three scenes presumably at the behest of Victoria and Albert, who were desirous of a record of the 'sad, solemn, affecting & most impressive sight' of the funeral procession (fig. 92).[51] These were mounted in the sixth View Album and varied significantly from those reproduced in print. That of the procession, showing the highly decorated funeral car bearing the coffin wrapped in crimson velvet, gives a strong sense of the scale and spectacle of the occasion. In addition to the temporary wooden stands erected on the far right, in the foreground are people who have scrambled up lampposts and atop carriages in order to secure a view. As Victoria wrote in her journal the evening of the funeral, it was as though 'the whole nation seemed to join in bearing the great Duke, with all honours & respect, to the grave.'[52]

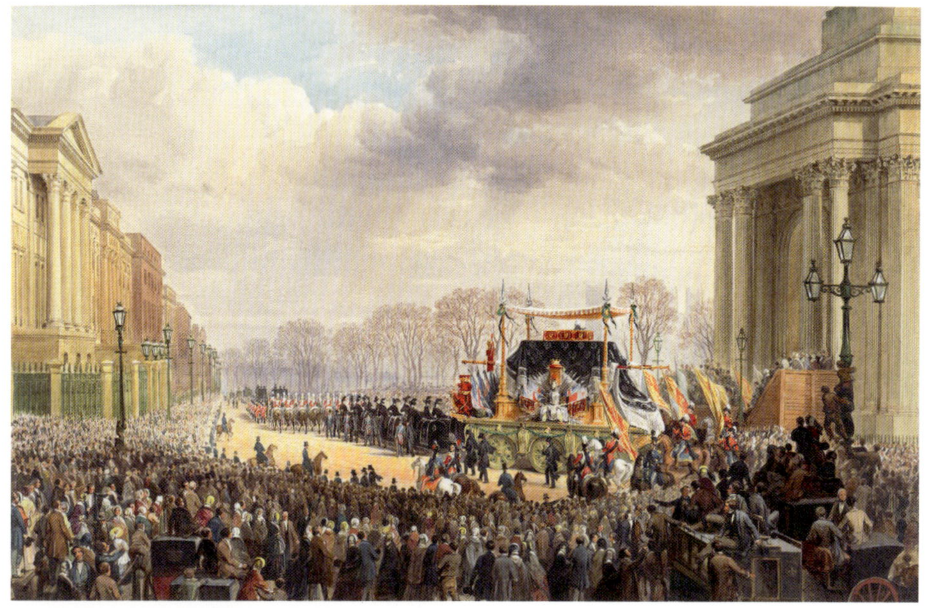

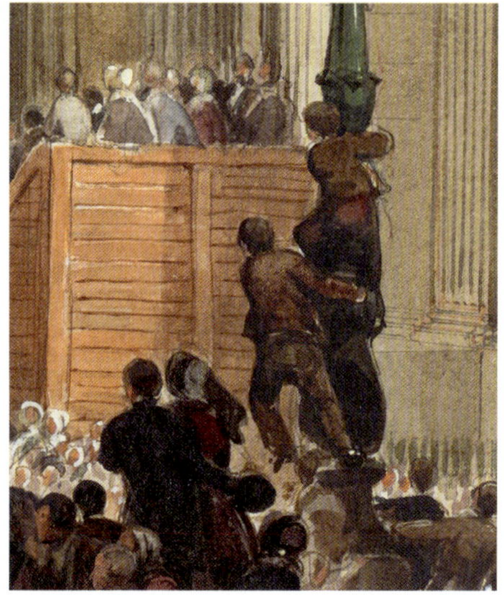

Fig. 92

LOUIS HAGHE

The funeral procession of the Duke of Wellington passing Apsley House, 18 November 1852, 1854

Pencil, watercolour and bodycolour with gum arabic, 30.0 × 47.5 cm

RCIN 916697

'The whole nation seemed to join in bearing the great Duke, with all honours & respect, to the grave.'

– Queen Victoria

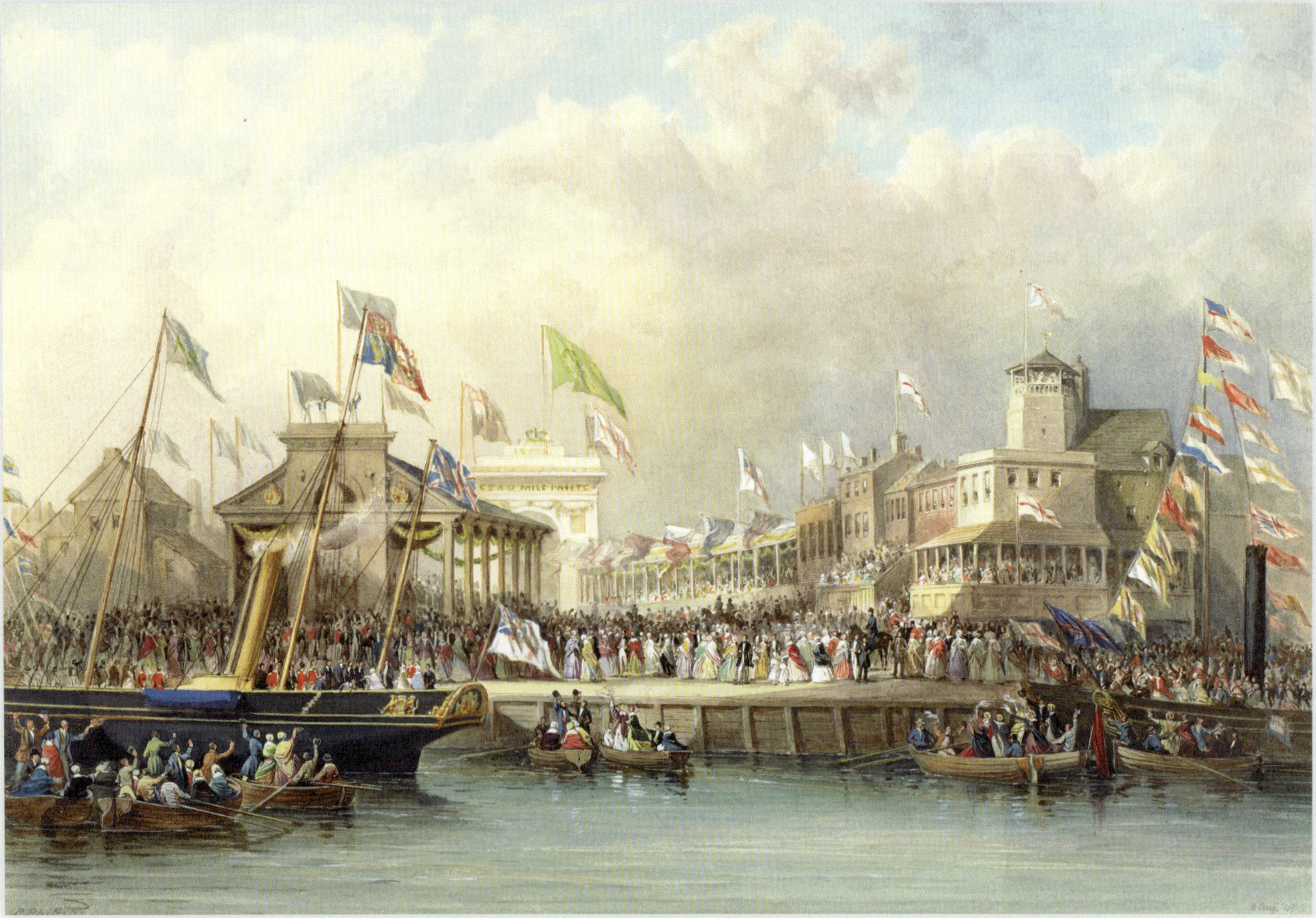

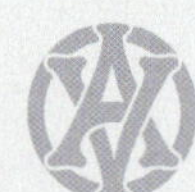

Fig. 93

PHILIP PHILLIPS (d. 1864)

Queen Victoria knighting the Mayor of Belfast, 1849

Watercolour and bodycolour, 25.0 × 37.4 cm

RCIN 920214

Although Prince Albert rode in the Duke of Wellington's funeral procession and attended the service at St Paul's, the Queen did not play any official role in the ceremony. There are, however, View Album watercolours that illustrate scenes of Victoria undertaking public duties, as we have already seen in relation to the unveiling of the Crimean monuments. Another such depicts the knighting of the Mayor of Belfast (fig. 93), which took place in August 1849 on a visit to the city during her first tour of Ireland, and was painted by Philip Phillips, a landscape and panorama painter who often collaborated with his artist wife Elizabeth (*fl.* 1832–78). Phillips made another four views of different places on the royal itinerary, all of which were incorporated in the fifth View Album.[53] In this watercolour the act of knighting itself is taking place on the royal barge to the left of the scene; the figures of Victoria and the mayor are small and distant. As with many of the other illustrations of Victoria and Albert's public and private travels, the approach here is more panoptic – demonstrating the warm and joyful reception they received from the city of Belfast – than focused on the specific event taking place. The watercolour is full of bright colour and incidental detail, with flags fluttering in the breeze, small boats crowding close to the scene of the action to enable their occupants to get a better view, and ladies waving handkerchiefs and men doffing their hats in the direction of the royal barge. Prominent in the centre background is a triumphal arch inscribed with the Gaelic phrase '*céad míle fáilte*', meaning 'a hundred thousand welcomes'.

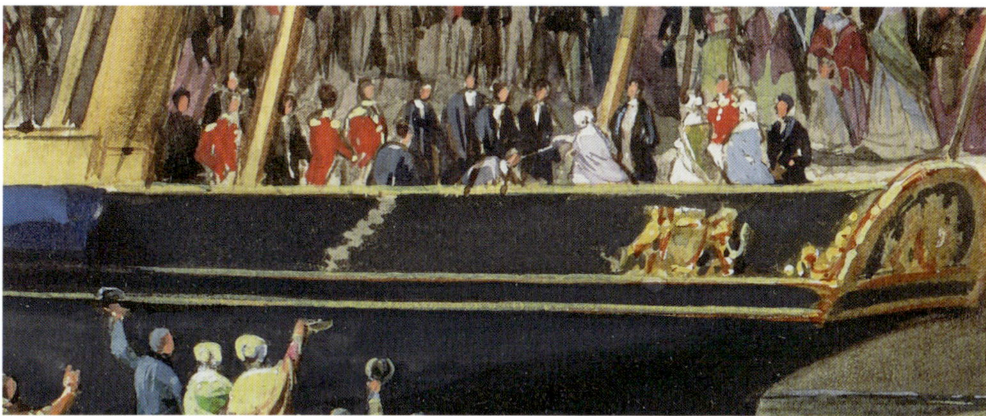

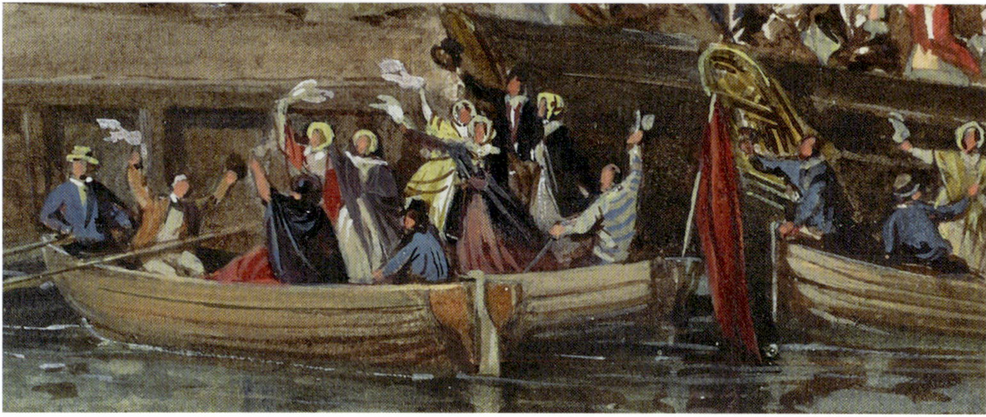

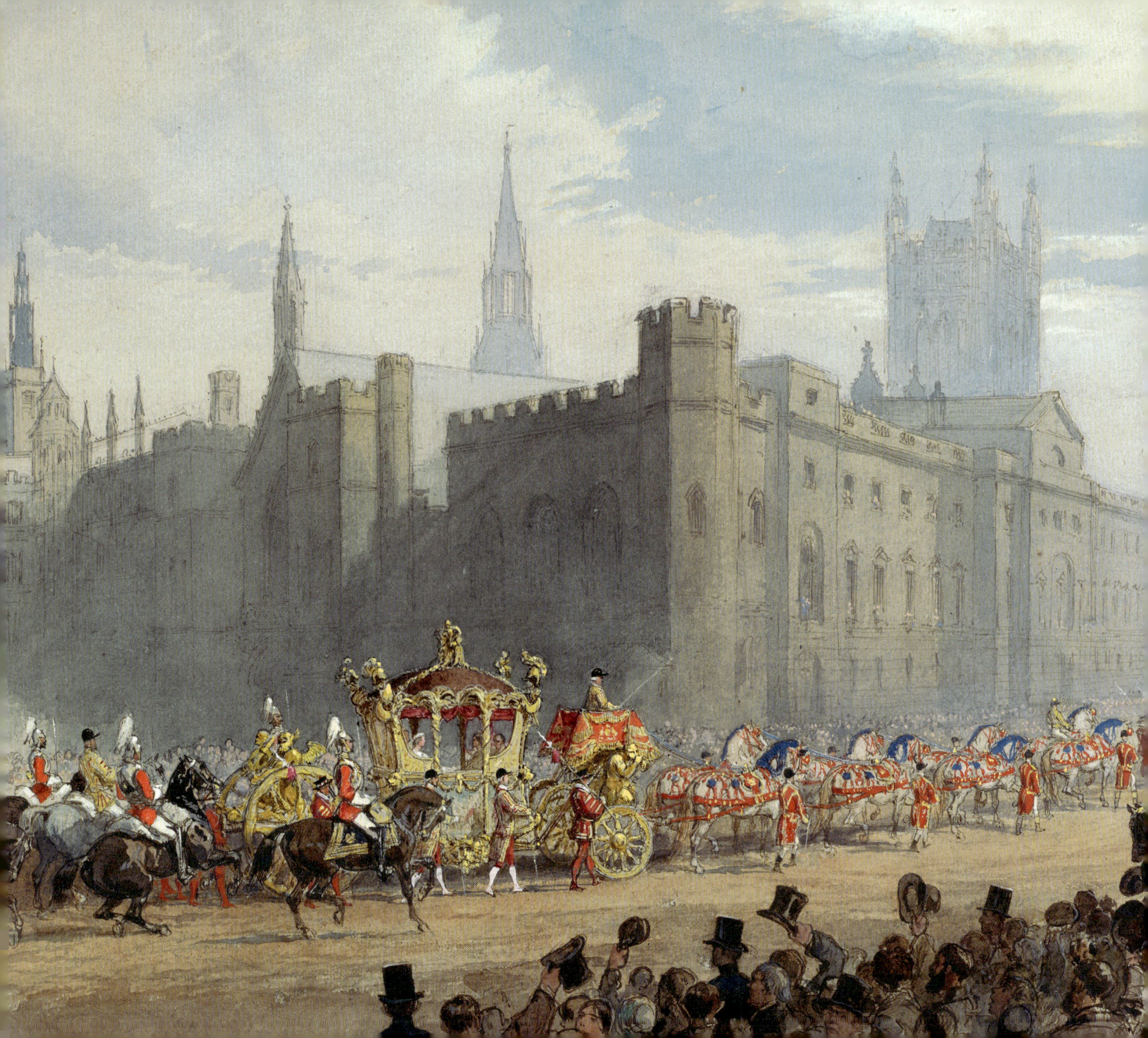

The last View Album contained a watercolour depicting Queen Victoria travelling in the Gold State Coach to carry out another of her very public duties – the opening of Parliament (fig. 94). George Housman Thomas represented the scene with great skill. The rich gilding and glamour of the coach, built for the Queen's grandfather George III (1738–1820) and first used by him for the state opening of Parliament in 1762, the smart livery of the escort of Life Guards and the colourful harnesses of the horses pop out in contrast against the almost monochromatic buildings in the background. Thomas also adeptly utilised the heavily textured, off-white paper as a mid-tone for much of the cloudy sky, and the dry white highlights which accentuate the clouds, the grey-blue tone of the patches of sky showing through and the bare branches of the tree at the far right perfectly evoke a clear but cool February day in London. The suggestion of deep crowds lining the processional route, despite the cold, accords with Victoria's observation that there were 'many people out'.[54]

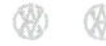

In many of the watercolours capturing scenes of public events attended by Victoria and Albert, they themselves are rather small figures, with arguably more emphasis on their often grand surroundings and the ceremony taking place than on their personal participation. This can, to a degree, be explained by the likely vantage point the artist responsible would have been accorded – possibly at a height, and at some distance from the central dais that the royal party would occupy. Victoria and Albert, though, were clearly receptive to illustrations that offered a wider view of an occasion, rather than being focused solely on them and their actions. It may also be that they saw watercolours of ceremonials (and indeed those depicting the enthusiastic receptions they received on their domestic and international travels), in which they are small figures within a larger narrative scene, as nevertheless demonstrating their unequivocal status and power. After all, the attraction of such a spectacle for the spectators was, usually, the presence of the Crown.[55]

Fig. 94

GEORGE HOUSMAN THOMAS

Queen Victoria driving to open Parliament, 1861

Pencil, pen and ink, watercolour and bodycolour, 30.3 × 45.5 cm

RCIN 920251

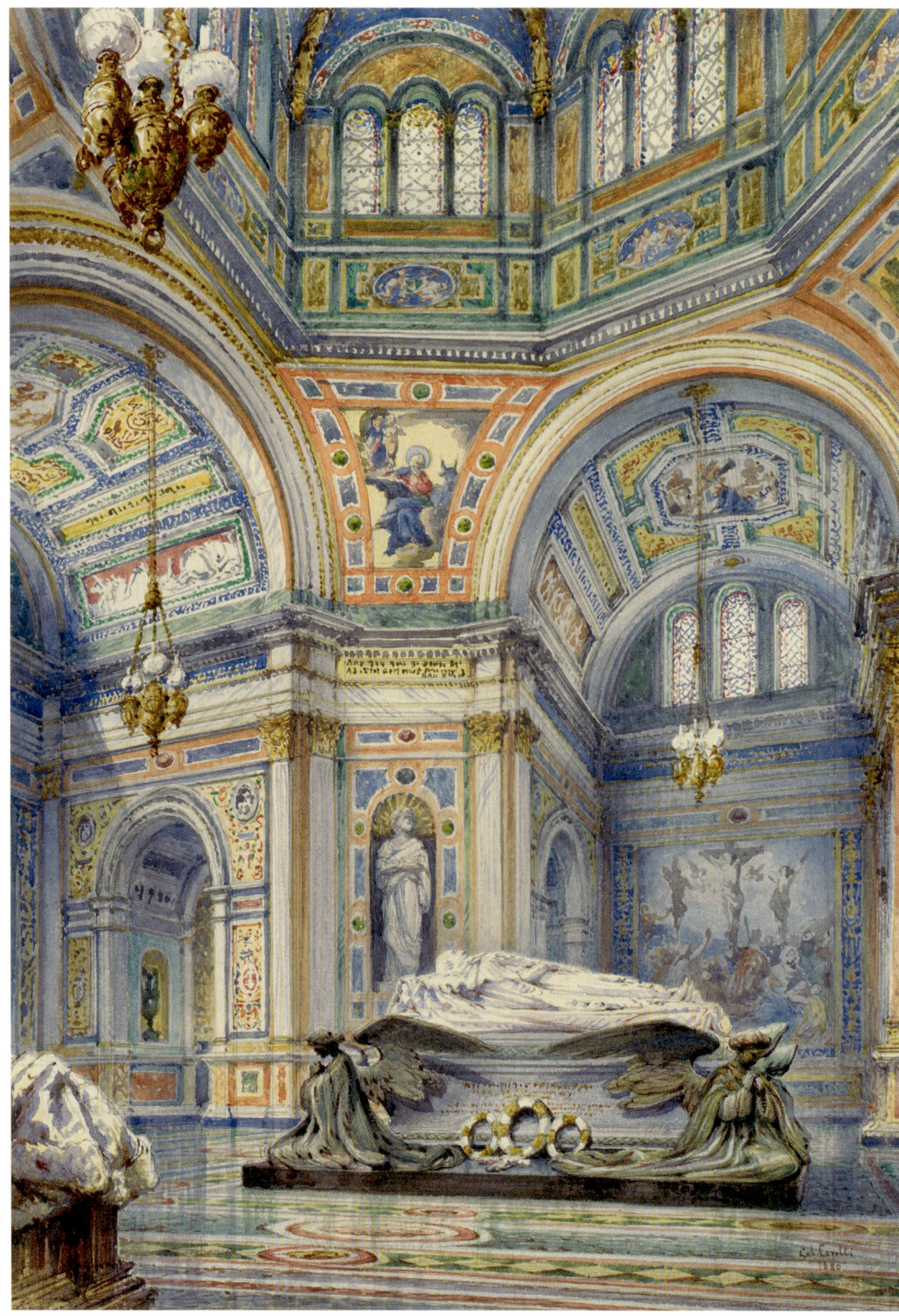

Fig. 95

GABRIELE MARIANO NICOLAI CARELLI (1821–1900)

The Royal Mausoleum, Frogmore, 1883

Pencil and watercolour, 45.4 × 33.1 cm

RCIN 919746

Conclusion

'*I shall end them, for ever with last year.*'[1]

– Queen Victoria

So wrote Victoria about the View Albums in January 1862, just a few weeks after Albert's death. With the exception of a small group of watercolours commissioned by the Queen which related to the royal couple's activities in the last year of Albert's life, no further works were ever added to this very personal sequence of albums. While Victoria did continue to evince an interest in the arts, much of her patronage focused on perpetuating Albert's memory publicly and privately, for example, in the design and decoration of the mausoleum in which he was interred (fig. 95).

However, as the *Art-Journal* speculated in 1876 (clearly with some degree of knowledge), despite their abrupt discontinuation the albums Victoria and Albert compiled during their marriage held great historical and art-historical significance, as well as being deeply personal: 'The series, which must now be pretty extensive, ranging over so many years, forms, as it were, an illustrated history of her Majesty's reign.'[2] Surveying this body of material as a whole, it is possible to draw out some broad themes in Victoria and Albert's collecting approach as well as in their taste for watercolour painting.

The artists

There were clearly several different ways in which Victoria and Albert were introduced to the work of contemporary British and continental artists. Personal recommendation, either verbal or in the form of gift-giving, played a key role, facilitating important patronage networks. Artists such as Franz Xaver Winterhalter, Eugène-Louis Lami, William Leighton Leitch and Carl Haag came to the attention of the royal couple through relatives or members of their court, such as Charlotte Canning. Family ties created a different opportunity for network building; the sons of both Leitch and Joseph Nash received royal commissions, presumably recommended by their fathers.

Another method by which Victoria and Albert sourced artists was through agents. There is evidence that Dominic Colnaghi (1790–1879), of the firm of P. & D. Colnaghi, worked in this capacity for the royal patrons. Lami, for example, wrote to Colnaghi in 1848 to solicit information about the Queen's response to a watercolour he had sent for her approval (probably that of the Grand Staircase; see fig. 82). It seems that this letter was forwarded on to Marianne Skerrett, the Queen's dresser and another significant intermediary between the royal couple and artists, as it is with her papers in the Royal Archives, but no record of the reply survives.[3] According to William Wyld's friend and biographer Philip Hamerton (1834–94),

Wyld's Balmoral commission in the autumn of 1852 (see figs 25 and 26) also came about via Colnaghi: 'It happened that Mr. Wyld had already executed several commissions for the Queen, so that Mr. Colnaghi, who was entrusted by Her Majesty with the duty of finding a competent artist, suggested the project to him.' Hamerton recorded elements of the process of selection of an artist in this context, noting that Wyld had to submit sketches in advance for consideration.[4]

It also appears likely that the illustrated press played a role in bringing some artists to royal attention. George Housman Thomas may have come to Victoria and Albert's notice in this way, whether through the reproductions of his works in the *Illustrated London News* or his physical attendance (presumably, visibly sketching) at royal events – or indeed a combination of the two. It is perhaps unsurprising that Thomas became a particular favourite of the royal couple given that the newspaper for which he worked was reliably and emphatically pro-royal in its coverage.

Victoria and Albert engaged directly with the artists they employed.[5] They were quick to discuss matters of technique and composition with the painters working around them, and Carl Haag was even given the use of the Queen's own painting materials when he mislaid his on the train up to Balmoral on his first visit.[6] Many artists found them exacting patrons who emphasised their desire for prolificacy and veracity, but loyalty was rewarded. The royal couple were generous in their recommendations of the artists who pleased them – William Ross gained his introduction to the Belgian and French courts thanks to Victoria, and she also promoted Leitch's career as a watercolour tutor: as she told Lady Canning, '[Leitch] is an excellent Master & I recommend him whenever I can.'[7] Moreover, Victoria and Albert gave some artists additional financial support in times of need. Ross appears to have been receiving payments from the privy purse after 1857, when he had a stroke and was probably not producing any new works, and Victoria later paid towards the school fees for Edward Corbould's son for several years.[8]

Coverage and choice of subjects

It is notable that the View Albums do not comprehensively document the lives of the royal family. Depictions of only four of the christening ceremonies of the nine royal children were included, for example, in addition to the watercolour illustrating the banquet held on the occasion of Prince Leopold's christening (see fig. 16); this latter event took place on the fifteenth anniversary of Victoria's coronation, which may have prompted the decision to commission a watercolour of this particular banquet for her album and not any of the others.[9] Similarly, Eugenio Agneni's watercolour of the same prince's birthday ball (see fig. 17) is the only one in the View Albums to show a birthday party, and there are no representations of the birthday tables prepared for Prince Albert. The only wedding to be included was that of the Princess Royal (see fig. 69). In that case, however, Vicky's marriage was the only one of the royal children's to take place before the

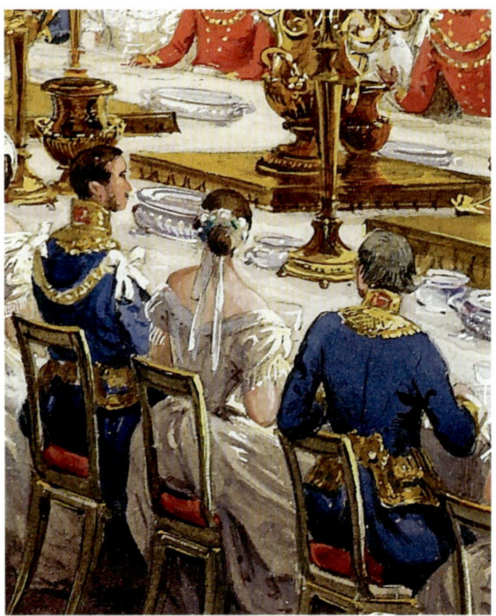

Fig. 16 (detail)

death of Prince Albert in 1861, which explains the lack of any other watercolours of such occasions in the albums.

As regards Victoria and Albert's travels, for both pleasure and duty, they were so numerous that to have attempted to record them all would have been a Herculean task. Furthermore, the Queen and Prince also kept another series of albums that related to this particular aspect of their lives known as the 'Journey albums' (see pp. 45–6). One of these albums remaining in the Royal Collection relates to the state visit to Paris in 1855 and has a title-page inscribed and signed by Queen Victoria.[10]

Similarly, had the couple tried to include representations of all the events, ceremonies and balls that they attended in the View Albums, the series would have expanded to unwieldy proportions. There was, therefore, a process of selection to determine what was represented in the albums and what was not. Lack of inclusion in the View Albums did not always mean absence of a visual record within Victoria and Albert's wider collection, of course – oil paintings, sculpture and, later on, photographs may have been commissioned instead, and sometimes they were themselves given albums of watercolours as mementoes of visits (see pp. 94 and 102). In some instances, too, watercolours were acquired later in Victoria's reign, such as those by Louis Haghe of the christening of the Prince of Wales and the inauguration ceremony of the Royal Exchange, though these were framed and hung, not added to any of the albums.[11]

It is also noticeable that in Victoria and Albert's repeated patronage of certain artists there is a correlation with the types of subjects commissioned. Lami, for example, painted many of what might be termed the 'society' watercolours, or scenes of balls and court spectacle. James Roberts was only ever commissioned to produce views of rooms in royal residences, though this brief broadened to include the complex interiors of the Great Exhibition in 1851.[12] Winterhalter's skill lay in portraiture and he, therefore, was the artist the royal couple turned to first for accurate likenesses of themselves or members of their family; the same was often the case with William Leighton Leitch, whose specialism was landscape. It may also have been that, at times, the relationship was reversed, and the types of scenes Victoria and Albert commissioned were influenced by the artists they particularly admired.

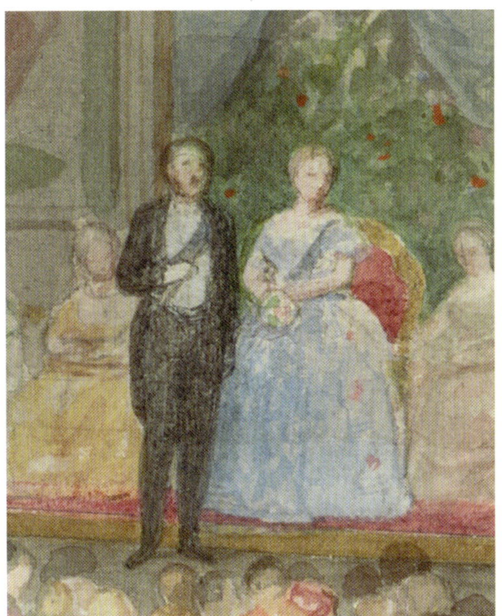

Fig. 17 (detail)

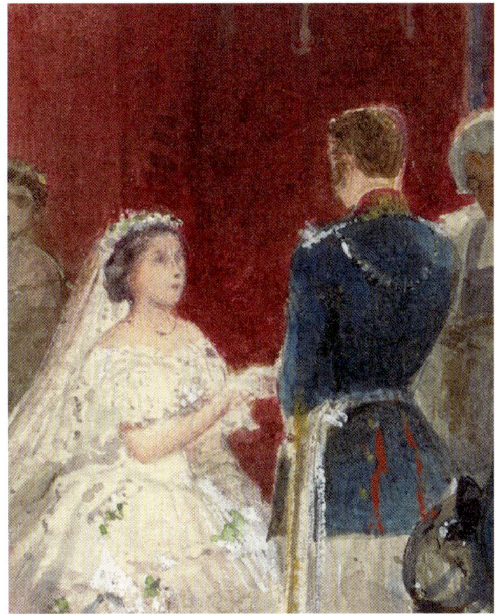

Fig. 69 (detail)

Style, accuracy and the relationship with photography

Above all, Victoria's particular requirement of any artwork was veracity. A portrait or a depiction of an event was only truly approved if it was an accurate likeness of the appearance of a person or accorded with the Queen's memory of an occasion. Egron Lundgren, who painted a number of scenes from plays seen by the royal family, recorded in his diary that the Queen 'took his watercolours with her to the theatre and compared them on the spot with the productions he illustrated'.[13] This goes some way to explaining why Victoria and Albert did not commission or collect the works of arguably the most famous watercolour and landscape painter of the first decade of their marriage, J.M.W. Turner (1775–1851). Though Turner did sketch subjects that were undoubtedly of interest to them, including views of the Rosenau and the arrival of Louis-Philippe, King of the French, at Gosport for his visit to Windsor in 1844, his rendering of such scenes would have been far too nebulous in character for Victoria, and with nowhere near enough of the literal transcription of places and people for her taste.[14]

Connected to the theme of accuracy is the reportage-like quality of many of the View Album watercolours. Though the majority of the artists Victoria and Albert commissioned would have worked up a final painting for presentation from sketches made on the spot, many of the works retain a sense of first-hand observation and spontaneity. In some instances, this was achieved through close-up framing that cut off figures at the edges of the scene (see fig. 85), whereas other artists, such as George Housman Thomas, worked in a bravura, painterly style particularly appreciated by the Queen.

That Victoria and Albert sustained their interest in collecting watercolours throughout their marriage is perhaps surprising given the competition from photography as a medium for recording people, places and events, especially as the technology developed and improved in the mid-1850s and grew in popularity.[15] This may have been due to some of its remaining technical limitations; it was unable to capture scenes in colour (though photographs could be, and often were, hand-coloured) or without good lighting, and exposure times were long. A finished watercolour, created from a number of different sketches made on the spot, could also synthesise and harmonise multiple elements of an occasion in a single image. From 1853, though, the royal couple demonstrated a sustained enthusiasm for collecting and commissioning photographs and created a number of photograph albums together. Unlike the View Albums, these were not organised chronologically but rather classified mainly by subject.[16] The two media were clearly not in competition for Victoria and Albert's attention.

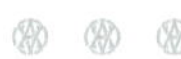

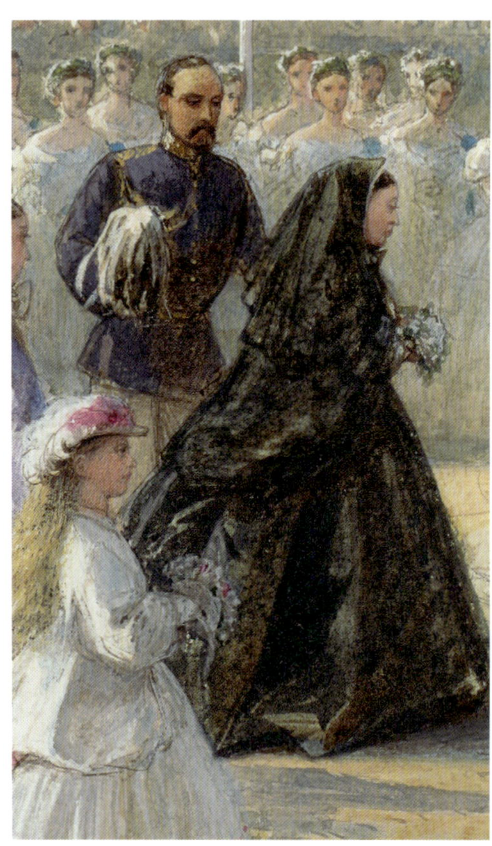

The View Albums that Albert and Victoria jointly created contained works by many well-known artists of the period whose talents were widely esteemed. The royal couple played a role in publicising the work of some of these artists – and presumably enhancing their reputations – through allowing the reproduction of certain watercolours in their collection as prints. The public were, therefore, able to see and indeed own in print form some works in the View Albums commissioned by the royal couple.

Nevertheless, the albums were deeply private and of great significance and emotional resonance for Queen Victoria, serving as visual repositories of important memories after Albert's death. As she told her eldest daughter in 1893, Victoria enjoyed and drew comfort from surrounding herself with 'my favourite pictures, my portraits & views'.[17] Leafing through the pages of colourful watercolours depicting happy times of the past, the Queen kept her beloved husband's image and memory alive.

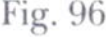

Fig. 96

GEORGE HOUSMAN THOMAS

Queen Victoria at the statue of the Prince Consort, Coburg, 1865

Pencil, watercolour and bodycolour, 44.5 × 34.6 cm

RCIN 914747

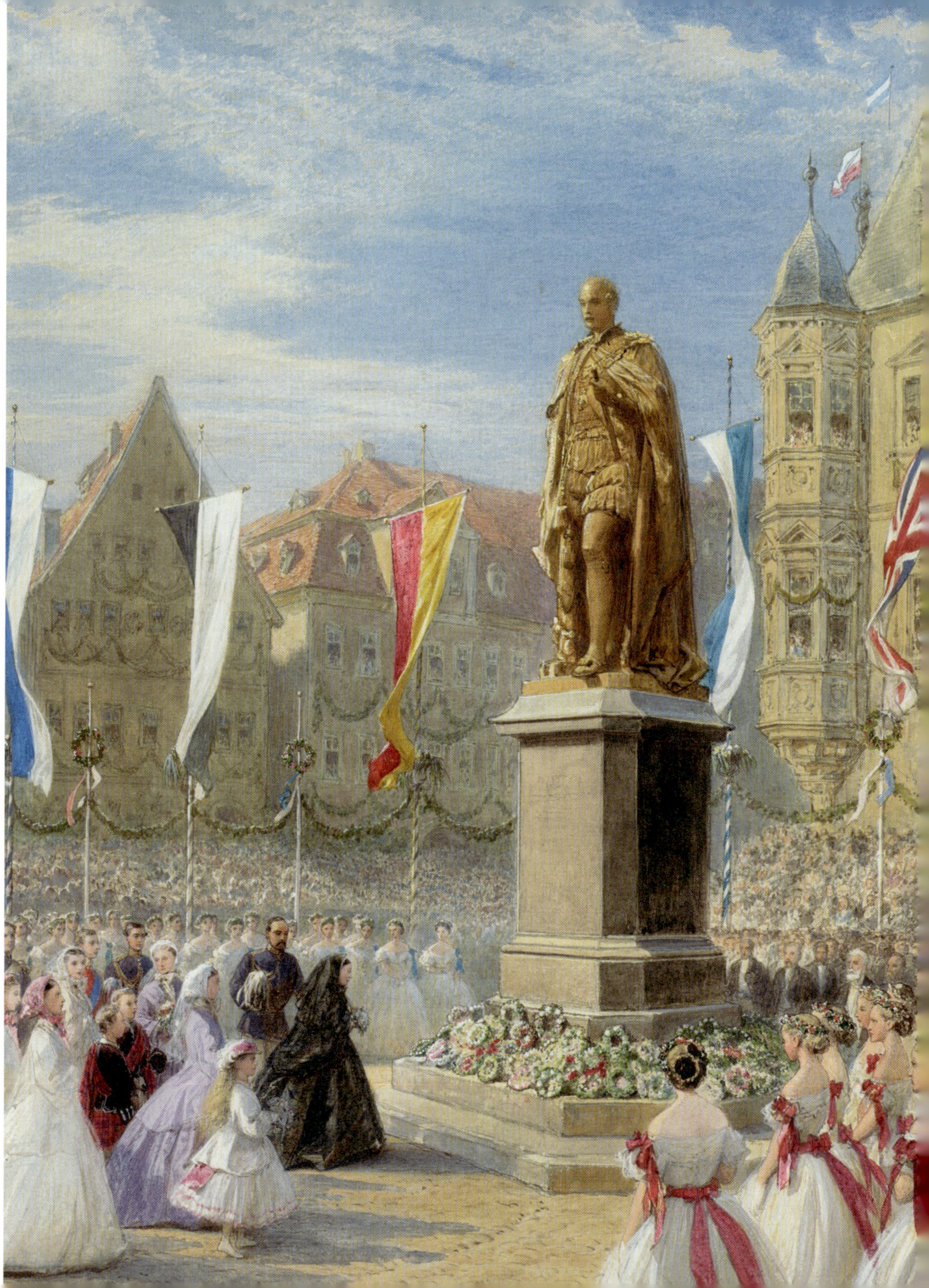

Notes

Introduction

1 The manual was written by Theodore Fielding (1781–1851), brother of the esteemed watercolour painter and President of the Old Watercolour Society Anthony Vandyke Copley Fielding.
2 Simon 2014.
3 There are payments to Ackermanns recorded in Queen Victoria's private accounts during the 1840s, but without specific reference to what was purchased.
4 See Irwin 1995 for another discussion of this frontispiece and Victoria as an amateur artist.
5 Redgrave 1860, p. 6. Paul Sandby (1731–1809) is traditionally referred to as the 'father of English watercolour'; from the mid-eighteenth century onwards the medium increased in importance and was practised by leading artists such as J.M.W. Turner (1775–1851) and John Sell Cotman (1782–1842), engaging the interest of patrons and connoisseurs. The first exhibiting watercolour societies were established in Britain in the early nineteenth century to celebrate and promote the skill and achievements of British artists in the discipline.
6 For a recent and comprehensive exploration of Victoria and Albert's deep engagement with the arts across multiple disciplines, see Marsden 2010.
7 Queen Victoria's journals were digitised by the Royal Archives in partnership with the Bodleian Library in 2012; they are freely available online (within the UK) at <http://www.queenvictoriasjournals.org> (accessed 11 January 2019).
8 RA QVJ 14 April 1841, 31 December 1843 and 21 February 1844. For more on Victoria's interest in and custodianship of the miniatures and Albert's many curatorial endeavours, see Remington 2010, I, pp. 21–8, and the introduction to Millar 1992 respectively.
9 For a full listing of the gifts Victoria and Albert commissioned, bought and gave one another throughout their marriage, see Appendix II in Marsden 2010, pp. 456–62. See also pp. 27 and 28 for watercolours by James Roberts recording Victoria's birthday and Christmas tables in 1861 and 1850 respectively.
10 Studies of Albert's many and varied contributions to nineteenth-century British industry and culture include Steegman 1950 and Hobhouse 1983.
11 RA VIC/MAIN/Z/261, fol. 227r.
12 Fewer than 50 watercolours by Albert's hand survive in the Royal Collection, compared to almost 1,000 created by Victoria before 1861.
13 For Westall, see Westall 1984. For a study of Victoria as an amateur artist, see Roberts 1987, ch. 3.
14 'Obituary – Richard Westall, Esq., R.A.', *Gentleman's Magazine*, VII, 1837, pp. 213–14.
15 RA QVJ 27 June 1833.
16 See Spender 1987, p. 16. The annual exhibition of the Associated Painters in Water-Colours (then also known as the New Watercolour Society, but now the Royal Institute of Painters in Water Colours) at Old Bond Street was under the patronage of Queen Adelaide; the alternative was the exhibition of the Old (now Royal) Watercolour Society, at Pall Mall.
17 RA QVJ 22 April 1836.
18 RCIN 913601 (by Tayler); the works by Copley Fielding, Prout and De Wint are no longer in the Royal Collection. Victoria showed these to her prime minister and close confidant Lord Melbourne on their arrival at Buckingham Palace on 22 July (QVJ). Prout was appointed Painter in Water-Colours in Ordinary to George IV (1762–1830) and continued in the same position under William IV (1765–1837) and then the new queen.
19 Cundall 1908, p. 107.
20 Roget 1891, II, p. 10.
21 Spender 1987, p. 16.
22 Quoted in Millar 1995, I, p. 14.
23 RCIN 451108. Victoria and Albert went on to patronise Corbould frequently: for his admission to Victoria, see RA QVJ 15 January 1863.
24 A comment made by the artist Clarkson Stanfield on seeing a finished watercolour by the Queen in the studio of landscape painter William Leighton Leitch – without knowing the identity of the artist; quoted in MacGeorge 1884, p. 63.
25 See Scott-Elliot 1961 for a discussion and catalogue of the prints produced by the royal couple.
26 For Victoria painting in oils, see RA QVJ 11 May 1840. She also recorded Albert doing so twice around the same time (8 May and 5 July 1840). Roberts (1987, pp. 107–8) discusses Landseer teaching the Queen. For Albert and photography, see Gordon 2014, p. 110. There are no known photographs by Albert.

27 Grey 1867, pp. 98, 107 and 350.
28 She also referred to Albert helping her with a watercolour copy of her own; see RA QVJ 20 December 1848.
29 RA QVJ 15 July 1846. Victoria was aware of Lear's own landscapes through the recent publication of the first volume of his *Illustrated Excursions in Italy* (1846).
30 See Warner 1979 and Roberts 1987, ch. 3. Queen Victoria's drawings in the Royal Collection have been digitised and are available at <http://www.rct.uk> (accessed 11 January 2019).
31 Sell 1884, p. 58.
32 RA VIC/MAIN/Z/491, fol. 1r.
33 Ibid., fols 20v–21r.
34 Marsden 2010, p. 33.
35 RA VIC/ADDT/275.
36 RA QVJ 10 October 1844.

Chapter 1: Home & family

1 Letter from Queen Victoria to her uncle Leopold I, King of the Belgians, dated 29 October 1844; Benson and Esher 1907, II, p. 27.
2 Marsden 2010, no. 25.
3 RA VIC/MAIN/Z/491, fol. 21r.
4 See, for example, RA QVJ 1 July 1842 and 27 January 1852.
5 Letter from Leopold I, King of the Belgians, to Victoria, dated 15 December 1843; Benson and Esher 1907, I, p. 511.
6 RA QVJ 17 August 1839. Stanley's Windsor views are RCINs 919751, 919752, 919754 and 919766.
7 Davidson 2008, p. 8.
8 Marsden 2010, no. 110. See Roberts 2004, ch. 4, for more on Pyne's publication.
9 Millar 1995, II, p. 635. A reviewer noted the similarities between the endeavours of Pyne and McLean and was complimentary about Nash's work: 'Windsor Castle', *Literary Gazette*, 15 May 1847, p. 370.
10 *Morning Chronicle*, no. 24,201, 18 May 1847, p. 1.
11 See Millar 1995, II, pp. 636–42.
12 'Fine Arts – The Watercolour Exhibitions', *Athenaeum*, no. 811, 13 May 1843, p. 468.
13 RA QVJ 19 June 1844.
14 RCIN 919785. See Millar 1995, II, no. 3978.
15 Beecher Stowe 1854, II, p. 41. The spontaneity of many of the interior views commissioned by Victoria and Albert is noted in Cornforth 1991.
16 RA QVJ 12 November 1847.
17 Marsden 2010, no. 118.
18 See the introduction to Millar 1992 and nos 401, 402, 414 and 415 for examples; and the introduction to Millar 1995.
19 RA VIC/ADDC4/73, dated 16 June 1848.
20 For Roberts's interior views and their associated payments (where known), see Millar 1995, II, nos 4605–4651. The other watercolour included in the payment of June 1852 was probably RCIN 926518, *Queen Victoria's birthday table at Osborne 1852.*
21 RA QVJ 31 March 1847.
22 My grateful thanks to Alex Buck for identifying a number of the portraits depicted in this watercolour.
23 For Victoria and Albert's fascination with dynastic portrait schemes, see Millar 1992, pp. xv–xvii.
24 Millar 1995, I, pp. 9–10.
25 RA QVJ 23 July 1850.
26 Marsden 2010, nos 153–5.
27 Stanley 1916, pp. 155–6. For an impression of the lithograph, see RCIN 606043.
28 Quoted in Millar 1995, II, p. 750.
29 Millar 1995, I, p. 398. See also Ballantine 1866 for numerous references to Haghe; David Roberts (1796–1864) and Haghe were close friends, and made frequent sketching tours together on the Continent.
30 Taylor 1857, pp. 24–5.
31 RA QVJ 26 June 1850, 23 April 1852, 18 April 1856 and 2 May 1860. For the report on the opening ceremony, see 'Her Majesty's visit to Manchester', *The Times*, 1 July 1859, p. 5.
32 Millar 1995, I, no. 2357.
33 For example, Victoria recorded in her journal (RA QVJ 9 June 1845) that she looked at 'a charming sketch of our Ball' (the 1745 costume ball, which had taken place three days previously) by Haghe; the finished watercolour is RCIN 919907.
34 The Italian press recorded Agneni's arrival in London that January and (rather hyperbolically) described the English public rushing to admire his five paintings in the opera house before they were even finished; 'Eugenio Agneni a Londra', *Lo Spettatore*, 4 July 1858, p. 313.
35 A comment Elphinstone made in his diary on 6 February 1860 regarding a children's ball held by the Duchess of Kent; quoted in Howard McClintock 1945, p. 40.
36 'Messrs Caldesi and Montecchi … attended, by command of Her Majesty, at Buckingham Palace, to execute a series of photographs of their Royal Highnesses the Princes and Princesses, in the costume which they wore on the occasion of the recent fancy ball'; 'Metropolitan News', *ILN*, 23 April 1859, p. 398. See RCINs 2900163–2900169 and 2914284–2914289 for the photographs.
37 Agneni fought under Garibaldi both before and after his residency in London; Luzio 1937, p. 137.
38 In the same letter, dated 18 December 1860 and addressed to Emma Herwegh, Agneni also described the children of the aristocracy in attendance at the ball in less than complimentary terms; Luzio 1937, pp. 137–8.
39 Millar 1995, II, no. 4625.
40 Ibid., no. 4633.
41 Morton 1991, no. 19, and Marsden 2010, no. 297.
42 The Duchess died on 16 March 1861. The two watercolours she commissioned are landscapes of Fife scenes by George Greig (d. 1867), RCINs 450625

and 919592, and the copy by Marshall Claxton (1813–81) after Winterhalter is RCIN 408955.

43 Kensington was where Queen Victoria had grown up with her mother; Claremont, the residence of Uncle Leopold (the Duchess's brother), was a happy holiday home during Victoria's childhood and into her marriage; and Frogmore House was the Duchess's residence from 1840, and the place where she died.

44 For Nash's watercolours, see Millar 1995, II, nos 3996–3999, for the years 1846–9, and p. 735 for a discussion of Roberts's prices.

45 RCIN 919807.

46 Translated in Jagow 1938, p. 76.

47 Stanley 1916, p. 157.

48 RA QVJ 24 December 1850.

49 Prince Albert paid 300 guineas for the Corbould, compared to the £22 Roberts was paid for three watercolours.

50 'Vice-Chancellor's Courts', *The Times*, Wednesday 17 January 1849, p. 6.

51 Letters from Victoria to Leopold I, King of the Belgians, 17 October 1844 and 25 March 1845; Benson and Esher 1907, II, pp. 25 and 35.

52 RA QVJ 19 February 1845.

53 For more on the building and decoration of Osborne, see Marsden 2010, pp. 22–4 and 194–8.

54 RA QVJ 26 August 1850, and Stanley 1916, p. 211.

55 Letter from Eleanor Stanley to her mother, dated 28 July 1848; Stanley 1916, p. 173.

56 Rappaport 2003, p. 55.

57 For more on Balmoral, see Marsden 2010, pp. 25 and 205–19.

58 RCINS 920223 and 920219 – see pp. 58 and 61.

59 Letter from William Wyld to an unidentified correspondent, dated 25 September 1852; RA VIC/ADDJ/1575.

60 RA QVJ 11 October 1852.

61 See note 59 above.

62 Roget 1891, II, p. 404.

63 RA QVJ 22 September 1859.

64 Marsden 2010, p. 24.

65 RA VIC/ADDU/32.

66 RCIN 917108.

67 Marsden 2010, nos 128 and 129.

68 Clayton 2004, no. 64.

69 For a more detailed account of Haag's technique and innovations, see Millar 1985, appendix, pp. 144–5.

70 Ibid., p. 144.

71 RA QVJ 29 July 1854.

72 Winsor & Newton colour book 20, p. 19.

73 RA QVJ 1 October 1873.

74 RA QVJ 28 April 1883 and 21 June 1884 respectively.

Chapter 2: Travelling the kingdom

1 Letter from Victoria to Leopold I, King of the Belgians, 3 August 1841; Benson and Esher 1907, I, pp. 295–6.

2 Letter from Albert to the Dowager Duchess of Gotha, 11 June 1840; translated in Grey 1867, p. 346.

3 'Royal visits', *ILN*, 31 August 1844, p. 129.

4 RA QVJ 31 July 1841.

5 RA VIC/MAIN/Z/491, fols 21r–22v. See Plunkett 2003, ch. 1, on the relationship between Victoria, the press and the public, during her marriage.

6 Victoria and Albert were often presented with views of houses they visited either by professional artists or by amateurs (generally female members of the host family). Lady Catherine Vernon-Harcourt, daughter-in-law of the Archbishop of York, probably presented her two watercolours of Nuneham House (RCINS 920146 and 920147) to Victoria as a souvenir.

7 RA QVJ 26, 29, 30 and 31 July 1841.

8 *The Times*, 31 July 1841, p. 4.

9 Letter from Victoria to Lady Barham, later the Countess of Gainsborough, dated 8 August 1841; RA VIC/ADDU/29/7.

10 RA QVJ 2 February 1842.

11 A guide to the house published in 1838 states that the walls of the State Drawing Room were then yellow; *Stowe* 1838, p. 70.

12 Letter from Prince Albert to Frederich William IV of Prussia, dated 1 October 1842; translated in Jagow 1938, p. 82.

13 Tyrell and Ward 2000.

14 RA QVJ 1 September 1842. Letter from Queen Victoria to Lord Melbourne, dated 10 September 1842; Benson and Esher 1907, I, p. 430.

15 Murray 1843, p. 8.

16 'The Royal visit to Scotland', *ILN*, 3 September 1842, p. 259.

17 Victoria, describing the scene on her arrival, noted that Edinburgh was 'wrapped in fog'; RA QVJ 1 September 1842.

18 Translated in Jagow 1938, p. 95.

19 RA QVJ 24 September 1844; Millar 1995, II, no. 3384.

20 Millar 1995, I, pp. 518–30; Millar 1992, pp. 136–57.

21 RA QVJ 9 August 1832. For public expectations, see Tyrell and Ward 2000, p. 114; Parry 1850, pp. 465–7.

22 RA QVJ 15 August 1847; Parry 1850, p. 467.

23 Roget 1891, II, p. 285.

24 RA QVJ 9 May 1854 and 5 May 1855.

25 Marsden 2010, no. 288.

26 'The Royal visit to the Britannia Bridge', *ILN*, 23 October 1852, pp. 331–2.

27 RA QVJ 14 October 1852.

28 Millar 1995, I, no. 1556.

29 Victoria and Albert first visited Ireland in August 1849 (see the discussion of fig. 93, p. 131).

30 Quoted in Millar 1995, I, no. 2731.

31 RA QVJ 30 August 1853.

32 *The Times*, 29 August 1861, p. 12. By the time of the royal visit there were a number of published guides devoted solely to Killarney; in the preface to his own (1822), the Revd G.N. Wright claimed it as the first guidebook to concentrate entirely on the area.

33 RA QVJ 28 August 1861.
34 *The Times*, 30 August 1861, p. 8; RA QVJ 27 August 1861.
35 Hare 1893, I, p. 299.
36 For a catalogue of Mary Herbert's works, see Butler *et al.* 1999.
37 RCIN 980035.v.
38 RCINs 920253 and 920255.
39 See Hobhouse 1983.
40 Letter from Prince Albert to Baron Stockmar, dated 17 December 1843; translated in Jagow 1938, p. 87.
41 See, for example, Princess Victoria's journal entry giving a dramatic description of the urban scenes she witnessed as she travelled from Birmingham to Wolverhampton: RA QVJ 2 August 1832.
42 RA QVJ 11 October 1851.
43 'The Royal Pictures', *Art-Journal*, III, 1857, p. 204.
44 RA QVJ 9 October 1851.
45 RA QVJ 7 September 1858.
46 Millar 1995, II, p. 635.
47 See RA QVJ 29 and 30 September 1848.
48 No views relating to the first of Victoria and Albert's cruises along the south coast (28 August–2 September 1843) were mounted in the View Albums, but thereafter seventeen watercolours were incorporated in the fourth album (August–September 1846, south coast and Channel Islands, and August 1847, south coast and Isles of Scilly); one in the sixth (August 1854, visit to Alderney); three in the seventh (August 1856, south coast); and another three in the eighth (August 1859, Channel Islands).
49 Stanley 1916, p. 119.
50 Letter from Victoria to Leopold I, King of the Belgians, dated 7 September 1846; Benson and Esher 1907, II, p. 100.
51 RA VIC/ADDT/232/182.
52 Roget 1891, II, pp. 352–4; Pottle 2004 (rev. 2011).
53 'Her Majesty's visit to Guernsey', *ILN*, 5 September 1846, p. 149. Naftel's home and studio was Millmount, St Peter Port. Six pencil sketches by the artist showing the royal arrival and celebratory processions were sold at auction at Cheffins, Cambridge, 30 November 2016, lot 716.
54 'Landing of Her Majesty at Guernsey', *ILN*, 7 November 1846, p. 295.
55 RA QVJ 24 August 1846.
56 RA QVJ 23 August 1846.
57 Their name for these tours; Millar 1985, pp. 103–5.
58 RA QVJ 4 September 1860. For more watercolours illustrating the Great Expeditions, see Millar 1995, II, pp. 553–5.
59 Millar 1985, p. 103.
60 RA QVJ 10 October 1861.

Chapter 3: France & Germany

1 RA QVJ 3 November 1836.
2 Grey 1867, p. 55.
3 Quoted in Millar 1995, I, p. 13.
4 Letter from Victoria to Leopold I, King of the Belgians, dated 26 September 1843; Benson and Esher 1907, I, p. 493.
5 Victoria's phrase; quoted in Queen Victoria 1880.
6 'The Queen's visit to France', *ILN*, 2 September 1843, p. 145.
7 'Our weekly gossip', *Athenaeum*, no. 885, 12 October 1844, p. 927.
8 'Album offert à la reine d'Angleterre', *L'Illustration*, 12 October 1844, p. 82 (this author's translation); and 'Miscellaneous', *Spectator*, 12 October 1844, p. 968 (quoting the *Gazette des Beaux-Arts*).
9 RA QVJ 8 October 1844. The watercolours were removed from the album in the first half of the twentieth century as part of the reorganisation of the Victorian works on paper in the Royal Collection, but the original listing of works in the album survives.
10 RA QVJ 24 December 1838. The painting is RCIN 405132.
11 Millar 1992, p. 284.
12 Bloomfield 1883, I, p. 87.
13 Janin 1844, p. 241.
14 Ibid. A number of paintings were made for the gallery, but it had not been completed by the time of the revolution in 1848.
15 Razzall 2016, p. 4.
16 RA QVJ 2 September 1843, and 'Landing of Queen Victoria', *ILN*, 16 September 1843, p. 179.
17 RA QVJ 2 September 1843.
18 Bloomfield 1883, I, p. 80.
19 Letter from Queen Victoria to Leopold I, King of the Belgians, dated 4 June 1844; Benson and Esher 1907, II, p. 13.
20 RA QVJ 10 October 1844.
21 Letter from Victoria to Leopold I, King of the Belgians, dated 4 September 1843; Benson and Esher 1907, I, p. 490.
22 Razzall 2016, p. 6.
23 Translated in Martin 1875–80, III (1878), p. 123.
24 RA QVJ 7 September 1854.
25 Storey *et al.* 1993, p. 410.
26 'The late G.H. Thomas', *ILN*, 22 August 1868, p. 177.
27 These qualities were enumerated as common to the best artists who worked for the illustrated journal the *Graphic* by its founder W.L. Thomas (1830–1900), George Housman Thomas's brother; Thomas 1888.
28 RA QVJ 16 April 1855.
29 Haswell Miller and Dawnay 1970, no. 2377/3.
30 RA QVJ 20 April 1855.
31 'Visit to England of the Emperor and Empress of the French', *ILN*, 28 April 1855, p. 398.
32 Aldrich 1988.
33 There are two listed as being on display at the Crystal Palace in Philips 1854, nos 312* and 312A.
34 Letter from Victoria to Leopold I, King of the Belgians, dated 29 August 1855; Benson and Esher 1907, III, p. 138.

35 Letter from Albert to the Duchess of Kent, dated 29 August 1855; translated in Jagow 1938, p. 233.
36 Winterhalter's correspondence on this topic was with Marianne Skerrett, Victoria's dresser. Letter from Winterhalter to Skerrett, dated 3 July 1855; RA VIC/ADDC4/263.
37 Razzall 2016, pp. 15–16.
38 RA QJV 18 August 1855.
39 A similar manipulation was adopted by Eugène Guérard, who painted an arrival scene for Victoria at the command of the Emperor and Empress. See Razzall 2016, no. 4.
40 Le Vert 1857, II, pp. 315–8.
41 Letter from Victoria to her half-sister Feodora, Princess of Hohenlohe-Langenburg, dated 19 September 1855; quoted in Millar 1995, II, no. 5440.
42 RCIN 405111.
43 RA QVJ 10 May 1859.
44 RA QVJ 24 August 1855.
45 For a catalogue of all the watercolours relating to the 1855 Paris visit acquired and presented to the Queen, see Razzall 2016.
46 Letter from Victoria to Napoleon III, dated 30 December 1855; quoted in translation in Razzall 2016, p. 15.
47 'Notes of the month – New Year's Gift of the Emperor Napoleon to Queen Victoria', *Gentleman's Magazine*, XLV, 1856, p. 164.
48 Letter from Victoria to Leopold I, King of the Belgians, dated 23 August 1855; Benson and Esher 1907, III, p. 136.
49 Hare 1893, I, p. 290.
50 Letter from Albert to Ernest, Duke of Saxe-Coburg and Gotha, dated 23 May 1845; translated in Bolitho 1933, p. 80.
51 RA QVJ 19 August 1845.
52 RA QVJ 15 August 1845. Lady Canning's words quoted in Millar 1995, I, p. 164.
53 RA QVJ 11 September 1845.
54 *The Times*, 26 August 1845, p. 4.
55 RA QVJ 20 August 1845.
56 Millar 1995, II, no. 3934.
57 Ibid., p. 626.
58 As advertised in the *Athenaeum*, no. 930, 23 August 1845, p. 825.
59 Millar 1995, II, no. 3670.
60 Letter from Albert to Baron Stockmar, dated 5 February 1858; translated in Jagow 1938, p. 289.
61 RA QVJ 16 August 1858.
62 Ibid.
63 Millar 1995, II, no. 3827.
64 RA QVJ 21 August 1858.
65 Millar 1995, II, no. 2191.
66 RA QVJ 24 August 1858.
67 Marsden 2010, p. 359.
68 RA QVJ 12 October 1860.

Chapter 4: Public spectacle in peace & war

1 RA QVJ 28 February 1854.
2 'A Royal Album', *Art-Journal*, XV, 1876, pp. 349–50.
3 RA QVJ 14 October 1851.
4 For a thorough account of the Great Exhibition, see Hobhouse 1983, ch. 7.
5 Letter from Albert to Ernest, Duke of Saxe-Coburg and Gotha, dated 15 July 1849; translated in Bolitho 1933, p. 110. Letter from Winterhalter to Skerrett, dated 8 March 1850; RA VIC/ADDC4/175 (the original in French, this author's translation).
6 Letter from Albert to Prince William of Prussia, dated 29 December 1850; translated in Jagow 1938, p. 175.
7 Letter from Victoria to Leopold I, King of the Belgians, dated 3 May 1851; Benson and Esher 1907, II, p. 317.
8 Millar 1995, I, pp. 16, 27, 29, and RA PPTO/PP/QV/4/4041.
9 I am grateful to Puneeta Sharma who first discovered this evidence while conserving one of Nash's Great Exhibition watercolours and shared the information with me.
10 For more on the Indian Court, see Bryant and Weber 2017, pp. 3–14.
11 'The Queen's Visit to the City', *ILN*, 12 July 1851, pp. 41–2.
12 'Grand State Ball at the Guildhall', *ILN*, 12 July 1851, p. 58.
13 Ibid. Letter from Victoria to Lord John Russell, dated 10 July 1851; Benson and Esher 1907, II, pp. 319–20.
14 Le Vert 1857, I, p. 31. The subsequent quotations in this paragraph come from the same account.
15 Lemoisne 1912, p. 136.
16 RA QVJ 13 June 1849.
17 'Fine Arts – Royal Academy – Architectural drawings', *Athenaeum*, no. 1178, 25 May 1850, p. 560.
18 RA QVJ 26 January 1846. A landscape-format depiction of the same scene by Lami now in the Fogg Art Museum, Harvard University, Cambridge, MA, may be a first version rejected by Victoria and Albert.
19 Le Vert 1857, I, p. 31.
20 RCINS 920037 and 913165.
21 RCIN 919915.
22 Marsden 2010, no. 298.
23 RCIN 404540.
24 RA QVJ 13 June 1851. Letter from Albert to Prince William of Prussia, dated 18 June 1851; translated in Jagow 1938, p. 177.
25 See the account given in the 'The Queen's Costume Ball', *ILN*, 21 June 1851, p. 584.
26 RA QVJ 13 June 1851.
27 RA QVJ 24 February 1840. The dancing master was Joseph Lowe, who wrote in his journal on 5 October 1852 that Albert was 'beautifully turned for a dancer'; Thomas 1992, p. 30. For the Queen dancing, see Stanley 1916, p. 79.
28 See Schoch 2004, especially pp. 37–60.
29 RA QVJ 28 December 1848.
30 Stanley 1916, p. 249.

31 RCINs 913000, 913001 and 921323 respectively.
32 Letter from Victoria to Lord Panmure, dated 5 March 1855; Benson and Esher 1907, III, p. 114.
33 Letter from Victoria to Leopold I, King of the Belgians, dated 14 November 1854; Benson and Esher 1907, III, p. 52.
34 See RA QVJ 20 and 21 December 1854 for reports in person – 'It seemed quite strange & such a novel experience, to have a wounded Gen: for dinner. Poor Mrs Bentinck looks dreadfully worn' – and 27 October 1855, when she and Albert were reading the diary of General Codrington.
35 Eleanor Stanley wrote to her father on 12 January 1855 that she and other ladies of the household were 'knitting socks for the Crimea, by the Queen's desire'; Stanley 1916, p. 286.
36 For example, RA QVJ 23 February 1855, when 34 wounded men came to the palace. Victoria wrote that the experience made her 'still more anxious for them all & to be able to do something to assist them'.
37 RA QVJ 3 August 1868.
38 Letter from Victoria to Leopold I, King of the Belgians, dated 28 February 1854; Benson and Esher 1907, III, p. 14.
39 Quoted in Massie 2005, p. 5.
40 Ibid.
41 Martin 1875–80, III (1878), ch. LIX.
42 Letter from Eleanor Stanley to her mother, dated 30 July 1856; Stanley 1916, p. 315.
43 RA QVJ 17 July 1856.
44 Ibid.
45 Letter from Victoria to Leopold I, King of the Belgians, dated 1 April 1856; Benson and Esher 1907, III, p. 185.
46 RCINs 913683, 913684 and 916783.
47 RA QVJ 9 May 1856.
48 Letter from Victoria to Leopold I, King of the Belgians, dated 17 September 1852; Benson and Esher 1907, II, p. 394.
49 Benson and Esher 1907, II, p. 393.
50 Millar 1995, I, no. 2338.
51 RA QVJ 18 November 1852.
52 Ibid.
53 RCINs 920209, 920210, 920212 and 920213.
54 RA QVJ 5 February 1861.
55 I am indebted to Michael Hatt for this observation.

Conclusion

1 RA VIC/MAIN/Z/491, fol. 21r.
2 'A Royal Album', *Art-Journal*, XV, 1876, pp. 349–50.
3 Letter from Lami to Colnaghi, undated; RA VIC/ADDC4/23.
4 Hamerton 1877, p. 194.
5 For more on this subject, see Remington 2012.
6 Millar 1985, p. 85.
7 Millar 1995, II, p. 750. Letter from Victoria to Charlotte Canning, dated January 1847; quoted in Roberts 1987, p. 100.
8 Millar 1995, II, p. 750 and I, p. 226.
9 The other christenings depicted were those of Prince Alfred (RCIN 919800), Princess Helena (919913), Prince Arthur (919915) and Princess Beatrice (919914).
10 RCIN 808993. This album was bequeathed by Victoria to her son Arthur, Duke of Connaught, who gave it to Queen Mary in 1935.
11 RCINs 921522 and 923135 respectively.
12 He also produced some copies after works by other artists (see RCINs 919991 and 920055).
13 Millar 1995, II, no. 3637.
14 Turner sketched the Rosenau during a German tour in 1840 and exhibited an oil view of it (now Tate, inv. no. TW0359) at the Royal Academy in 1841. Tate also holds two large unfinished oil paintings by Turner of the French king's arrival (inv. nos N04660 and N02068) and a sketchbook known as the 'Louis-Philippe at Portsmouth' sketchbook (Turner Bequest CCCLXII).
15 For more on the capabilities and limitations of photography in this period, see Mackenzie 2001, p. 232.
16 Gordon 2014.
17 Quoted in Millar 1995, I, p. 11.

Bibliography

Abbreviations

ILN: *Illustrated London News*
QVJ: Queen Victoria's Journal
RA: Royal Archives

Primary Sources

RA PPTO/PP/QV/PP2
Privy Purse accounts, 1853–69

RA VIC/ADDC4
Marianne Skerrett's correspondence, on behalf of Queen Victoria, with artists, 1838–70

RA VIC/ADDJ/1575
Miscellaneous correspondence, mostly non-royal, concerning the royal family, *c.*1838–1910

RA VIC/ADDT/232
Queen Victoria's Account Book for purchases of jewellery, pictures, presents, etc., 1851–61

RA VIC/ADDT/275
Queen Victoria's instructions regarding albums of paintings to be deposited in the Royal Library

RA VIC/MAIN/Z/261
Memoranda by Queen Victoria ('Conversations, Remarks, Reflections') on isolated events, 1857–62

RA VIC/MAIN/Z/491
Queen Victoria's reminiscences concerning Albert, the Prince Consort, with modern transcript, 1840–61

RA VIC/ADDU/29
Copy letters from Queen Victoria to Lady Jocelyn, 1837–55

RA VIC/ADDU/32
Copy extracts from letters from Queen Victoria to the Empress Frederick, 1858–1900

Published Sources

Aldrich 1988
M. Aldrich, 'Fit for an emperor at Windsor', *Country Life*, 182/49, pp. 56–9

Ballantine 1866
J. Ballantine, *The Life of David Roberts, R.A.*, Edinburgh

Beecher Stowe 1854
H. Beecher Stowe, *Sunny Memories of Foreign Lands*, 2 vols, London

Benson and Esher 1907
A. Benson and R. Esher, *The Letters of Queen Victoria: A Selection from Her Majesty's Correspondence between the Years 1837 and 1861*, 3 vols, London

Bloomfield 1883
Georgiana, Baroness Bloomfield, *Reminiscences of Court and Diplomatic Life*, 2 vols, London

Bolitho 1933
H. Bolitho (ed.), *The Prince Consort and His Brother: Two Hundred New Letters*, trans. by Mrs Laurentzen, London

Bryant and Weber 2017
J. Bryant and S. Weber (eds), *John Lockwood Kipling: Arts & Crafts in the Punjab and London* (exh. cat.), Victoria and Albert Museum, London, and Bard Graduate Center Gallery, New York

Butler *et al.* 1999
P. Butler, S. McCoole and C. Briggs, *Mary Herbert of Muckross House*, Killarney

Clayton 2004
Martin Clayton, *Holbein to Hockney: Drawings from the Royal Collection*, London

Cornforth 1991
J. Cornforth, A Room of One's Own, *Country Life*, 195/45, pp. 50–60

Cundall 1908
H.M. Cundall (ed.), *William Callow: An Autobiography*, London

Davidson 2008
G.S. Davidson, *House Proud: Nineteenth-century Watercolour Interiors from the Thaw Collection* (exh. cat.), Cooper-Hewitt National Design Museum, New York

Gordon 2014
S. Gordon, 'Queen Victoria's private photographs', in Anne M. Lyden (ed.), *A Royal Passion: Queen Victoria and Photography* (exh. cat.), The J. Paul Getty Museum, Los Angeles

Grey 1867
C. Grey, *The Early Years of His Royal Highness the Prince Consort*, London

Hamerton 1877
P.G. Hamerton, 'Sketches in Italy', *The Portfolio: An Artistic Periodical*, 8, pp. 193–6

Hare 1893
A. Hare, *The Story of Two Noble Lives*, 3 vols, London

Haswell Miller and Dawnay 1970
A.E. Haswell Miller and N.P. Dawnay, *Military Drawings and Paintings in the Collection of Her Majesty The Queen*, London

Hobhouse 1983
H. Hobhouse, *Prince Albert: His Life and Work*, London

Howard McClintock 1945
M. Howard McClintock, *The Queen Thanks Sir Howard: The Life of Major-General Sir Howard Elphinstone*, London

Irwin 1995
F. Irwin, 'Amusement or instruction? Watercolour manuals and the woman amateur', in C. Campbell Orr (ed.), *Women in the Victorian Art World*, Manchester and New York, pp. 149–66

Jagow 1938
K. Jagow (ed.), *Letters of the Prince Consort, 1831–1861*, trans. E. Dugdale, London and New York

Janin 1844
J. Janin, *The American in Paris during the Summer*, London

Lear 1846
E. Lear, *Illustrated excursions in Italy*, London

Lemoisne 1912
P.-A. Lemoisne, *Eugène Lami, 1800–1890*, Paris

Le Vert 1857
Octavia Le Vert, *Souvenirs of Travel*, 2 vols, New York

Luzio 1937
A. Luzio, *Felice Orsini e Emma Herwegh*, Florence

MacGeorge 1884
A. MacGeorge, *William Leighton Leitch, Landscape Painter: A Memoir*, London

Mackenzie 2001
J. Mackenzie (ed.), *The Victorian Vision: Inventing New Britain* (exh. cat.), Victoria and Albert Museum, London

Marsden 2010
J. Marsden (ed.), *Victoria & Albert: Art & Love* (exh. cat.), The Queen's Gallery, London

Martin 1875–80
T. Martin, *The Life of His Royal Highness The Prince Consort*, 5 vols, London

Massie 2005
A. Massie, *The National Army Museum Book of the Crimean War: The Untold Stories*, London

Millar 1985
D. Millar, *Queen Victoria's Life in the Scottish Highlands, Depicted by her Watercolour Artists*, London

Millar 1995
D. Millar, *The Victorian Watercolours and Drawings in the Collection of Her Majesty The Queen*, 2 vols, London

Millar 1992
O. Millar, *The Victorian Pictures in the Collection of Her Majesty The Queen*, Cambridge

Morton 1991
T.-M. Morton, *Royal Residences of the Victorian Era: Watercolours of Interior Views from the Royal Library, Windsor Castle* (exh. cat.), Edinburgh, Manchester, Windsor and London

Murray 1843
J. Murray (publisher), *Queen Victoria in Scotland 1842*, London

Parry 1850
E. Parry, *Royal Visits and Progresses to Wales, and the Border Counties*, London

Philips 1854
S. Philips, *The Portrait Gallery of the Crystal Palace*, London

Plunkett 2003
J. Plunkett, *Queen Victoria: First Media Monarch*, Oxford

Pottle 2004 (rev. 2011)
M. Pottle, 'Naftel, Paul Jacob (1817–1891)', *Oxford Dictionary of National Biography*, 2004 (rev. 2011) <https://doi.org/10.1093/ref:odnb/19719> (accessed 15 January 2019)

Queen Victoria 1880
Leaves from a Journal, being a record of the visit of the Emperor and the Empress of the French to The Queen and of the visit of the Queen and H.R.H. The Prince Consort to the Emperor of the French, privately printed

Rappaport 2003
H. Rappaport, *Queen Victoria: A Biographical Companion*, Santa Barbara and Oxford

Razzall 2016
R. Razzall, *Queen Victoria in Paris*, Compton Verney, Warwickshire

Redgrave 1860
R. Redgrave, *Inventory of the British Watercolour Paintings in the Fine Arts Collection at South Kensington*, London

Remington 2010
V. Remington, *The Victorian Miniatures in the Collection of Her Majesty The Queen*, 2 vols, London

Remington 2012
V. Remington, 'Queen Victoria, Prince Albert and their relations with artists', *Victoria & Albert: Art & Love* study day e-publication <http://www.rct.uk> (accessed 26 September 2018)

Roberts 1987
J. Roberts, *Royal Artists: From Mary Queen of Scots to the Present Day*, London

Roberts 2004
J. Roberts (ed.), *George III and Queen Charlotte: Patronage, Collecting and Court Taste*, London

Roget 1891
J.L. Roget, *A History of the 'Old Water-colour' Society now the Royal Society of Painters in Water Colours*, 2 vols, London and New York

Schoch 2004
R. Schoch, *Queen Victoria and the Theatre of Her Age*, Basingstoke

Scott-Elliot 1961
A. Scott-Elliot, 'The etchings by Queen Victoria and Prince Albert', *Bulletin of the New York Public Library*, 65.3, pp. 139–53

Sell 1884
K. Sell, *Alice, Grand Duchess of Hesse, Princess of Great Britain and Ireland*, trans. Princess Christian, London

Simon 2014
'Rudolph Ackermann' and 'Rudolph Ackermann junior' (updated September 2018) in J. Simon, 'British artists' suppliers, 1650–1950', 3rd edn, National Portrait Gallery, <http://www.npg.org.uk/research/programmes/directory-of-suppliers> (accessed 30 March 2018)

Spender 1987
M. Spender, *The Glory of Watercolour: The Royal Watercolour Society Diploma Edition*, Newton Abbot

Stanley 1916
E. Stanley, ed. Mrs S. Erskine, *Twenty Years at Court*, London

Steegman 1950
J. Steegman, *Consort of Taste*, London

Storey *et al.* 1993
G. Storey, K. Tillotson and A. Easson, *The Letters of Charles Dickens. Vol. 7: 1853–1855*, Oxford

Stowe 1838
Stowe. A description of the house and gardens … of the Duke of Buckingham and Chandos, London

Taylor 1857
T. Taylor, *A Handbook to the Drawings, Watercolours and Engravings in the Manchester Exhibition*, London

Thomas 1992
A. Thomas (ed.), *A New Most Excellent Dancing Master: The Journal of Joseph Lowe's Visits to Balmoral and Windsor …*, New York

Thomas 1888
W.L. Thomas, 'The making of the graphic', *Universal Review*, 2, pp. 80–93

Tyrell and Ward 2000
A. Tyrell and Y. Ward, 'God Bless Her Little Majesty: the popularising of the monarchy in the 1840s', *National Identities*, 2.2, pp. 109–25

Warner 1979
M. Warner, *Queen Victoria's Sketchbook*, London

Westall 1984
R.J. Westall, 'The Westall Brothers', *Turner Studies*, 4/1, pp. 23–38

Wright 1822
Revd G.N. Wright, *A Guide to the Lakes of Killarney*, London

Index

Acknowledgements

The author would like to thank the following Royal Collection Trust colleagues for their many significant contributions towards this publication and the accompanying exhibition:

Martin Clayton, Kate Heard, Lauren Porter, Rosie Razzall and Rhian Wong in the Print Room; Jenny Foot, Sam Harris, Samantha Johnson and Theresa-Mary Morton in Exhibitions; Martin Grey, Sarah Laing, Lachlan Marshall, Clara de la Peña Mc Tigue, Puneeta Sharma, Rachael Smith, Kate Stone and Emma Turner in Paper Conservation; Lynnette Beech, Allison Derrett, Laura Hobbs and Colin Parrish in the Royal Archives; Emma Stuart and Oliver Urquhart-Irvine (formerly Royal Librarian) in the Royal Library; Glenn Bartley, Ted Bennett, Laura Hollingworth, Emily MacMillan, Andreas Maroulis, Philippa Räder and Matt Stockl in the Royal Bindery; Alex Buck, Lucy Peter and Vanessa Remington in Pictures; Sophie Gordon, Catlin Langford and Helen Trompeteler in Photographs; Caroline de Guitaut in Decorative Arts; Karen Lawson, Daniel Partridge and Eva Zielinska-Millar in Photographic Services; Katie Buckhalter in Press; Andrew Davis in Collection Online; and Georgina Seage and particularly Polly Atkinson in the Publishing section.

I am also most grateful to Alison Effeny and Jane Roberts for their considerable assistance with the research for and preparation of this publication. My work on Victoria and Albert's watercolour collection has been underpinned by the seminal catalogue of the Victorian drawings and watercolours in the Royal Collection by Lady Delia Millar, the product of more than twenty years of research in the Print Room and Royal Archives. I very gratefully acknowledge my debt to Lady Millar's catalogue.

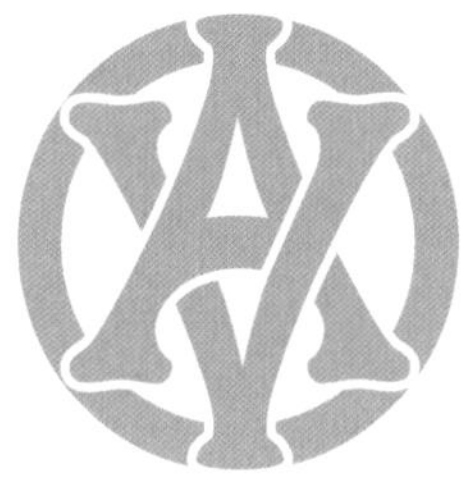

This catalogue was published to accompany the touring exhibition at:

Laing Art Gallery, Newcastle upon Tyne: 29 June – 15 September 2019
Poole Museum, Dorset: 26 October 2019 – 5 January 2020
Wolverhampton Art Gallery: 7 March – 31 May 2020